SOUTHERN LITERARY STUDIES
Fred Hobson, Editor

THE

UNREGENERATE

SOUTH

MARK G. MALVASI

THE

UNREGENERATE

SOUTH

THE AGRARIAN THOUGHT OF
JOHN CROWE RANSOM, ALLEN TATE,
AND DONALD DAVIDSON

LOUISIANA STATE UNIVERSITY PRESS
Baton Rouge and London

Copyright © 1997 by Louisiana State University Press
All rights reserved
Manufactured in the United States of America
First printing
06 05 04 03 02 01 00 99 98 97   5 4 3 2 1

Designer: Amanda McDonald Key
Typeface: Bembo
Typesetter: Impressions Book and Journal Services, Inc.
Printer and binder: Thomson-Shore, Inc.

Library of Congress Cataloging-in-Publication Data

Malvasi, Mark G., 1957–
    The unregenerate South : the agrarian thought of John Crowe
Ransom, Allen Tate, and Donald Davidson / Mark G. Malvasi.
        p.   cm. — (Southern literary studies)
    Includes bibliographical references and index.
    ISBN 0-8071-2143-6 (cloth : alk. paper)
    1. American literature—Southern States—History and criticism.
    2. Literature and history—Southern States—History—20th century.
    3. Ransom, John Crowe, 1888–1974—Knowledge—Southern States.
    4. American literature—20th century—History and criticism.
    5. Davidson, Donald, 1893–1968—Knowledge—Southern States.
    6. Tate, Allen, 1899–1979—Knowledge—Southern States.   7. Southern
States—Historiography.   8. Agrarians (Group of writers)   I. Title.
    II. Series.
    PS261.M28   1997
    210.9'975'09041—dc21   97-10950
                                                                      CIP

For my father and mother
Sempre con amore

Have I forgotten

The dead young men whose flesh will not reflower

But in this single bloom which now I pluck,

Weaving it into my spirit as victors weave

A chaplet, gathered from mould, for honor's sake?

This is my body, woven from dead and living,

Given over again to the quick lustration

Of a new moment: This is my body and spirit,

Broken but never tamed, risen from the bloody sod,

Walking suddenly alive in a new morning.

—*Donald Davidson, "The Sod of Battlefields"*

CONTENTS

Preface

The quest to discern meaning in history has been characteristic of Western thought for more than five hundred years. This enterprise carries two inherent dangers: first, that human beings will attribute ultimate purpose to historically provisional ambitions and values; and second, that they will confuse the historical with the divine and seek to abolish time, to repeal contingency, and at last to establish the kingdom of heaven on earth. In their efforts to reclaim southern history and to revitalize the southern tradition, the Southern Agrarians of the 1920s and 1930s had constantly to restrain themselves from making the City of God out of a City of Man. They were not entirely successful.

This study explores the thought of John Crowe Ransom, Allen Tate, and Donald Davidson on a wide range of related issues, including the meaning of southern history, the purpose of literature and the role of the man of letters in society, the nature of tradition, and the complexities and perils of the modern world. In the pages that follow I argue that, despite their shared commitment to the South as an antidote to the crisis of modernity, differences arose among Ransom, Tate, and Davidson precisely over their interpretation of southern history and over how much meaning that, or any, history could bear without a transcendent reference. I contend that these differences point toward a more fundamental tension that afflicts southern conservative thought as a whole: the tendency to divinize the secular, to replace the piety for God with a piety for history, society, and tradition.

Southern conservative thinkers since the Agrarians have never fully resolved these problems, and I make no attempt to do so here. If I have world enough and time, I propose to follow this study with another that analyzes principally the efforts of a later generation of southern conservative thinkers to confront the discordant legacy of Agrarianism. The conclusion to the present study, in which I examine the work of Richard M. Weaver and M. E. Bradford, anticipates what I hope is to come.

Andrew Lytle is the most obviously overlooked figure in this study. Lytle was engaged in a venture similar to that of Ransom, Tate, and Davidson. He saw civilization in the South as an extension of the Christian civilization that had originated with Charlemagne, if not earlier. My reason for excluding Lytle from this study, other than that considering his thought would have added significantly to an already long book, is that his version of Agrarianism is too complete and refined. His statement of the Agrarian world view, developed over many years, goes far beyond the original articulation of it by Ransom, Tate, and Davidson during the 1920s and 1930s. I will take up Lytle's thought at length at another time. If there is a resolution to the tensions within the southern conservative tradition, I expect to find it mainly in Lytle's work, for he seems to have definitively and unequivocally subordinated human history to divine revelation.

I hope and believe that I have written the present book without polemical excess, but it would be dishonest to assert that I wrote with utter impartiality. Whenever I have discovered in the thought of Ransom, Tate, and Davidson virtues that may aid us in resolving our current political, cultural, and spiritual crises, I have emphasized them with approbation. Similarly, whenever I have uncovered vices that formerly gave rise to evils, I have emphasized them also in the interest of determining what injury they may yet do.

I have thus not hesitated to wound the feelings of both opponents and partisans of the Southern Agrarians and the tradition that they represented. In so doing, I have often felt regret but never remorse. I hope that any aggrieved persons will know that I have sought only to tell as much of the truth as my abilities permit me to understand.

For my own part, I have found much to admire in the thought of Ransom, Tate, and Davidson and, indeed, in the southern conservative tradition itself. In an age when many, if not most, narratives had already become ironic, tending only to reveal the contradictions, shortcomings, and malevolence of the values, beliefs, and traditions of Western civilization, the Agrarians sought to establish a basis for piety and faith. If at times they erred in their defense of southern society and history, so that the South became for them an embodiment of the City of God on earth, they also knew that it was better to go to the grave believing in something rather than in nothing.

At their finest, the Agrarians and their followers testified to the afflictions of modern civilization and exposed as nonsense the idea that political remedies alone could mend its crumbling spiritual foundations. They associated the decline of the South and the southern tradition with the decline of Christendom. In their view, that commonly meant a fall from the belief in a divine order of the universe into a belief in history, that is, into a belief in man judging man as the final authority in this life and the next. Of this sin, they sometimes recognized themselves to be guilty.

As an alternative, they offered, however inconsistently and inadequately, a vision of transcendence and immortality that encompassed humanity, society, and history but that located ultimate meaning beyond time. This unbroken chain, they believed, had been there from the beginning and would endure throughout the ages to come.

ACKNOWLEDGMENTS

I have always followed the preoccupations of my own mind, wherever they have led me. It is thus now not false modesty that prompts me to say that I am surprised some of the results of these private deliberations have interested others enough to be published. I am both flattered and grateful for their kind attention.

John Easterly of Louisiana State University Press made the process of completing a book manuscript considerably less arduous than I had been led to believe it would be. His patience, encouragement, and insight are apparently without limit. Catherine Landry and Christine N. Cowan ably guided the book to publication. Fred Hobson, the editor of the Southern Literary Studies series, and the anonymous reader for the press offered thorough and rigorous commentaries of the manuscript that have rendered it an immensely better book than it would otherwise have been. I am deeply indebted to each of them.

The archivists and librarians at the Firestone Library at Princeton University, the Beinecke Rare Book and Manuscript Library at Yale University, and especially the Department of Special Collections in the Jane and Alexander Heard Library at Vanderbilt University made research a joy. I can imagine no more congenial places to work.

Samuel McSeveney, Dewey Grantham, Paul K. Conkin, William Havard, and William Bandy, all of Vanderbilt University, extended to me courtesies that far exceeded professional obligation. C. Vann Woodward and the late Cleanth Brooks of Yale University took the time to advise me about southern history and the Southern Agrarians at an early stage of my work. The late Christopher Lasch compelled me always to write clearly and to argue forcefully. Stanley Engerman read the entire manuscript and offered his invariably thoughtful criticisms, as he has long done, and continues to do, for so many others. Lenore Thomas Ealy also read the book at an early stage and offered a number of helpful suggestions, most of which I have been pleased to incorporate.

The late M. E. Bradford, of the University of Dallas, graciously consented to answer all my questions about the Agrarians. His counsel served me well, even when I disagreed with him. His magnanimity will, I hope, serve as a model of professional courtesy and personal conduct for me in the years ahead.

I wish also to thank William Franz, associate dean of Randolph-Macon College, and the members of the Committee on the Faculty, who awarded a Rashkind Fellowship during the summer of 1994 that enabled me to complete additional research and writing on this book. The Earhart Foundation provided funds during the summer of 1995 to complete final revisions on the manuscript. I am grateful to Antony Sullivan, who supervised the application of the grant.

Four people have not only helped me write a better book but have made me a better scholar and, I may hope, a better person.

David Bovenizer, formerly of Willie Pie's Store in Crozier, Virginia, and at present of Indianapolis, Indiana, enlightened me with his vast knowledge of the Southern Agrarians in particular and of southern history in general. I am as obliged to him for his persistence in trying to educate me as I am for his friendship and his concern for my immortal soul.

Clyde N. Wilson, of the University of South Carolina, Columbia, read the entire manuscript and subjected it to exacting criticism. If I may pay him but a single compliment, it is that he is a historian's historian.

To Eugene D. Genovese and Elizabeth Fox-Genovese I owe extraordinary obligations. They were never too busy to field my inquiries or to help me solve the problems that arose with the work. Eugene Genovese made the most careful and considered criticism of my work that I can ever hope to receive. In his own way, he also offered encouragement. I kept my mouth shut, took his threats seriously, and did as I was told. I am a better man for it. "Tu duca, tu segnore, e tu maestro." These two fine teachers and scholars have my gratitude; but more than that, they have my fidelity, my admiration, my respect, and my friendship.

Although I did not always listen, my wife, Meg, has never let me forget that there is more to life than work. For her insight, succor, and forbearance, she has my appreciation and my love.

My parents, Joseph and Ira Gene Malvasi, have made everything possible. I dedicate to them this book, the first fruit to ripen from the seed that they planted so long ago. I hope that the taste is as sweet as the love that nurtured it and watched it grow.

Abbreviations

Works by M. E. Bradford

BGR   *A Better Guide than Reason: Studies in the American Revolution.* La Salle, Ill., 1979.

RI   *The Reactionary Imperative: Essays Literary and Political.* Peru, Ill., 1990.

RWWA   *Remembering Who We Are: Observations of a Southern Conservative.* Athens, Ga., 1985.

Works by Donald Davidson

AL   *The Attack on Leviathan: Regionalism and Nationalism in the United States.* Chapel Hill, 1938.

LC   *The Literary Correspondence of Donald Davidson and Allen Tate.* Ed. John Tyree Fain and Thomas Daniel Young. Athens, Ga., 1974.

SRSY   *"Still Rebels, Still Yankees" and Other Essays.* Baton Rouge, 1972.

SWMW   *Southern Writers in the Modern World.* Athens, Ga., 1958.

Works by John Crowe Ransom

BB   *Beating the Bushes: Selected Essays, 1941–1970.* New York, 1972.

GWT   *God Without Thunder: An Unorthodox Defense of Orthodoxy.* New York, 1930.

NC   *The New Criticism.* Norfolk, Conn., 1941.

PE   *Poems and Essays.* New York, 1955.

SE   *Selected Essays of John Crowe Ransom.* Ed. Thomas Daniel
                Young and John Hindle. Baton Rouge, 1984.

SL   *Selected Letters of John Crowe Ransom.* Ed. Thomas Daniel
                Young and George Core. Baton Rouge, 1985.

WB   *The World's Body.* Baton Rouge, 1968.

WORKS BY ALLEN TATE

EFD   *Essays of Four Decades.* Chicago, 1968.

FD   *The Forlorn Demon: Didactic and Critical Essays.* Chicago, 1953.

JD   *Jefferson Davis: His Rise and Fall.* New York, 1929.

MO   *Memoirs and Opinions, 1926–1974.* Chicago, 1975.

RE   *Reactionary Essays on Poetry and Ideas.* New York, 1936.

RLA   *The Republic of Letters in America: The Correspondence of John
                Peale Bishop and Allen Tate.* Ed. Thomas Daniel
                Young and Thomas Hindle. Lexington, Ky.,
                1981.

RM   *Reason in Madness: Critical Essays.* New York, 1941.

OTHER WORKS

ITMS   Twelve Southerners, *I'll Take My Stand: The South and the
                Agrarian Tradition.* Baton Rouge, 1977.

STB   Richard M. Weaver, *The Southern Tradition at Bay:
                A History of Postbellum Thought.* New Rochelle,
                N.Y., 1968.

THE
UNREGENERATE
SOUTH

Introduction

The Southern Conservative Tradition in the Modern World

> No more the sound of guns. The silence drags
> Over the sunken breastworks and old graves
> Where bones forget their names, and only earth
> Utters fragments we know not how to reap.
> No sound of guns. A different thunder plagues
> The far-off streets where smokes recoil and languor
> Dogs the blue cannoneers who now too late
> Flinch from the lanyard. For the years take back
> The spoils, the laurels that they gave.
>   —Donald Davidson, "The Last Charge"

Contrary to old slanders and present distortions, the South has long been home to a vigorous intellectual tradition. That the principal intellectual tradition of the South is overwhelmingly conservative complicates matters. It obscures or, in some cases, discredits the contributions that southern thinkers have made to the most pressing debates about American politics, society, culture, civilization, and history.[1]

Sadly, today we have come increasingly to reinvent our past to suit the prejudices of the moment. Since antebellum southern conservative thinkers fashioned their tradition in defense of slavery and since their twentieth-century heirs often acquiesced in racism and segregation, their ideas, values, and convictions are now routinely portrayed as evils to be

---

1. *Cf.* Fred Hobson, "Surveyors and Boundaries: Southern Literature and Southern Literary Scholarship After Mid-Century," *Southern Review,* n.s., XXVII (1991), 739–55. Hobson invokes Howard Odum, Rupert Vance, W. J. Cash, Richard Wright, and Zora Neale Hurston to argue that the " 'southern tradition' is certainly not exclusively a conservative tradition" (745).

exorcised by means fair or foul. That liberals and radicals continue to denounce, if they even bother to acknowledge, the southern conservative tradition should not surprise us. It has ever been thus. That the repudiation of the southern conservative tradition has also become an ideological imperative among many conservatives is more arresting.

The reasons for this ideological warfare among conservatives are not hard to identify. The southern conservative tradition has long constituted the most impressive critique of American national development and, indeed, of the more disquieting aspects of the modern world. Since the antebellum period, southern conservative thought has evolved in ways that fundamentally challenge the celebration of the free market, of limitless material progress, and of the worldwide advance of democracy to which conservatives as diverse as William F. Buckley, Jr., Irving Kristol, Michael Novak, Francis Fukuyama, and Ronald Reagan have, in one sense or another, long been devoted.

Before the Civil War, southern thinkers' denunciation of free society was rooted in the emerging defense of slavery as a social system. Antebellum southern thinkers agreed with European socialists that the capitalist world was on the threshold of a protracted crisis from which it would not recover. From the perspective of the southern slaveholders and their spokesmen, slavery alone could ensure progress without the social dislocation, political upheaval, and moral confusion that tormented bourgeois society. For these men and women who took seriously the biblical injunction to be their brothers' keepers, slavery seemed the best means of preserving a Christian social order in the modern world.[2]

After the Civil War, this social, political, and moral vision proved impossible to sustain. Emancipation destroyed the social relations that nurtured the southern critique of free society and of the free labor system. Yet southern conservative thinkers since 1865, as before, continued to associate the deepening crisis of the modern world with the steady development of capitalism.

During the twentieth century the legatees of this conservative tradition, the Agrarians and their successors, have condemned the rise of the profit motive, the savagery of unrestrained economic competition, the growing obsession with material acquisition, the separation of the own-

---

2. See Eugene D. Genovese, *The Slaveholders' Dilemma: Freedom and Progress in Southern Conservative Thought, 1820–1860* (Columbia, S.C., 1992).

ership from the control of property, and the destructive exploitation of nature. They have viewed socialism of one form or another as the logical outcome of the ascendancy of corporate capitalism and the centralization of the power state.

With Karl Marx and Friedrich Engels, antebellum and twentieth-century southern conservative thinkers have regarded capitalism as the most revolutionary and destructive force in modern history. In its seemingly endless capacity for adaptation and accommodation, capitalism has been, these thinkers asserted, the force primarily responsible for the dissolution of traditional society. There, of course, the similarity ends. Marx and Engels applauded capitalism precisely for its destructive work; southern conservative thinkers to a man condemned it.

More important, twentieth-century southern conservative thinkers also denied that this imposing analysis of capitalism originated in the antebellum defense of slavery. They have been so intent to dissociate themselves and their tradition from slavery that they have denied it was the foundation of the antebellum southern social order.[3]

The legacy of slavery and racism is not the only affliction to trouble the heirs of this antebellum southern conservative tradition. The recent triumphs of conservatism—including what now passes for southern conservatism—in national politics have been engineered precisely in defense of the free market, the proliferation of consumer goods, the celebration of laissez-faire capitalism and the profit motive, and the pursuit of what C. B. McPherson identified as possessive individualism.[4] Southern conservative politicians might support legislation to impede the ravaging of nature as long as environmental interests do not interfere with making a profit. They are lyrical in their exaltation of multinational corporations. The recent emergence of a host of southern conservative politicians as leaders in the United States House of Representatives and the Senate

3. See Eugene D. Genovese, *The Southern Conservative Tradition: The Achievement and Limitations of an American Conservatism* (Cambridge, Mass., 1994), 79–80. Among the Agrarians, Allen Tate long struggled with the question of slavery. John Gould Fletcher acknowledged the centrality of slavery to southern social and political life. See John Gould Fletcher, *The Two Frontiers: A Study in Historical Psychology* (New York, 1930).

4. C. B. McPherson, *The Political Theory of Possessive Individualism: Hobbes to Locke* (New York, 1962). See also Elizabeth Fox-Genovese, "The Anxiety of History: The Southern Confrontation with Modernity," *Southern Cultures,* I (1993), 65–82, and Genovese, *The Southern Conservative Tradition,* 91–103.

does not promise a resurgence of the older brand of southern conservatism any more than did the election of Ronald Reagan.

Those who now identify themselves as southern conservatives remain conservative on certain cultural and social questions: gay rights, feminism, abortion, crime, immigration, welfare reform, family values, and similar issues. Philosophically, though, they are far removed from anything that resembles traditional southern conservatism. In one sense they are right-wing liberals who have departed from the historic conservatism of antebellum southerners as well as from that of the Agrarians.

These new southern conservatives espouse an optimistic view of human nature and emphasize human goodness and benevolence at the expense of the older Christian doctrine of human sinfulness. They continue to believe, with a naïve faith that is almost touching, in the inevitability of progress and in the efficacy of technology. In fact, Newt Gingrich is a disciple of the futurist Alvin Toffler and grows vertiginous in the presence of the technological gadgetry that he contends will at last not only improve but perfect society and the human race. The Agrarians would have been quick to identify and condemn his attitude as one more manifestation of the vain, false, sinful, and ultimately destructive desire to overcome the human condition in an effort to fashion a heaven on earth.[5]

Politically, too, the call for restrictions on federal power and the restoration of states' rights notwithstanding, these politicians are not conservative in the traditional sense at all. They combine elements of a reactionary populism and a radical nationalism that repudiates the brand of conservatism that has long appealed to southern thinkers. This odd conjunction reveals how easily radicalism and conservatism have come to coexist in the same movement and even in the same minds. As populists and nationalists, these politicians profess to put America first and actually show occasional sympathy for ordinary citizens in their struggle against a federal government that would oppress them with unresponsive bureaucracies, arcane regulations, and high taxes.

But as populists and nationalists, they also, in their quest for power, do not recoil from appealing to the worst fears, prejudices, and hatreds of the American people. In the end, they do not actually want to limit the power of the national government. It is, after all, so-called conser-

---

5. See Samuel Francis, "Gnostic Newt," *Chronicles: A Magazine of American Culture,* XIX (April, 1995), 8–9.

vatives who have advocated massive defense spending, promoted huge military bureaucracies, strengthened the police state, and burdened the American people for generations with "progressive" tax policies and the financial bailout of various corporations and banks.

Finally, in their views on foreign policy, Gingrich and company can hardly call themselves conservatives. They are, instead, revolutionaries of a sort, still intent on realizing their version of Woodrow Wilson's internationalist vision to remake the world in the American image. Their populism and nationalism have not bred in them isolationist sentiments. With few reservations, they are committed to the intervention of the United States everywhere around the world—and are devoted to the idea of American domination of the world—in the interest of advancing capitalism and democracy.[6] It is an empire that they seek, not a republic that they wish to preserve.

The defection of southern politicians from traditional southern conservatism both reflects and effects its rejection among ordinary southerners, who now embrace the prevailing conservative agenda almost without question. There are, in fairness, few alternatives available to them. The Agrarians and their successors have so far proven unable to craft and sustain a mass political following among their own people.

The inability to come to terms with slavery or to exercise much political influence has hampered but not paralyzed southern conservative thinkers. Since the late 1920s, the Agrarians and their successors have undertaken to reinterpret southern history, to reexamine the southern tradition, and to defend southern values when many Americans dismissed the South as a bastion of ignorance and a citadel of reaction. Their efforts have produced astonishingly original contributions to American social, cultural, political, and economic discourse—contributions that, nevertheless, remain incomplete and problematic.

Among the first and most gifted proponents of the southern cause in the twentieth century were John Crowe Ransom, Allen Tate, and Donald Davidson, who stood at the center of the Southern Agrarian movement and of the southern literary Renascence. This study focuses principally on their vision of southern history, their social and political thought,

---

6. See John Lukacs, *Outgrowing Democracy: A History of the United States in the Twentieth Century* (Washington, D.C., 1984), 327–41, and *The End of the Twentieth Century and the End of the Modern Age* (New York, 1993).

their confrontation with modernity, and their critique of its political and cultural expression in modernism.

According to the southern conservatives' reading of history, which Frank L. Owsley ably expounded, the yeomanry, not the slaveholding planters, dominated and shaped antebellum southern society, culture, and politics. In Owsley's view, which other southern thinkers such as Davidson, Andrew Lytle, and M. E. Bradford adopted, slavery was an unfortunate and unavoidable contingency that encumbered the development of the South and offered nothing essential to the order of southern society or to the character of its people.

Following Owsley, Davidson, for example, understood the South not as a slave society at all but as a traditional, agrarian society inhabited by "plain folk" who had created a unified, homogeneous culture: a kind of extended family, clan, or tribe. Similarly, Ransom and Tate, with somewhat different emphases, remained convinced that slavery had prevented the South from becoming the kind of society it should have been. Tate, in particular, could not have been clearer. The South, he argued, should have become a modern feudal society composed of southern lords and southern serfs who would assume the stewardship of traditional European values: hierarchy, duty, chivalry, reverence, piety, and faith.

These interpretations of southern history, influential as they have been among southern conservatives, will not suffice. Both obscure the greatest insight of antebellum southern thinkers, who recognized the plight of the modern world arising directly from the system of free labor and the character of free society. Southern conservative thinkers in the twentieth century have wanted nothing to do with slavery or its legacy, which has embarrassed and horrified them. But as Eugene D. Genovese has pointed out on more than one occasion, "they have yet to figure out how to defend and develop a world view the roots of which have been severed." [7]

The Southern Agrarians were dispossessed of the foundations upon which to construct a social and political alternative to capitalist society. The defeat of the Confederacy and the abolition of slavery shattered any hopes that antebellum southern conservative thinkers had of constructing a social, political, economic, and moral alternative to a capitalist social

---

7. Eugene D. Genovese, "Critical Legal Studies as Radical Politics and World View," *Yale Journal of Law & Humanities,* III (1991), 131–56, esp. 153.

order. Yet it did not diminish the commitment of their intellectual and spiritual descendants to formulate such an alternate society in the modern world.

The heirs to the southern conservative tradition in the twentieth century, particularly Ransom, Tate, and Davidson, saw the vast economic, political, social, and technological changes sweeping the modern world as detrimental not only to the regional integrity of the South but also to the future of civilization in the West. The Agrarian credo called for measures that "might promise to stop the advances of industrialism, or even undo some." If they could not prevent the defection of an entire generation of southerners to the "American industrial ideal," the Agrarians argued that the South would become an undifferentiated replica of the filthy industrial cities of the Northeast and the Midwest. Ransom, Tate, Davidson, and their compatriots believed that the South stood or fell upon southerners' willingness to resist the encroachments of industrialism and the allure of the market. They held little hope for survival of the southern tradition in a world governed by industrial councils and chambers of commerce.[8]

The Southern Agrarians refused to divest themselves of their cultural heritage, to define the southern tradition with reference to its defects, or to conform to the dictates of modernity. The South, they asserted, was not a moral abomination among the nations of the earth. Old-fashioned, homemade, long discredited southern ways might yet halt the threatened emergence of a new barbarism.

For the Agrarians, the southern tradition, even in defeat—perhaps especially in defeat—counseled restraint and humility before nature and God. Southern history, as they interpreted it, represented a moral alternative to the national myths of innocence, omnipotence, and invincibility. They exalted the mystery and contingency of life and admonished men and women to accept the conditions and limitations that God had imposed on them. They denounced all schemes to liberate human beings from history, society, family, and self and to remake them into "New Men" and "New Women" poised to enter a perfectly engineered earthly paradise. By contrast, they emphasized the experience of the South to expose the reality of sinfulness, depravity, evil, and tragedy in all human

8. All quotations in this paragraph come from "The Statement of Principles" in *ITMS*, xxxvii–xlviii.

affairs amid the growing conviction of American purity, righteousness, and power that characterized the 1920s.

Disparaging the American legend of unimpeded success, progress, and happiness, the Agrarians tried to dispel the illusion that virtue, morality, rectitude, and honor were confined within regional boundaries or national borders. They cautioned the victors not to revel too heartily in the defeat of their enemies, for they could be next. There was no guarantee of ultimate triumph, no assurance of inevitable victory, no matter how deep the conviction of righteousness. The abyss of history, Tate warned, was large enough for all.

In the end, the Agrarians struggled to confront the tragedy of their own history, which was embodied most fully in slavery and civil war. They were too honest and too honorable not to do so. The slaveholding class, its frauds and ogres notwithstanding, boasted a multitude of extraordinary men and women who were courageous, socially and morally responsible, God-fearing, and tough. Yet these same men and women were culpable for one of the greatest enormities of the nineteenth century, and their commitment to slavery doomed their world to ruin.

Southerners thus knew defeat intimately. They had witnessed the destruction of their world and, almost alone among citizens of the United States, understood what it meant to lose all that they cherished. As Tate put it, southerners had placed their faith in history, and in 1865, history had disappointed them.[9]

But Ransom, Tate, and Davidson did not revel in the defeat of the South or celebrate the lost cause. To fashion an image of the South as the good society, which could provide a moral if not always a concrete social and political alternative to the modern world, they set out to discredit the romantic vision of the Old South that emerged with emancipation and defeat. In broad outline the particulars of this romantic fantasy are familiar: the fragile southern belle dressed in a hoop-skirt emerging onto the veranda of the big house, her beguiling face partially concealed behind a Japanese fan; the breathtakingly handsome cavalier skilled in politics, dueling, warfare, and horsemanship, pledging all in defense of honor and country; the happy darky, undyingly loyal to master

---

9. See *MO*, 35–38. See also C. Vann Woodward, *The Origins of the New South, 1877–1913* (Rev. ed.; Baton Rouge, 1971), and *The Burden of Southern History* (3rd ed.; Baton Rouge, 1993).

and mistress, content to live out his days on the old home place as their servant and bondman. The creation of the romantic Old South by the generation who survived the Civil War was one southern response to the frustration, anger, shame, insecurity, and fear that arose from defeat.

Fifty years later, Ransom, Tate, and Davidson explicitly rejected the portrait of the Old South as the land of moonlight and magnolias. They renewed the attack of antebellum southern thinkers on the destructive power of capitalism and on the perils of unfettered individualism. They struggled to recover the complex history of the South that the postbellum generation of southern writers and thinkers had sentimentalized, distorted, or repressed. The Agrarians sought to use the history of the antebellum South not to console a people anguished by military defeat, economic collapse, political tumult, and social discord. They hoped instead to find in that history a vision of order that would enable them to resist the chaos of the modern age.

Because they could no longer ground their critique of modernity in the humane social relations of a traditional society, however, they had to confront modernity on its own terms. The Agrarians accepted what they could not change. Modernity, as it turned out, was one of the afflictions of life about which they could do nothing, or next to nothing. They had long ago lost the means to advance an effective critique and thus found themselves in the awkward position of having to accept much of the modern world, as Ransom wrote, "with a very bad grace" (*ITMS,* 22).

Before the Civil War, southern thinkers displayed every confidence that their society embodied the finest attributes of Western civilization. They thus tried to prevent the transformation that industrialism, capitalism, and individualism had effected in the North and in Western Europe from intruding on their world. Antebellum southern conservative thinkers were not alienated from society, as many of their northern and European counterparts were from theirs. Rather, southern conservatives identified closely with the social order of the South.

Southern conservative thinkers during the twentieth century have not been immune to the spiritual disease of the modern age: individualism. Torn loose from family, community, civic responsibility, history, and tradition, individualism has degenerated into a narcissism or a solipsism that has inhibited belief in any cause outside the self. For all their determination to imagine an alternative to modernity, the Southern Agrarians could not surmount the condition of man in the twentieth century. They were prisoners of their own psyches, and they knew it.

Trapped in a world in which the messianic cults of rationalism and scientism had fragmented traditional spiritual values, they had to resign themselves to lives without piety and faith. Even Davidson, who remained devoted to the Agrarian cause throughout his life, had reluctantly to acknowledge this crippling spiritual disability. The predicament of modern man, Tate reminded him, could not be ignored or willed out of existence. It was the spiritual milieu of the age. Although Davidson never gave up the fight, he was, at times, a solitary warrior. His was a private civil war waged against the excesses of this "century of no belief." [10]

Since at least the eighteenth century, the autonomous individual has stood at the center of the universe as the measure of all things. Antebellum southern thinkers did not reject individualism per se, but they did denounce the triumph of a radical subjectivity that threatened to demolish objective standards of value, judgment, and morality. Indeed, the defense of slavery was predicated on the renunciation of such radical subjectivity as the proper basis for civilized social order. Individualism in the antebellum South was reserved to white, male property owners. No one not fully a proprietor of himself could be the proprietor of another. Slave society thus required the acceptance of social stratification, legitimate authority, and mutual obligations among people of different social classes, *i.e.,* masters and slaves.

Southern conservative thinkers in the twentieth century have concurred with their antebellum forebears that the prevailing effect of modern thought has been the destruction of objectivity. The collapse into subjectivity in knowledge, belief, and morality, they have contended, has produced social atomization and individual estrangement from God, nature, and one's fellow human beings. The conflicts between man and God, man and nature, and man and society are the substance of much modern literature and thought. Southern thinkers and writers, including the Agrarians and their followers, have had to concede, and to take as their subject, the triumph of individualism and subjectivity and the ensuing disintegration of faith, piety, and order. They no longer enjoyed the luxury of criticizing modernity from the outside or of painstakingly

10. Donald Davidson, "Woodlands, 1956–1960," in *Poems, 1922–1961* (Minneapolis, 1966), 20.

considering other options. They have been compelled by events to describe, understand, and explain the modern world or at least to find a way of living in it.

Antebellum southern writers and thinkers, by contrast, could assert that no one was anyone by himself. To become fully human, everyone had to belong to a community, and obedience, discipline, and submission were the price of belonging, the price of being human. They believed that men and women could establish their individual identities only by fulfilling their prescribed roles within a stable, hierarchical, and duly constituted society. Writing of antebellum southern literature, Elizabeth Fox-Genovese has suggested the social character of its heroes: "Antebellum southern literature does not offer stories of heroes wracked by anxiety or beset by existential dilemmas. The function of the southern hero is to embody a special kind of socially grounded individual excellence, the very antithesis of the rootless bourgeois individualism. Typically, the southern hero owes his identity to his identification with society, rather than his struggles against it."[11]

Caught in the maelstrom of the twentieth century, Ransom, Tate, and Davidson struggled to fashion and articulate an ideal that Richard M. Weaver labeled "social bond individualism." By the late 1930s, however, other tendencies had already emerged in southern literature and thought. These alternate inclinations are perhaps best exemplified by the work of Robert Penn Warren.

A student at Vanderbilt University during the early 1920s (he graduated in 1925), Warren early came under the influence of Ransom, Tate, and Davidson.[12] He remained devoted to his Agrarian friends and consistently identified with their movement and their cause. Warren maintained throughout his life an abiding interest in and commitment to the South and its history, but by the early 1930s, he had already begun to separate himself in decisive ways from the fundamental principles and premises that the Agrarians espoused.

Unlike Ransom, Tate, and Davidson, Warren concluded that to overcome the spiritual anarchy of the twentieth century, modern men had to endure it alone. They could not draw a sense of identity, value, and

11. Fox-Genovese, "The Anxiety of History," 76.
12. See Daniel Joseph Singal, *The War Within: From Victorian to Modernist Thought in the South, 1919–1945* (Chapel Hill, 1982), 340–49.

meaning from the society in which they lived, for, properly speaking, the social bonds that had once provided such cohesion no longer existed. Rather, modern men, severed from the past and the future, could only create a place, a purpose, and an identity for themselves in the present.

For Warren, the past existed only in the consciousness of the individual, to do with as he would. It carried no more meaning than men were willing to ascribe to it. By contrast, Tate may have viewed modern men as isolated from the heroic dignity and magnificence of the past, but the past remained the repository of all that was once noble and heroic. Davidson's sense of history demanded continuity between the past, the present, and the future. History, for him, provided access to tradition: the timeless and unchanging source of identity, order, and meaning in the modern world.

Warren, on the contrary, understood history as provisional, relative, and contingent. Knowledge of history, like knowledge of the self, was a human construct that offered no innate value or meaning. If modern men wanted history to mean something, if they wanted to locate themselves in time and mold their identities, they would have to do so themselves. Yet Warren insisted that, whatever the disabilities under which they labored, modern men were obliged to create values and meaning if they hoped to transcend the essential chaos of the modern world. It was simply that society, history, tradition, and faith tendered little help or solace in this endeavor. Modern men lived without certainty, subject to, and striving against, anxiety, anomie, rootlessness, subjectivity, and loneliness.

The themes of modern alienation and the quest for meaning in a fragmented world distinguish Warren's most important fiction, especially his masterpiece *All the King's Men*. These ideas found their way into much of his other writing as well, most notably perhaps his meditation on the Civil War. In *The Legacy of the Civil War*, published in 1961, Warren acknowledged that the war marked for Americans the "Homeric period" of national history, in which the figures "loom[ed] up only a little less than gods."[13] Although the book attests to Warren's enduring interest in the South, the interpretation of war that he proposed could hardly have delighted many of his fellow Agrarians.

13. Robert Penn Warren, *The Legacy of the Civil War: Meditations on the Centennial* (New York, 1961), 82, hereinafter cited parenthetically by page number in the text.

Abraham Lincoln, Warren intimated, stood out as the modern hero of the war. Lincoln's ethical pragmatism and intellectual flexibility enabled him to impose meaning on the indeterminacy and chaos of events. Unlike the doctrinaire abolitionists and the rigid fire-eaters, both of whom believed that they had a monopoly on truth and, as a consequence, could not adjust to rapid changes in circumstance, Lincoln advocated a "tentative, experimental, 'open' approach to the life process." Following the historians David Donald and T. Harry Williams and the philosopher Sidney Hook, to whom the work is dedicated, Warren argued that Lincoln's thought and conduct were distinguished by an essential pragmatism (41, 17−18).

The New England abolitionists tolerated no challenge to their opposition to slavery and were unwilling to submit their views to the arbitration of reason. They believed their actions to be guided by Providence. All virtue and righteousness were theirs, as they prepared for "the arbitrament of blood," even if it required the universal slaughter of victim and oppressor and the dissolution of society itself. Warren affirmed that the abolitionists' cause was just and that they often pursued it from admirable motives, but he was equally distressed "by the picture of the joyful mustering of the darker forces of our nature in that just cause" (20−23).

The abolitionists, Warren argued, appealed to a "higher law" that denied the very concept of society. Individual conscience, not custom, tradition, or piety, was foremost in determining social action. The Transcendentalists, who contributed the philosophical underpinnings of abolitionism, had renounced society. They abdicated not conscience but the intellectual and social responsibility that must accompany every act of conscience. According to Warren, they sensed that as men of letters they were losing their status and power to merchants, manufacturers, and financiers. Although determined to reform society, these men sought at the same time not to contaminate, defile, or compromise themselves by becoming involved with business or politics. Instead, they maintained their innocence by withdrawing from society into "the infinitude of the individual." Warren wrote: "Having lost access to power and importance in the world of affairs, these men repudiated all the institutions in which power is manifested—church, state, family, law, business. . . . For all things were equally besmirched and besmirching to the ineffable and quivering purity" (29, 27).

After the defeat of the Confederacy and the supposed reconstruction of the South, northern society as a whole developed what Warren called the "Treasury of Virtue." In triumph, northerners could feel redeemed by history for all the sins of mankind, past, present, and future. This self-righteousness, this moral narcissism was, Warren declared, a "peculiarly unlovely and unlovable trait" (71). It encouraged in northerners an arrogance and self-assurance that made them reckless and irresponsible, willing to act without giving thought to the consequences. Since their intentions were good and their hearts were virtuous, every enterprise, northerners congratulated themselves, would automatically be rewarded with success. The North and its people were morally unassailable.

Nothing in Warren's critique of the North would have drawn fire from even the most staunch defenders of the Agrarian creed. The South, however, did not escape Warren's critical attention. If he condemned the individual absolutism of the abolitionists, according to which each man constituted his own majority and his own law, he also chastised the fire-eaters who exalted the moral authority of society over the individual.

Antebellum southern thinkers did not deny the concept of society. Instead, Warren wrote, they denied "the very concept of life" in their defense of an "anachronistic and inhuman" social system (34). While northern opponents of slavery believed that they were carrying out God's will on earth, southern defenders of slavery ceased to engage in self-criticism. The South became, in Warren's analysis, a closed society, silencing condemnation of its values, institutions, and way of life. After the debates over slavery that took place in the Virginia legislature during 1831 and 1832, southern thinkers could operate only as apologists for the South. "If in the North the critic had repudiated society," Warren concluded, "in the South society had repudiated the critic." In the southern apologia, "there was little space for the breath of life, no recognition of the need for fluidity, growth, and change which life is" (36–39).

Southerners, too, developed their own rationalization for the outcome of the war. Warren defined it as the "Great Alibi," for it permitted southerners to declare their innocence. It released them from the responsibility for illiteracy, poverty, racism, violence, and corruption, enabling them to transform vices into virtues and defeat into victory. It eroded the will to face the complex and intractable problems that dominated southern life after the war. So grim, traumatic, and devastating were the effects of the war that southerners evaded the reality of them. They preferred instead the fanciful contemplation of hopeless valor and lost glory.

Both the "Treasury of Virtue" and the "Great Alibi" facilitated the escape from self-criticism and historical reality that human beings, in their weakness, craved. The "Treasury of Virtue" and the "Great Alibi" thus prevented the contemplation of the tragedy of civil war, essential to a deeper understanding of the human condition. Neither the victors, the vanquished, nor their descendants had the fortitude to accept the truth that life is ambiguous, indeterminate, and unpredictable. "We fear . . . to lose the comforting automatism of the Great Alibi or the Treasury of Virtue, for if we lose them we may, at last, find ourselves nakedly alone with the problems of our time and ourselves," Warren wrote. "Where would we find our next alibi and our next assurance of virtue?" (76).

The continuing appeal of the Civil War, for Warren, derived from no simple piety of blood, kin, region, or cause. The war gripped the national imagination because of its haunting complexity. Historians could not easily sort it out into a simple conflict between good and evil. The war, because it divided a nation against itself, acted a private drama for Americans. The "dark inner conflicts" that tormented Abraham Lincoln and Jefferson Davis, Ulysses S. Grant and Robert E. Lee, reflected the deeper agonies of a nation tearing itself apart.

The Founding Fathers, from Warren's perspective, were strong, practical, intelligent, and confident. The heroes of the Civil War were men of a different sort. They attained fortitude and wisdom not only from their military and political exploits but also from their encounters with the tumultuous convulsions of the soul. These were modern men, and the attraction that the Civil War held for subsequent generations of Americans derived from the interiority of the experience. In their efforts to overcome strife and division, to establish a clear purpose, and to fashion an identity amid the riot of events, the men who fought the war mirrored the aspirations, disappointments, and fears of Americans in the late twentieth century.

For Warren, southern history in general, and the history of the Civil War in particular, became utterly personal and individual. He acknowledged the importance of community and collective identity, but in the end, he believed, the anguish and fascination of southern history and the Civil War reduced "to problems of our personal histories and individual acts." In their contemplation of the war, contemporary Americans, Warren hoped, might confirm their common humanity and affirm the tragic dignity of life. If Americans were to find any meaning in the war beyond its "monstrous inhumanity," however, they would have to create it themselves "from the complex and confused motives of men and the blind ruck of event" (102, 108).[14] If individual men and women did not bring such order out of chaos, they condemned themselves to live always in the brutal confusion and the fatal ambivalence of the moment.

Those who have accepted the inherent ambiguity of modern life may find alluring Warren's vision of history and the self, but in important ways that vision represented the antithesis of Southern Agrarianism. Ransom, Tate, and Davidson sought to locate and ground meaning, or at least to find refuge, in a collective, not an individual, sensibility and experience. Of course, though all three shared many of the same commitments and apprehensions, they also differed sharply among themselves in their interpretations of the southern tradition and in their responses to the modern world.

By 1937, when Ransom departed Vanderbilt for Kenyon College in Gambier, Ohio, he, like Warren, had begun to edge away from the Agrarian movement. He found that economic analysis and political agitation compromised his identity as a poet and a critic. Ransom had to choose between the life of an activist and reformer, committed to realizing an ideological vision, and the life of a poet and critic, committed to seeing the world in all its stubborn contingency. Yet, again like Warren, Ransom carried with him a dedication to certain aspects of the Agrarian philosophy that he never relinquished. More fully than Davidson, Ransom made his peace with the modern world of cities and factories, but he insisted at the same time that science and reason were not the sole repositories of truth and, in fact, obscured as much as they revealed and explained. He proposed instead an aesthetic vision of reality in which the whole of experience was beyond the compass of reason or the senses.

The aesthetic appreciation of the "world's body," Ransom's description of the abundance and substance of reality, would restrain the unwholesome appetites and destructive passions of humanity. It would force civilized men to savor and cherish the things of this world, not merely to take, dominate, or exploit them. Ransom's Agrarianism and his aesthetic flowed into and out of each other. They were, at crucial junctures,

14. See Fox-Genovese, "The Anxiety of History," 79–80.

mutually conditioning and reinforcing. Ransom jettisoned much of the political and economic content of Agrarianism or, at least, ceased to concern himself with it. Yet he remained determined to prevent the unqualified triumph of the scientific and industrial world view, even as he could do little to halt the advance of science and industry themselves.

The South proved less accommodating and congenial to Ransom's aesthetic than he originally imagined. Nonetheless, he did not abandon the notion that sensitive men and women, especially artists and writers not easily at home in the world of science and industry, had to live somewhere. Unlike Warren, he was not ready to plunge humanity into the vortex of time and change in the perilous quest for meaning and identity. Truth, for Ransom, may not have resided in history, tradition, or faith any more than it did in reason and science, but the aesthetic experience of life had to be refined. Civilized men and women had to keep their distance from the world.

To that end, Ransom envisaged a "community of letters" growing up naturally among the wise and humane souls whom the "real" world would have humiliated, tortured, and destroyed. This independent community of letters offered freedom, encouragement, inspiration, and solace to writers, whose allegiance, in turn, liberated them from the burdens of patriotism, piety, history, and tradition. For Ransom, men of letters thus existed outside of society and occupied a special realm. He may have posited the community of letters as an antidote to the most remorseless aspects of the modern scientific-industrial world, but his assertion of an independent realm of letters occupied by writers shorn of their primary loyalty to any history, tradition, society, or faith owed much to the triumph of bourgeois individualism and modern subjectivity that southern conservative thinkers had long disclaimed.

Allen Tate never retreated from his Agrarian principles. He thought the South distinct from the rest of the United States and argued that it represented the last and greatest flowering of medieval European civilization. Both the European and the southern traditions he saw as standing fast against the emerging capitalist world order.

Tate came to believe, however, that the Agrarians had confounded secular and sacred history, exalting the South as a holy nation, the embodiment of God's will on earth. The Agrarians, he concluded, like their antebellum forebears, mistakenly judged the South to be constitutionally unique among nations. The South, they resolved, was a divinely ordained, redemptive community that would save mankind from the disappointment and torment of history.

Tate's letters reveal that he sensed this problem in the Agrarian movement as early as 1929. Not until his conversion to Roman Catholicism in 1950, however, did he describe clearly and fully what theologians identify as the gnostic heresy: the belief that men, through the possession of some secret knowledge, can alter the nature of being and transform the human condition. Unwittingly and unintentionally, Tate suggested, the Agrarians had exalted the contingent and the historical over the divine and the eternal. The Agrarians were themselves guilty of misconstruing the South as the source of redemptive power and the instrument of God's will and grace. They entertained the beguiling possibility, which they always criticized in their opponents, that the South might escape the burdens of original sin.

At their finest, Tate reminded his fellow Agrarians, southerners had long been wary of such utopian designs. They believed that they lived in a fallen world, which rendered impossible the expectation of heaven on earth. They also believed in the sinfulness of man, which saved them from disregarding the complications of human nature and the human condition. The benefits of the traditional southern way of life, Tate understood, were many. Men and women born and raised in the South knew who they were and where they belonged. Consequently, they knew where they were going or at least where they ought to be going.

The temptation to see the world as ultimately fathomable, ultimately rational, and thus ultimately pliant and controllable, was, Tate pointed out, as old as mankind. It had assumed a special virulence in an age of mass communication and advanced technology. Whatever the form, the dream had always been the same: the achievement of power, progress, and perfection in this world. The Agrarians, like their antebellum counterparts, failed to realize that the nearer the South approached its moment of perfection, the nearer it came to beginning its decline.

The death of individuals and societies was the condition of life on earth after exile from the Garden. The unique history of the South and the common misfortune of its people were not enough, Tate maintained, to deliver southerners from the fate that all nations and peoples had to endure. Redemption came not through fidelity to a particular history, culture, or tradition, as important as those might be in revealing man's proper relations to nature and to God and in sustaining an image of the transcendent. The transformation of history, culture, and tradition into objects of worship was, Tate asserted, an act of idolatry. Severed from their connection to the divine and the eternal and set up as ends in themselves, even the most decent and virtuous of human constructs would disintegrate.

For Davidson, on the contrary, the history, culture, and tradition of the South alone afforded a set of images and principles by which to live. Davidson never relinquished his stalwart opposition to pragmatism, rationalism, industrialism, and science. He was convinced that together these outrages had diminished the efficacy of poetry, destroyed the primacy of myth, and eroded the traditional social order of the South. Davidson mourned the loss of a distinct sense of family and place that attended the rise of science and industry and brought a deadening conformity and an appalling bewilderment to modern life. Yet he, too, often felt helpless and frustrated before these mighty and imponderable forces of change.

Davidson set himself a difficult task. He sought to transmute the history of the South into myth. Critics and colleagues alike accused him of indulging in caprice, fancy, romantic nostalgia, even "mystical secularism." They had a point but were too quick to dismiss Davidson's efforts as frivolous, misguided, or illusory. Davidson looked upon the modern world with a discerning eye. He saw its suffering and its sorrow. To compensate for the miserable state of the modern world, Davidson tried to devise a way, not of avoiding, but of dealing with reality by infusing the life of his community with purpose and hope.

The myth of the South that Davidson attempted to recover would, he believed, redeem time, place, and world, for the myth emphasized constancy over change and rendered ordinary life meaningful by linking it with ancestral memory. Davidson's myth was secular and thus risked imputing spiritual authority to a commonly revered culture and history, to flesh, blood, and bone, rather than to God. Piety for the South did in some sense replace in Davidson's thought the sacred, transcendent dimension of meaning. The myth, like the society that it represented, was thus subject to the merciless vicissitudes of time.

Davidson fought a courageous rear-guard action against an encroaching modernity. The Scopes trial of 1925 represented the intrusion of science into the South. It posed a direct threat to Christian fundamentalism, to say nothing of encouraging outside interference with southern customs, values, and institutions. Although the Scopes trial did not prompt Davidson or the other Agrarians to take up arms against an insurgent modernism, it did provide a convenient symbol on which to fasten their disgust and anger at the national mockery of the South and its people.[15]

World War I had a subtler and more enduring influence on Davidson's thought and, perhaps, on the development of Southern Agrarianism in general. Not only was World War I the first industrial war in which technology was systematically applied to the slaughter of human beings. It was also a cataclysmic event that pushed the world into the twentieth century. Yet, ironically, at the outbreak of war Europeans on both sides of the conflict welcomed it as an adventure that would release them from the petty materialism of the nineteenth century. War would create moral men and a moral society by ridding the world of selfishness, greed, and ambition. Initially, many Europeans regarded this war as perhaps the greatest exaltation of the human spirit in history.

Disillusionment set in quickly and was devastating. The war, rather than offering an adventure that exalted the human spirit, proved dull, tedious, bureaucratic, and unheroic. At the same time, the war was an unprecedented festival of mechanized violence and death. For the postwar generation of European writers and thinkers, World War I destroyed the ideals of enlightenment and the belief in the inevitability of material and moral progress that had characterized the eighteenth and nineteenth centuries. The French poet and essayist Paul Valéry captured the mood of his generation in 1919: "We modern civilizations have learned to recognize that we are mortal. . . . We feel that a civilization is as fragile as life."[16]

Southerners who took part in World War I, as Davidson and Ransom did, were less apt to suffer the same disillusionment. Within recent memory, their ancestors had lost a great war. They were conditioned to accept defeat and were thus not predisposed to imagine a blissful future. They could not look back on centuries of matchless glory or look forward to centuries of uninterrupted progress. History had not vindicated their aspirations to independence or sanctioned their convictions of superiority. They knew that civilization was tenuous and intermittent.

15. See Singal, *The War Within*, 200–201, 398 n. 5.

16. Quoted in Hans Kohn, "The Crisis in European Thought and Culture," in *World War I: A Turning Point in Modern History*, ed. Jack J. Roth (New York, 1967), 28.

In 1930, when the Agrarians took their stand, portions of the traditional South remained relatively untouched by science, capitalism, and individualism, the solvent forces of modernity. The Agrarians' original objective was not only to perpetuate and revitalize the southern tradition but to forge it into a weapon with which to combat the absurdity and meaninglessness of a faithless world.

In practical terms, of course, they failed. They never organized an Agrarian political party or even secured control of a wing of the Democratic party, as Ransom once suggested they try to do. The Agrarians, like later generations of southern conservative thinkers, encountered huge difficulties in organizing a mass political movement. Frequently, they also came close to making themselves look foolish by appearing to be the enemies of science, industry, and, indeed, of reason itself.

But the Agrarians never intended politics to define their undertaking. Their principal concern was with the spiritual condition of man in the modern world. Nor did they mindlessly repudiate reason, science, or even industry. Rather, they questioned the messianic cults of rationalism, scientism, and industrialism. Whatever contradictions obscured the Agrarians' interpretation of southern history, they agreed, at least for a time, that the southern tradition offered another, and better, way of ordering modern life.

The essence of Agrarian thought lies in its persuasive challenge to the assumption that heaven can be made immanent, can be established on earth. The Agrarians forcefully exposed the treachery, persecution, violence, and tyranny that informed the millennial ambitions of modern man. Modern men, the Agrarians recognized, claimed for themselves a knowledge, and thus a power, to which they had neither right nor entitlement. Ransom, Tate, Davidson, and their colleagues knew where such declarations would lead.

Their analyses read like a summary of the contemporary predicament. They anticipated the rejection of Christian pessimism and the acceptance of the idea that human nature is innately good or at least is a "blank slate" on which social scientists and behavioral therapists can inscribe an appropriate personality. They foresaw the decline in education, so that today American schools, colleges, and universities are at best intellectual factories to prepare students to produce and consume a dizzying array of goods and services. They predicted the degradation of nature and the degeneration of freedom into license and knew the calamity that the autonomous self could visit upon the rest of humanity when liberated from a sense of responsibility to society, to nature, and to God.

By focusing on the Agrarian thought of John Crowe Ransom, Allen Tate, and Donald Davidson, we can see more clearly the origins and development of southern conservatism in the twentieth century. Their contributions expose the lines of argument and of tension within the southern conservative tradition itself, for they rarely agreed on what kind of society the South had or what southern history meant. Indeed, their analyses of southern history differ so markedly from one another that it is difficult, if not impossible, finally to confirm a single image of the South to which they were devoted.

Although the basis of the southern tradition proved more elusive than Ransom, Tate, and Davidson imagined during the 1920s and 1930s, they nonetheless regarded preserving it as the best way to save the rudiments of Christian civilization in the West. They defined the nature of that civilization as the continual struggle for discipline, self-control, and order against latitude, excess, and chaos.

At the end of the twentieth century, we endure the consequences of a total emancipation from the moral heritage of Christianity. We have at last achieved the "rights of man." Two centuries of technological progress have brought us access to such a quantity and quality of goods and services that we enjoy a level of material comfort and security inconceivable only a few generations ago. Yet we now also believe that luxury, leisure, and unlimited freedom in the selection of pleasures are the epitome of "the good life."

Ransom, Tate, Davidson, and the tradition they honored stood against the notion that the pursuit of power and prosperity ought to be the sole, or even the principal, aim of life. They set themselves at odds with the champions of that kind of progress and endorsed what Richard M. Weaver called "*the last non-materialist civilization in the Western World*" (*STB*, 391). As one not southern by birth or conservative by conviction, I have come to admire their deep reverence for, and their brave devotion to, the South. In the end, history may prove them to have been more right than wrong, for the celebrated achievements of science and technology and the apparent triumph of democracy and individualism will not redeem the enormities of the twentieth century.

1

Ransom's Agrarian Aesthetic:
What These Have Done in Love

The sons of the fathers shall keep her, worthy of
What these have done in love.
— John Crowe Ransom, "Antique Harvesters"

THE THIRD MOMENT

Science, according to John Crowe Ransom, brought the modern world
to the level of civilization enjoyed by a refined caveman. Modern scientists entertained grandiose fantasies of subjugating nature; they appealed to men's base predatory impulses. Indeed, the logic of science was
not entirely human, Ransom thought, but paralleled the instincts of the
beasts. Biology relentlessly determined animal needs and animal desires.
Businessmen, inspired by scientists, devised sophisticated and efficient
economic mechanisms to gratify those same purely animal cravings
in men.

A starving man, for example, performed an animal act in looking for
food. He was, Ransom supposed, unlikely to develop a special attachment to, or a sentimental fondness for, the food set before him. As an
animal, and a starving animal at that, the man instinctively activated his
scientific and economic inclinations. He sought only a series of commodities (bread, meat, potatoes, wine) within an infinite range of variety
and substitution. He longed for no particular kind of food prepared in a
special way. Any morsel that filled his stomach and ended his hunger
pangs, no matter how tasteless and unsavory, would do.[1]

Ransom certainly did not begrudge a meal to a starving fellow.
"Work-forms," as he called them, like science and economics, were in-

1. See *WB*, 221–24.

dispensable to the welfare of society. They were recipes for maximum efficiency, shorthand formulas for the attainment of natural pleasures and necessary comforts. Scientific and economic labor, he conceded, enhanced the production and distribution of goods requisite to security and survival, enabling men to indulge their aesthetic sensibilities without disregarding the necessary business of life.

But men could not live by bread alone, any more than they could live in a perfectly rationalized, scientific utopia. Few were content to submit to the fastidious authority of scientists, businessmen, and economists bent on eradicating inefficiency from the human condition. The ideal of efficient animality, Ransom contended, was not good enough for human beings. The traditional complications of human nature ensured that men would cultivate irrational affinities for "precious objects" that had no practical utility or market value whatsoever: an old house, an old horse, an old wife. Any attempt to alter this arrangement, however scientifically advantageous or economically lucrative, would bring not bliss but misery.[2]

Scientists and businessmen necessarily repressed the subversive aspects of experience that resisted easy analysis, classification, and use. They thus projected an incomplete and superficial understanding of nature. Ransom detected in their work no expression of love for that stubborn complex of particular things that made up the "world's body." Instead, he discerned only an endless sequence of experiments, deliberations, and adjustments undertaken to confirm their own oversights, miscalculations, and prejudices.[3]

What incentive prompted artists to write, to paint, to sculpt, or to compose? Artists were first, but perhaps not foremost, men. As men confronting the world, Ransom insisted, artists, like scientists and businessmen, were tempted to confine it immediately to functional proportions. They reverted quite as naturally as other men to the disposition to acquire and exploit. But artists, again like scientists and businessmen, had fashioned a discipline of their own. Poets, painters, sculptors, and composers adhered to a hard doctrine that enabled them to resist their instinctive preferences. Art restrained the natural man in the artist. The aesthetic sensibility was intentionally inefficient. "Aesthetic forms . . . do

2. See *ibid.,* 30–32, 37–38, 222–27.
3. See *ibid.,* 63–68, 120–28, 208–11.

not butter our bread," Ransom wrote, "and they delay the eating of it" (*WB*, 31). The exercise of the aesthetic sensibility deliberately inhibited and hindered men, facilitating their journey from nature to culture.

The purpose of society was not to confirm the existence of natural men in a natural environment but to nourish those qualities that made humane life possible. "The object of proper society," Ransom asserted, "is to instruct its members how to transform instinctive experience into aesthetic experience" (*WB*, 42). Custom, ritual, and tradition, honor, friendship, and romance, all complicated human action.

The "natural man," whom Ransom feared was becoming more prevalent in the modern world, insistently asserted his rights as an individual and regarded everything and everyone as objects of prey. He led a stupidly appetitive, brutally economic existence. The "social man," by contrast, willingly submitted to the restraint of convention and code. Contemplative and dignified, the social man veered from the severely logical course in pursuit of his objectives and thus realized the joys of the aesthetic life. He was fit for more than primitive diversions and animal pleasures.[4] By extending the aesthetic sensibility beyond the realm of art, Ransom hoped that all men could apprehend the invincible, inexhaustible, indissoluble contingency of nature that would not countenance human domination. The world, according to Ransom's aesthetic, was a diffuse assemblage of discrete, unique, and particular objects. To know an object aesthetically was to know it in all its characteristic particularity as an individual thing. To know an object scientifically was to know it in its abstract universality as a categorical idea, which, for Ransom, meant not to know it at all. Aesthetic cognition accepted reality in all its contingency and knew it in all its heterogeneity without anticipating the dialectical resolution of conflict or contradiction.[5]

Poetry embodied this reality. The poet represented it. The critic made it intelligible. Without poetry and its critical exegesis, Ransom contended, men's knowledge of reality was fragmented and incomplete. Poetry, he argued, "will always undertake to tell more truth about the world

4. See *ibid.*, 46–54, 212–20. See also Louis D. Rubin, Jr., "A Critic Almost Anonymous: John Crowe Ransom Goes North," in *The New Criticism and After*, ed. Thomas Daniel Young (Charlottesville, 1976), 1–21, and *The Wary Fugitives: Four Poets and the South* (Baton Rouge, 1978), 267–92.

5. See *WB*, 111–42, 231–32. See also *NC*, 279–336; *PE*, 88–108; and "Criticism as Pure Speculation," in *SE*, 128–46.

of its discourse than science cares to tell, or with its limited purpose needs to tell" (*NC,* 93). Poetic truth revealed a world that exceeded easy definition. Scientific inquiry lost sight of the complex objectivity of the world and fashioned a false world after its own likeness. Ransom would no doubt have approved the homely image of science as a tautological dog chasing its own tail in a meaningless circle.

Only through poetry could men recover "the body and solid substance of the world." Poetry, in Ransom's unusual chronology, came after science and restored the world of whole and infeasible objects that science had destroyed. The poem provided an organic model of reality, sheltering men from the analytical incursions of science that impaired their ability to recall the original fecundity of the world out of which poetry itself was born. The "world's body" had retreated into memory and longing. But from the fullness of memory men made poetry, which was the aesthetic counterpart to the fullness of nature.[6]

The intolerable disorder of modern times required a governing principle. Neither politics nor economics, neither morality nor philosophy, neither religion nor science could provide it. The aesthetic sensibility expressed in the structure and the content of poetry alone, Ransom thought, would supply the necessary vision of order. He contemplated an order so radical and iconoclastic, though, that the scientist would find it incomprehensible.[7] The knowledge that men would attain and record through poetry would be a kind of knowledge fit only for a new kind of world.

As early as 1925, Ransom had contemplated a philosophical analysis of poetic experience. He wrote to the British poet, critic, and novelist Robert Graves that he hoped to secure a Guggenheim Fellowship for 1926 or 1927 that would enable him to travel to England, where he could write in a more stimulating environment than Nashville provided.[8] Ransom's ideas, as his letters to Graves show, were as yet unfocused and inchoate. He failed to win a Guggenheim but obtained a sabbatical from Vanderbilt University that made possible six months of uninterrupted writing.

6. See *WB,* x. See also René Wellek's insightful "John Crowe Ransom's Theory of Poetry," in *Literary Theory and Structure: Essays in Honor of William K. Wimsatt,* ed. Frank Brady, Jon Palmer, and Martin Price (New Haven, 1973), 184–86.

7. See *WB,* 45.

8. See *SL,* 142–49.

During the summer of 1926, Ransom, along with his wife Robb and their children Reavill and Helen, left Nashville not for England but for Indian Hills, Colorado, a small town located in the foothills of the Rocky Mountains approximately twenty miles southwest of Denver. When he returned to Nashville in December, Ransom carried with him a manuscript of over two hundred pages that represented, as he had earlier written to Edwin Mims, the chairman of the Department of English at V anderbilt, and to Allen Tate, a first attempt to treat systematically "a great mass of observations I have to make about literature."[9]

Early in 1927 Ransom submitted "The Third Moment" to Harper and Brothers, which returned the manuscript to him with recommendations for extensive revision. For years, according to his biographer Thomas Daniel Young, Ransom kept the manuscript on his desk, always intending to make the changes that Harper and Brothers required. He never did. In the preface to *The World's Body*, published in 1938, Ransom finally disclosed the fate the manuscript met at his hands. The manuscript was, he had concluded, beyond recovery. Abstract and ponderous, it would never do as a general theory of aesthetics. Ransom thus granted himself "the pleasure of consigning [it] to the flames" (*WB*, vii).[10]

"The Third Moment" contained the essence of the aesthetic theory that Ransom would later elaborate in more than one hundred essays and in his three most important critical texts: *God Without Thunder: An Unorthodox Defense of Orthodoxy, The World's Body,* and *The New Criticism,* published in 1930, 1938, and 1941, respectively. Although Ransom destroyed "The Third Moment," he supplied a detailed synopsis of its contents in a series of remarkable letters written to Allen Tate during the period of its composition.

On September 5, 1926, about a month after he and his family arrived at Indian Hills, Ransom wrote to Tate to define the "three moments in the historical order of experience" on which he focused his aesthetic vision. The "first moment" constituted the original experience of perception that was preconceptual, unreflective, and unique. The first moment, Ransom declared, was "pure of all intellectual content." The experience of the first moment was not the act of a sophisticated, mature,

---

9. See *ibid.*, 157–63. The Reavills, Mrs. Ransom's family, were from Denver.
10. See also Thomas Daniel Young, *Gentleman in a Dustcoat: A Biography of John Crowe Ransom* (Baton Rouge, 1976), 174.

adult mind. The experience may have been intense, perhaps overwhelming, but once the moment passed, the feeling of exhilaration died away and the subject returned to a careless stupor or was distracted by some other external stimulus.

The "second moment" in the historical order of experience distinguished human beings from beasts. For the cows grazing in yonder field, the original first moment was sufficient. They had neither the need nor the capacity for contemplation beyond the original experience. Not so with man. Human beings, Ransom noted, were rational creatures. In the second moment reason asserted itself and cognition took place. Men, in the second moment, formulated concepts that recorded the experience of the first moment that had just transpired. The second moment marked the beginning of science. The ends of cognition and science were practical and utilitarian; the means were analytical. Science and cognition abstracted portions of the original experience from the organic, preconceptual whole.

Although the second moment made possible language and knowledge, it was, for Ransom, ultimately an unsatisfying basis for aesthetic experience. During the second moment, Ransom told Tate, "experience becomes History, conceptualized knowledge, in respect to a part, and Unconscious Knowledge, lost knowledge, in respect to the vast residue of the unconceptual." He continued: "So also is generated the cognitive or scientific habit; which is that which disposes us to shorten the subsequent First moments of our experience to the minimum, to dwell upon subsequent fresh experiences only long enough to reduce them as here; and which is so powerful when formed that many of us unquestionably spend most of our waking lives in entertaining or arriving at concepts" (SL, 155). History and science, though, provided an inadequate transcript of reality. In the "third moment" men became aware of the deficiency of the scientific and historical record. Indeed, science and history left out the majority of experience or at least neglected the most important aspects of it. "All our concepts and all our histories put together," Ransom maintained, "cannot add up into the wholeness with which we started out" (SL, 155). Experience was vaster and more complex than the constructs of the human mind could encompass.

History and science, however formidable as analytical tools, could not reduce experience to manageable proportions without violating its integrity and thereby falsifying it. "Philosophical syntheses do no good . . .

when they try to put Humpty-Dumpty together again by logic," Ransom went on. "They only give us a Whole which, as Kant would say, is obtained by *comprehensio logica* and not by *comprehensio aesthetica*—a Whole which it is only necessary to say fails to give us satisfaction" (*SL,* 155–56).

The first moment marked the time of innocent childhood, in which the mind could know only "pure experience." The second moment was the period of youthful adolescence, in which the mind could analyze and categorize experience according to the rules and methods of science. The rational, scientific world view that the adolescent mind had so laboriously constructed from the second moment was predicated upon an illusion, however. Sounding every bit the radical empiricist, Ransom asserted that science rested on a theoretical infrastructure the reality of which no one could demonstrate or verify. Science necessarily presented an artificial version of experience, the absolute truth of which men accepted at their peril. The mature mind of adulthood recognized the deficiencies of science and sought to recover and to reconstitute the fugitive first moment.

Through dreams and daydreams, religion and morality, and, most important, art and poetry, men could create the third moment. This act of creation was regressive, as much an act of recovery as an act of innovation, for through the aesthetic experience of the third moment men attempted to retrieve the "pure experience" of the first moment, which they had lost. The connections between Ransom's developing aesthetic theory and his nascent agrarianism emerged clearly in his image of this third moment.

Science and technology, however indispensable, remained fundamentally instruments for the conquest of nature. But Ransom was not categorically opposed to science "except as it monopolises and warps us" (*SL,* 156). Only fools, he admitted, could think of doing away completely with science and technology. To deny their efficacy would be irrational, if not suicidal. Ransom offered an alternate proposition, which soon became embodied in his defense of the South. The aesthetic, like the southern ethos, restrained the unmitigated impulse to use and exploit nature and instead taught respect for and appreciation of its mysteries.

Men could still use science and technology, which became increasingly undifferentiated in Ransom's thought, to transform nature and to satisfy their material wants. Art, however, compelled them to submit to the special particularities and tough contingencies of nature. Science could not achieve uncontested dominance over nature; men could never analyze nature into tidy categories or reduce it to a series of artificial classifications. The complexity of nature remained beyond full human comprehension. Men had to become more modest in their aspirations.

A life lived close to the soil, in harmony with the vast forces of nature, offered a practical compromise between the exploitative sophistication of the modern and the abject ignorance of the primitive. In an agrarian society, men could extract a living from the land they loved without raping it. They could develop elaborate rituals, like art, to recall their original innocence, expunge their present guilt, and reconcile themselves to nature and nature's God.

Men were instinctively willful and cognitive, Ransom asserted, but art prevented them from calculating the world out of existence. In an agrarian society, with its aesthetic sensibility, men could fashion images that represented their proper relations with each other, with nature, and with God. They could not escape cognition altogether, but they could consciously limit its power and effectiveness. "What we really get, therefore, by this deliberate recourse to images," Ransom wrote to Tate, "is a mixed world composed of both images and concepts; or a sort of practicable reconciliation of the two worlds" (SL, 156).

From the beginning, poetry afforded Ransom his best and purest model of reality. Poetry always exhibited a combination of both conceptual and formal elements, such as meter, and particular and concrete elements, such as metaphor. Although these poetic devices distinguished poetry from prose, they stood in tension and attempted to dominate one another. In a meticulously crafted poem, however, neither the conceptual and formal nor the particular and concrete elements could eclipse or eliminate the other. They coexisted. A poem dramatized the opposition between, but effected the reconciliation of, the formal, conceptual, and cognitive and the particular, concrete, and contingent aspects of experience. The body of a poem, Ransom argued, revealed the dual nature of reality that science, by itself, obscured and discredited.

The paramount service that men of letters could render to modern civilization was to expose the fictions of science. To that end, Ransom declared that poets and critics must have done with architectonic philosophical systems and cosmologies and instead explore and exhibit in their work "the infinite quality that is in every situation anywhere, anytime."

In place of system and cosmology, poets should simply refer concept to image and show how the abstract concept is lost in the particular image, how the categories of science are subsumed in the multiplicity and complexity of reality, how, as Ransom put it, "the determinate is drowned in the contingent, and how, ultimately, the world can neither be understood nor possessed" (*SL,* 161).

Poetry revealed that despite the repeated onslaught of men's rational capacities, scientific acumen, and technological prowess, nature remained intractable. However bold their plans, however magnificent their powers, men were doomed to failure in their war on nature. At its best, poetry captured the eternal struggle between men and nature and revealed the tragic dimensions of the human condition. As poetry approached the tragic, it constrained men to admit the folly of their arrogance, yet it held out the hope of a reconciliation with nature by displaying the mysterious and fragile composition of reality in its own structure.

Poetry, Ransom thought, would teach men that nature could not be had on their terms. The bounty of nature would come to them only if they assumed a posture of reverence, humility, and awe, only if they proceeded by indirection and inefficiency to reap the fruits of their labor. He explained to Tate: "I think that serious poetry always approaches tragedy. In tragedy we admit to the impertinence of the whole possessive attitude, to the failure of our effort to grasp and to dominate the world. But in tragedy also we return to another very fundamental and very healing attitude which is the attitude of Respect. Such is our native dualism" (*SL,* 161–62).

Poetic reality implied the boundless multiplicity and complexity of experience, what Ransom called "inexhaustible quality," as opposed to the finite quantity of scientific calculation. Scientific methods, formulas, hypotheses, theorems, and axioms, like their philosophical counterparts, attempted to make the world agreeable and compliant. They were the source of men's delusions of power over creation. The State, the Soul, the World, the Cosmos, God were the kinds of elegant fictions that the rational, scientific mind perpetuated. These "Supersensibles," as Ransom called them, existed beyond the realm of the senses and, therefore, had no aesthetic quality and no ontological reality.

Poetry demanded a return to the sensible world in all of its stubborn individuality, contingency, and unpredictability. Reliance on the senses without reference to some transcendent, supersensible fiction would not provide men with a more certain understanding of how to tame their world, but Ransom was sure that it would supply a more accurate image of the human condition.

The man of letters who emphasized the sensible at the expense of the rational occupied a special place in Ransom's heart. "The artist is the man who keeps his eyes open," he wrote to Tate, "and is not afraid to look" (*SL,* 163). All the reality that the poet needed stood just outside his front door. Poets, Ransom declared, were confirmed nominalists, sensationalists, and skeptics. Nonetheless, he conceded, no perceptions remained untouched and unconditioned by conception and cognition. Ransom professed to Tate his belief in "universals" but at the same time voiced his objection to universal concepts that were "constructed and not found." He continued, "In other words, I object to those universals which are supersensible, which are mathematically infinite and grasped by reason rather than sense" (*SL,* 165). The expansive, synthetic power of the imagination had to constrain and recast the fragmenting, analytical power of reason if the aesthetic was to triumph over the scientific, if the beautiful was not to succumb to the pragmatic.

Ransom failed to develop his thesis sufficiently to bring "The Third Moment" to completion, but he did incorporate the insights scattered in the manuscript and in his letters to Tate into *God Without Thunder.* In his early discussion of aesthetic experience, Ransom never discovered the formula that would have enabled him to organize the vast amount of material he had accumulated. By his own admission, he could not focus his study. He salvaged many of the ideas contained in his discarded manuscript and in his letters to Tate only by abandoning the direct examination of aesthetics and undertaking the study of religion.

ART AS RELIGIOUS EXPERIENCE

Ransom discerned in religion the same preconceptual experience that he associated with the first moment. "Religion is fundamental," he wrote to Tate in 1929, "and prior to intelligent (or human) conduct on any plane" (*SL,* 180). Religious experience, for him, thus assumed a character formerly reserved for aesthetic experience alone. Religion became a bastion against the messianic cult of science, technology, and progress, against capitalism, socialism, and imperialism, or against "any other political foolishness." Religion provided a guarantee of security in a transient world and the only source of joy in temporal life. Fear of God was the beginning of wisdom, and love was the end.

Religion represented for Ransom the most popularly disseminated aesthetic experience. Certainly, more people knew something about religion than knew anything about poetry. The religious and the aesthetic became, he confessed to Tate, virtually indistinguishable in his mind. "Since last February," he wrote on July 4, 1929, "I've been writing a hot & hasty book on religion which I hope to complete this summer—an interlude in my aesthetic interests, and far from disconnected with them,—it can't possibly be a really finished & permanent book under the circumstances, but nevertheless it's a sincere book and one that somebody ought to write" (*SL,* 181). Initially titled "Giants for Gods," Ransom finished his book on religion in late 1929 and published it, revised and retitled, as *God Without Thunder* in 1930.

As was his habit, Ransom outlined and polished his ideas in his letters to Tate. Western civilization, he began in his letter of July 4, faced the most serious crisis of faith in its religious history, for in the West, religion had lost its capacity for myth and had become something akin to spirited public service. This unfortunate metamorphosis had occurred when the "soft-headed Western World" surrendered to the temptation, explicit in the New Testament, to envision God as a benevolent and loving Father who would not permit harm to come to his children. The spirit of the New Testament violated the essence of religious experience, to say nothing of poetic imagination, by denying the fundamental tragedy of human life.

Under the doctrine of love contained in the Gospels, the Epistles, and the Acts of the Apostles, the world became gentle, malleable, and comprehensible, effortlessly yielding its deepest secrets to men. The vision of the world according to the New Testament, Ransom concluded, foreshadowed the vision of the world according to modern science. The doctrine of the New Testament, insofar as it deviated from the Old Testament religion of the Jews, represented a grievous, and perhaps fatal, error in the history of Western Christianity. According to Ransom, "the N. T. has been a failure & a backset as a religious myth; not its own fault, as I think, but nevertheless a failure; it's hurt us" (*SL,* 181).

The central dilemma of the New Testament, which Ransom explored in *God Without Thunder,* emerged from the unwarranted elevation of Christ to the Godhead. Western mythology, at least since Homer's time, abounded with stories of "giants" who were the offspring of liaisons between gods and human beings. These giants were not deities but demigods who, nevertheless, believed themselves to be divine and behaved accordingly. Prometheus, who stole fire from Mount Olympus and gave it to mankind, was the prototypical embodiment of this motif. Ransom saw Satan as the Hebrew Prometheus. Christ, too, was a Promethean or Satanic figure who, like Prometheus and Satan, exemplified the power of reason: the *logos*.

Gradually but steadily, the God of Israel, the "God of Thunder," was reduced to the "Spirit of Science, or the Spirit of Love, or the Spirit of the Rotary" (*I.C.*, 181).[11] As a result, religious experience in the West lost its intense spirituality and became utterly secular, rational, and human. In the modern world, men had expelled God—at least any God with whom Ransom could identify—from the universe and proceeded to venerate themselves and their works. Havoc was loosed upon the land.

Reinvigorating the old, inscrutable God of Thunder presented a formidable task, for the marvels of science had gained ascendancy in the modern world. The revolution in science was subtle yet so pervasive that the scientists and their spokesmen hardly needed to engage the defenders of the old faith in open debate. Debate itself was frequently silenced. The interdiction against religious practice that the communist leaders of the Soviet Union imposed on their people represented for Ransom the extent to which the opponents of the old faith would go to eradicate the religious spirit. In the United States and Western Europe, the Scopes trial of 1925 revealed the depth and magnitude of the schism between science and religion that had ensconced itself in the public mind.

Despite its accomplishments, science left modern men stricken with an unanticipated and unimaginable poverty of mind and spirit. Mythic and aesthetic truths were not accessible to science but were incorporated into religious doctrine. The strategies of science were abundantly simple; the intricacies of nature were infinitely complex. The scientific explanation of natural phenomena, Ransom asserted, had disabused the modern world of the precious myths that had historically provided a rich spiritual and aesthetic life. Science had challenged and repudiated myth as quaint and antiquated, in Ransom's view, because scientists, committed to positivism and rationalism, objected that myths violated the detail and

11. See also *GWT,* 5.

reality of nature. With a circular logic that they would have scorned in the laboratory, scientists, Ransom declared, condemned myth because it was unscientific. He rejected their conclusion that myth was therefore false. In *God Without Thunder*, Ransom proceeded to delineate the nature and purpose of science and to confine science to its proper sphere.

Scientists concerned themselves exclusively with the natural world, but they had egregiously overestimated "the importance of . . . purely natural features" (*GWT*, 12).[12] Human life consisted of more than its natural aspects, which scientists could calculate, measure, define, and alter. God did not wholly reveal himself to scientists in nature any more than he did in the laboratory. Only the worst kind of arrogance and folly convinced scientists that God, since the creation of the universe, had been engaged by the same problems and at work on the same projects that had captured their interest and imagination.

Beguiled by the power of science to describe natural phenomena, scientists and positivists assumed that God had created a universe accessible to rational analysis and submissive to human will. The "first doctrine" of science stated that God himself was a scientist who had constructed the universe according to the principles, categories, and processes of science. The "second doctrine" of science was even more troubling and subversive. According to this seditious corollary, man himself was a god. God was the original scientist whose laboratory was the universe. He had created mankind and the rest of the universe for the profit of his beloved creatures. But men, rather than gratefully accepting the divine endowment, had cast themselves as "little scientists" who, with the advent of sophisticated technology, could improve upon God's handiwork. According to the second doctrine, men could now themselves perform God's work and do it more economically and efficiently. God thus became superfluous.

The only doubt that still clouded the happy destiny of mankind, Ransom scoffed, was how quickly men would comprehend the secrets of nature and thereby enhance their power and hasten their ascent. Scientists fantasized that human misfortune would one day become virtually inconceivable, for men already knew the most precious secrets of creation

12. For a review of the scholarly literature on *God Without Thunder*, see Mark G. Malvasi, "Risen from the Bloody Sod: Recovering the Southern Tradition" (Ph.D. dissertation, University of Rochester, 1991), 331–32 n. 64.

and doubtless the remainder awaited revelation in the near future. The God of Thunder had ignominiously become the modern scientist glorified. The modern scientist as god defined and activated those reliable scientific axioms by which the universe operated. He knew what worked and saw that it was good.

In former days, when men feared God's caprice, they worshipped him with humility, begging indulgence for their frailties and forgiveness for their sins. They set aside days of worship and seasons for prayer, fasting, penance, and celebration, often to the neglect of the practical business of life. Ransom argued that priests and prophets had invented these myths of God, officially legislating him into existence. Only those myths that captured the collective imagination of the entire society survived, dictating men's relations to God, to nature, to the universe, and to each other. Problems arose when unsophisticated believers forgot that men created the myth of God and attempted to alter the human condition by invoking the power of the deity through prayer, sacrifice, and ritual. Through these media, men did necessary homage to God, whose wrath they feared. Ransom, however, condemned the illusion that men could acquire God's grace by engaging in these good works.

Similarly, the new god of science was tame, amiable, and constant. He found no propriety in burnt offerings or blood sacrifices. The god of science was truly a god of man's own making. Modern men could feel tolerably at ease in their scientific Zion, Ransom surmised, for they venerated the reflections in the mirror that invited them to despoil the universe.

The doctrines of Christianity, and in particular those of Protestantism, offered no antidote to modern science. Protestantism was the religion of modern science. The Protestant God, in Ransom's analysis, was a gentle spirit who presided over an intelligible and tractable universe. By the twentieth century, he observed, Protestantism experienced a conversion to naturalism: "We wanted a God who wouldn't hurt us; who would let us understand him; who would agree to put away all the wicked thunderbolts in his armament" (*GWT,* 5). The emergence of Protestantism marked the demise of the original Judeo-Christian faith in all its tempestuous majesty. Protestantism, Ransom asserted, "has evidently been preparing itself to come at length to a completely naturalized religion—whatever anomaly that may be"(*GWT,* 28).

Religion in the modern world had thus been pressed into the service of humanity. The "modern religionists," who were merely scientists in another guise, wanted only a benevolent God who pampered and satisfied them. They recoiled from the stern and terrifying God of the Old Testament, the real and fearful God who would not reduce to the "God That is Good" (*GWT,* 49). Modern men deluded themselves that God's singular purpose was to promote the good of humanity. They were fools. How, Ransom asked rhetorically, did they explain evil, especially when confronted by vast testimony of its flourishing existence? He answered his own query: they could not. They simply pretended that evil was temporary, incidental, and negligible, that it did not inhere in the structure and composition of the universe. Ransom thought himself too much a realist to accept that easy conclusion.

Ransom's interpretation of modern Christianity hardly flattered the dreams of human omnipotence that the "Occidental" scientific mind entertained. The religion of the Old Testament promised the failure of all human endeavors. Human goodness and intelligence, long assumed to be a combination sufficient to generate success and happiness, did not universally and uniformly work their triumphant effect on the material world. Although militant Occidentals recognized no limits to their power or potential, in the end they had no choice but to surrender to the inevitable, for the world defeated them again and again.

Modern men grudgingly, but inescapably, had to accept reality. The universe was not entirely amenable to the laws of science, nor was it completely subservient to the aspirations of humanity. The ancient Oriental wisdom, far superior to the modern Occidental, considered the discrepancy between reality and fancy and made possible the difficult yet critical adjustment to reality once men realized that God was not committed to their moral vision of the world. "*The moral order is a wished-for order,*" Ransom wrote, "*which does not coincide with the actual order or world order*" (*GWT,* 47). Like Job, modern men could only take the world as they found it, without hope that God would relieve their earthly suffering or restore their earthly prosperity.

The misery that assailed Western civilization resulted from denying the tragedy of human existence that informed the Old Testament. From Ransom's perspective, the New Testament placed an unfortunate emphasis on the power of intellect. In the New Testament, God served man. Reason replaced the supernatural. The god of science, however, held dominion only over the intelligible aspects of experience, whereas the God of Israel encompassed both the rational and the contingent. "Therefore the old God was a whole God," Ransom maintained, "and the new God is half a God, or a Demigod" (*GWT,* 32). The estrangement from nature and God marked the tragedy of human ambition. Satan promised not only harmony with nature, which Adam and Eve had already attained in the Garden of Eden, but dominion over nature. Satan was a demigod, the "Spirit of Secular Science," who aspired to usurp God and to establish himself as the ruler of the universe. He charmed Adam and Eve, lured them into sin, and effected their expulsion from the Garden and subsequent life of toil, drudgery, struggle, and misery. Satan inspired men's fanatical devotion to the myth of progress, urging them to prey upon nature and, consequently, to become ever more alienated from it. He concealed the truth of human life: that tragedy, not progress, was the fate of mankind. The Old Testament had warned men to beware of Lucifer, the Bearer of Light, the Father of Lies, whose evil power was great.

In Ransom's "unorthodox defense of orthodoxy," Christ, like Satan, was also a demigod, but he represented an alternative to Satan. Christ was "*the Demigod who refused to set up as the God*" (*GWT,* 140). Like Satan, Christ, too, possessed the gift of reason, the *logos,* by which he could understand creation to the extent that it was intelligible to men. The principal difference between Satan and Christ, in Ransom's analysis, was that Satan disavowed the limitations of reason whereas Christ accepted them. Satan personified the ambition ingrained deeply in human nature. He worshiped Reason and encouraged his followers to do the same. Christ, though he was Reason incarnate, refused to yield to the blandishments of Satan. He understood the power and purpose of God and declined to pronounce himself divine. In accepting his role as a prophet who pointed toward One greater than he, Christ challenged the efficacy of Satanic power, redressed the sin of Adam, and reconciled mankind to God.

But it was as dangerous to worship Christ, Ransom declared, as it was to worship Satan. The transformation of Christ into God that took place in the New Testament obscured the tragic nature of human reality as much as did Satan's deceitful words and evil magic. The new god, Christ, became the messiah who offered salvation from the tragedy of sin and death. Although Christ taught that the kingdom of God lay within the hearts of the faithful, twentieth-century Christians misunderstood his teaching and concluded that evil was thus a figment of the imagination. If the kingdom of God were internal and subjective, Ransom explained, then sufficient intellectual and spiritual discipline would produce blissful serenity.

Ransom quickly pointed out that Christ did not come into the world to provide solace to anyone. Christian orthodoxy revealed not that evil was illusory but that happiness was a disposition of mind and spirit. Christ taught that men should find happiness even in their tribulations. They should attempt to sustain virtue and to glorify God without expectation of earthly reward; their effort should be to savor a world that did not devote itself to human contentment. But the sentimental Christianity of the twentieth century could tolerate nothing less than a loving God who promised gratification in this life and jubilation in the next.

Uncomfortable with the idea, to say nothing of the reality, of Hell, twentieth-century Christians simply dispensed with both. Modern Christians could not imagine that Christ, the new god of reason and love, would condemn any of his valued creatures to eternal torment. They soothed their troubled minds by contemplating universal salvation.

Ransom appreciated that the optimistic faith of Christianity had supplanted the tragic vision of the Greeks and the Hebrews. The reign of Christ marked the reign of *logos*. The grandiose and relentless secular project of Western civilization demonstrated that a rational and humane order of the universe must prevail. Modern men, led by the scientists and the positivists, wished for a world that was beneficent and thus decreed it to be so. The substitution of Christ as divine *logos* "for the whole of the Godhead," Ransom declared, "is a piece of thinking in which a wish has been father to the thought" (*GWT,* 162). The severe faith and the old, terrible God evinced that nature was neither rational nor humane, that, indeed, such an order was an imperious and sinful dream.

Christ as divine *logos* was the patron of science and Christianity, the religion of science. The divine *logos* forced nature into a system of classification that made it intelligible to the human mind. Ransom inferred that Christianity made modern science not only permissible but possible.

Horrified by the inordinate emphasis on science and infuriated by the excruciating repercussions of industrialism, Ransom did not feel at home in the modern world. The secular forces of modernity, he protested, alienated men from nature, each other, and God and deprived them of their native dignity. Worshipping the demigod Christ, the divine *logos,* brought men only illusory power and benefit. The cult of science, technology, and progress rendered men forgetful not only of the sorrow of life but of its joy. In the modern world, men continually reduced their expectations of happiness so that they could persuade themselves to be satisfied with the meager products of science and industrialism. They were enslaved to these rational, mechanized tyrants. Ransom concluded: "We will find that if we intend to enjoy the blessings of science, it will have to be by using the machines and machine-products that modern science has placed at our disposal, and then our existence will be mechanized, but not necessarily filled, not made more intelligent: we will have to spend much of it in doing what the machines dictate we should do" (*GWT,* 167).

Science flattered men's vanities and quieted their apprehensions. Like modern Christianity, science offered men hope that they could escape death. "The speeding driver in the car cannot afford to observe the infinite variety of nature," Ransom argued. "He must confirm his own sense of power." Hence, "he is deliberately practicing a technique of anesthesia" (*GWT,* 174). Such was the scientific habit of mind, the intellectual correlative to modern Christianity.

In Ransom's final appraisal both science and Christianity were thus deficient. Science blinded men to their own impotence and advised them to contemplate only problems that they could solve. By circumscribing the range of human thought and activity, science enabled men to bear false witness to the efficacy of their own power. They could conscientiously disregard those perpetual quandaries that lay beyond the realm of human capacity.

Science exaggerated the tendency within human nature to forsake the poetic and the spiritual for the mechanical and the material, the beautiful and the good for the practical and the functional. The substitution of mechanism and function for contemplation and meaning characterized life in the modern world and masked the social and spiritual bankruptcy of the rational, scientific, industrial order. Under the auspices of science and technology, life assumed the superficial appearance of success. Things worked. Beneath the surface, though, the multiplicity of creation escaped human reflection. Such ignorance, Ransom knew, was anything but blissful. He considered modern life a successful enterprise only if all discourse and analysis were limited to the severely restrictive and simplified language of science. He wrote: "Work, Power, Activity, Business, Industry,

Production—these are the great words of an age of applied science. They do beautifully for those who need them badly enough, and who are willing to abandon their deepest personal interests. They reflect power on those who cannot bear the sense of impotence. They are deeply Occidental—and they are quite scorned by Orientals, who insist upon their contemplation and their freest inner development regardless of what *impasses* they may find waiting for them on that road" (*GWT,* 177).

Christianity, which should have reacquainted men with the spiritual and poetic aspects of their nature, had in its modern form capitulated to the scientific world view. The logical development of Protestantism led to Christian Science, the current rage among modern "religionists." The Christian Scientist, like the natural scientists, instructed men that their tribulations and distress were temporary and even illusory. They had nothing to worry about. Human failures were insignificant and would be overcome in time. There were opportunities aplenty for human improvement; men had only to realize them.

Ransom decried scientific Christianity as unfit for a free people living fearlessly amid the complexity and confusion of modern life. Instead, though it operated as a palliative to guilt and suffering, Christian Science ironically revealed the dread and desperation of men and women who sought to escape a bleak reality. Modern men and women, even those who were professing Christians, feared an ample spiritual life, preferring the violent rush into action to the quiet repose of contemplation. For them, activity became an anesthetic.

In their anxiety and impotence, modern men and women built up an empty legend of power, which would crumble at the first disappointment. The modern world, for all its scientific acumen and technological prowess, was not an adult world. "The toys which science showers upon us," Ransom wrote, "are therefore amusements just a little more than innocent" (*GWT,* 174). Modern men and women had abandoned the maturity of their forebears and extended the period of youth. They were little better than spoiled children, worse perhaps, for they had accepted their pathological infantilism as normal behavior.

The persistence of evil constituted for Ransom the preeminent reality of human existence. No scientific discovery, no technological innovation could alter that fact. The physical sciences could not change the conditions that God had set to regulate life after the Fall. Technology could not eliminate labor, suffering, or death. The social sciences could not predict, discipline, or alter human conduct. The brutal contingencies of nature continued to wreck the most heroic projects of man, forever placing the world beyond human understanding and control. Men could only face contingencies and prepare for them as best they could.

The new cult of science, and the scientific Christianity that accompanied it, did not sanction these contingencies but vainly warred against them. Neither modern science nor modern Christianity was worthy of devotion, for, Ransom thought, neither provided a steady foundation upon which to construct a worthwhile social and spiritual order.

When he began writing *God Without Thunder,* Ransom intended to affirm the endowments of religion and to discredit the endowments of science. He could not have predicted that his unorthodox defense of orthodoxy would undermine the basis of religious faith. Both modern science and religion, in his view, denied the inexhaustible variety, the boundless plenitude, of nature. The theorems, formulas, and equations necessary to the operation of science were fictional. Just so, God, or at least the "Occidental God of the New Testament," was a fabrication. He was as abstract, as universal, and as ineffectual as the general laws of thermodynamics or the theory of evolution. Only Supersensibles, Ransom complained, seemed appropriate for scientific analysis or religious contemplation.

Despite Ransom's vigorous defense of religious orthodoxy, in the end the aesthetics of poetry displaced religion as the source of meaning, order, and being in the modern world. With its tendency to linger long over the objects within its compass, poetry prevented religion from degenerating into the pure *logos* of science. Only the aesthetic sensibility, by showing that men could neither define nor exhaust the fullness of God's creation, could save the religious imagination from self-destruction in its quest to attain direct knowledge of God.

Artists saw nature whole and, rather than attempt to master and use it, delighted in meditating on its beauty, majesty, and mystery. They questioned whether the assurances of modern science and the comforts of modern religion were not dangerously false, for these placebos provoked men to pretend that they had power over nature and, indeed, over God. If men followed the precepts of science and the doctrines of religion without the corrective that poetry offered, they would assuredly fall first into disappointment, then into perversion, and finally into madness.

Poetry, unlike modern science or religion, offered knowledge without desire. The modern scientist desired knowledge as power over nature; the modern religionist desired knowledge as power over human destiny. The poet alone could know without the desire to possess and exploit. Knowledge without desire ended in love. Only poetry, with its total respect for the object of contemplation, engendered feelings of love, whether for a woman, for nature, or for God.

But everywhere in the modern world poetry was under siege. Ransom worried that without the aesthetic influence, scientists, philosophers, and theologians would execute a compromise between positivism and religion to create a secular, naturalistic order in which Christ, personifying "the spirit of the scientific and ethical secularism of the West," reigned supreme (*GWT,* 320). Modern religion, having shed its orthodoxy, had not the wherewithal to resist the cunning of science.

Ransom doubted that any modern religion could lead men back to the "excellences of the ancient faith" (*GWT,* 325). He suspected that modern men had become too far removed from orthodoxy ever again to find the words of the prophets and psalmists congenial or meaningful. He conceded their alienation from the modern world: "Culturally their language and their images seem strange to us now. And we have heard so much fun made of them! There is a real effort required now to enter into them sympathetically even when we consider that metaphysically they are sound" (*GWT,* 324). Was there, Ransom wondered, the possibility of instituting a new faith that would revitalize the old myth of the God of Thunder? He thought such a development improbable at best.

In the end, Ransom could not reconcile the demands of religion with the requirements of poetry. Poetry needed both discipline and freedom, but aesthetic discipline had to be internal and sui generis. The poet could not be constrained by any discipline imposed on him from without. Religion ultimately failed to yield Ransom the insights that he required to formulate and clarify his interpretation of aesthetic experience. Instead of offering alternatives to science, modern religionists now justified their beliefs wholly in scientific terms. They stood prepared to serve the interests of science, for those interests were also their own.

Growing more personally alienated from organized religion, Ransom became less inclined to view it as the best analogue to aesthetic experience. Before he completed writing and revising *God Without Thunder,* however, he had located another model that he hoped would enable him to focus and develop his aesthetic theory: the traditional, agrarian South.

In the four years prior to the publication of *God Without Thunder*, Ransom's correspondence with Allen Tate, Donald Davidson, Andrew Lytle, and Robert Penn Warren was intermittently spiced with references to the "Southern question." In the spring of 1927, for example, Ransom wrote to Tate that their new cause was, "we all have sensed . . . at about the same moment, the Old South." He continued: "Our fight is for survival; and it's got to be waged not so much against the Yankees as against the exponents of the New South. I see clearly that you are as unreconstructed and unmodernized as any of the rest of us, if not more so. We must think about this business and take some very long calculations ahead" (*SL*, 166).[13] The southern tradition, Ransom contended, possessed an old and inviolable distrust of rationalism, science, and technology, which, under present circumstances, might remedy the dehumanizing tendencies of the modern world. The social relations of an agrarian society, instead of permitting men the luxury of illusory power over nature, continually reminded them that their lives were contingent upon the good offices of the Lord. Agrarians, unlike modern scientists, philosophers, and theologians, knew that men occupied a lowly place in the universe.

Ransom indicated the emerging connections between his aesthetic theory, his theology, and his nascent agrarian philosophy in the "Statement of Principles" that introduced *I'll Take My Stand*. There he wrote that religion could not flourish in an industrial setting, for religion demanded submission to the will of God, a concession that modern men, intoxicated by the false sense of their omnipotence, steadfastly refused to make. Ransom summarized his argument with a passage that could have come directly from *God Without Thunder:*

> Religion is our submission to the general intention of a nature that is fairly inscrutable; it is the sense of our role as creatures within it. But nature industrialized, transformed into cities and artificial habitations, manufactured into commodities is no longer nature, but a highly simplified picture of nature. We receive the illusion of having power over nature, and lose the sense of nature as something mysterious and contingent. The God of nature under these conditions is merely an amiable

13. See also *SL*, 173.

expression, a superfluity, and the philosophical understanding ordinarily carried in the religious experience is not there for us to have.
(*ITMS,* xlii)

If modern Christianity could not on its own resist the dictates of science,
perhaps the aesthetic sensibility could endure if nurtured in the premodern, antiscientific soil of the traditional South.

Even before he published *God Without Thunder* in 1930, Ransom had
embarked upon a quest to revitalize the southern way of life. During
much of the decade that followed, he attempted to realize his aesthetic
vision through the systematic defense of southern culture, history, and
tradition.

THE ANTIQUE HARVESTER

The agrarian philosopher cut an exotic and amusing figure even in his
native setting. A quaint anachronism, more to be pitied than feared, he
wandered village streets and country fields, proclaiming the glories of the
Lost Cause. There was scarcely a chance that anyone would follow him,
even at a respectable distance. He moved on, inevitably alone.

Such was the fate of a man, Ransom lamented, who backed an unpopular movement. Rather than condemnation or disgrace, he faced
ignorance and indifference. His neighbors, whose interests he tried to
serve, might even indulge what they saw as his eccentricities, congratu-
lating themselves on their patient concern for one of God's less fortunate
creatures. The antique conservatism of the South, Ransom well knew,
did not exert any great influence against the progressive doctrines of the
North, even below the Mason-Dixon line. In his day, he wrote, "the
Southern idea is down, and the progressive or American idea is up"
(*ITMS,* 3).[14] Could the South rise again? Ransom did not know. But he
felt confident that the southern, not the American or progressive, way
of life enjoyed the sanction of history and the blessing of God.

From Ransom's perspective the South represented an anomaly within
the United States, for the South resembled Europe in general and England in particular. In custom, manner, and disposition, southerners were
much indebted to Europeans, especially to Englishmen. Paramount

14. See also John Crowe Ransom, "The South—Old or New?," *Sewanee Review,*
XXXVI (1928), 139–47, and "The South Defends Its Heritage," *Harper's Magazine* CXIX
(June, 1929), 108–18.

among the many differences that separated England and the South from the rest of the United States was that the former were historically self-sufficient, conservative, and provincial communities whose citizens lived tranquilly on the endowment of their ancestors.

Englishmen and southerners had constructed stable economic orders by which they took their living from nature. Neither the English nor the southern economy was based fundamentally or permanently on exploration and conquest, as was the American system. Whatever modern Americans may have supposed, the life of the pioneer was neither the normal nor the natural estate of humanity. First the English and later the southern pioneers, Ransom argued, set the example that modern men would do well to imitate.

These provincial communities came long ago to settle accounts with nature. Antebellum southerners adapted to their natural environment and lived easily and conventionally in accordance with the traditions that they had inherited. They savored a leisure, a security, and a freedom that their pioneer ancestors would have envied. Southern life may have been provincial, but it was hardly provisional. Southerners, like Englishmen before them, willed their comfortable institutions and their modest prosperity to their descendants, who had the good sense to hold fast to them. Ransom, however, was silent on the enclosure acts, the rise of British industry, the establishment of the British Empire, and the practice of commercial agriculture in the South that depleted the soil.

The gospel of progress, on the contrary, did not reflect great credit on the intellectual and moral faculties of modern men. They conducted themselves like adolescent boys excited to flex their muscles, not like men who preferred the reflective, contemplative, aesthetic life. Modern men, propelled by an insatiable wanderlust, lived in a state of eternal flux, developing none of the attachments to the past that steadied old England and the antebellum South. Mistaking conquest and domination for progress, they were forever marching off on some new and magnificent adventure in their endless and aimless war against nature. "Our vast industrial machine," Ransom wrote, "with its laboratory centers of experimentation, and its far-flung organs of mass production, is like a Prussianized state which is organized strictly for war and can never consent to peace" (ITMS, 8). Once modern men had conquered nature, Ransom conjectured, they would no longer recall what they had wanted or why they had fought.

Modern men may have characterized themselves as ambitious, but that characterization was a mere euphemism. Ransom pronounced them belligerent, pathological killers, unhappy even in the midst of their slaughter. The scientist cloistered in his laboratory and the industrialist secluded in his office might seek fame and fortune, but they possessed no greater objective than vainly to trouble and torment the earth. They wished to grind nature under their heels.

The southern agrarian tradition offered at least a modicum of resistance to the modern philosophy of progress. The typical southerner never believed that the sole responsibility of a man lay in the work that he performed, nor did he think that his value could be measured by his material prosperity. "His business seemed to be rather to envelop both his work and his play with a leisure which permitted the activity of intelligence" (*ITMS*, 12). Although the southern temper, neither as jubilant nor as expansive as the northern, was realistic enough to accept defeat, it was, however, too undisciplined to remedy the consequences of that defeat. If twentieth-century southerners had indeed inherited a tradition from their ancestors worthy of preservation, then it was time to rally around the old flag once more.

The incessant hum of machines and the ecstatic convulsions of chambers of commerce shocked unregenerate southerners from their lethargy. Agrarianism was the most ancient and most humane of all modes of human livelihood, Ransom argued, and on that basis alone warranted a defense. But questions remained. Would southerners permit the South to lose its historic character in the ceaseless whir of the machine? Would they administer the acrid philosophy of progress to dissolve the historic conservatism that bound their lives to the past and inhibited their actions in the present? Did the political and economic reconstruction of the South necessarily entail a spiritual reconstruction of the southern people?

Ransom hoped southerners would give emphatically negative responses to each of these queries, but he remained uncertain about the exact political course they should chart to attain their objectives. Would it be most politic to revive the old sectional animosities and secure for the South a position analogous to that of Scotland in Great Britain: a section subject to the sovereignty of the Union, just as Scotland was subject to the sovereignty of the crown, but preserving its local customs, institutions, values, and culture? This tactic would be as effective as it was ruthless.

More gentlemanly and more diplomatic, if ultimately more difficult and frustrating, would be the determined reentrance of the South into American political life. Southerners should, for instance, pursue alliances with westerners, whose power and independence the industrial system had similarly eroded. The combination of western farmers and southern agrarians, Ransom maintained, would constitute a formidable opposition to "progressive forces." Perhaps such a unified bloc could seize control of the Democratic party and commit it to a conservative, agrarian, anti-industrial platform. If such a feat were possible, the rewards awaiting the South and her confederates would be extraordinary.[15]

Ransom realized, though, that more immediate problems demanded attention. The Agrarians could not salvage the traditional southern way of life or enlist the support of western allies to command the Democratic party if ordinary southerners could no longer make a decent living. Broken-down southerners sat on rotting fences, mangy hound dogs at their feet, and surveyed untidy fields, pondering the mysteries of existence. They were, Ransom knew, "trying to live the good life on shabby equipment" (*ITMS,* 16). Before they could revive the South politically and culturally, the Agrarians had to revive it economically. The attainment of economic autonomy would determine the future of the South, and the Agrarians' recommendations, he thought, were critical.

The fundamental economic problem of the twentieth century, Ransom concluded, originated in the industrial revolutions of the seventeenth, eighteenth, and nineteenth centuries. Technological advancement precipitated a steadily worsening crisis of overproduction that depleted the economies of the principal industrial powers of Western Europe. A similar fate awaited the United States, which, like her European counterparts, had come to rely heavily on foreign trade as an important source of wealth. The flood of commodities that overflowed the world market made it virtually impossible for any single nation to dominate international commerce. The competition for markets, which was nothing less than the struggle for national survival, erupted into fierce rivalries that threatened international security and portended worldwide disaster.[16]

15. See *ITMS,* 23–27.

16. See the following articles by John Crowe Ransom: "The State and the Land," *New Republic,* February 17, 1932, pp. 8–10; "Land! An Answer to the Unemployment Problem," *Harper's Magazine,* CLXV (July, 1932), 216–24; "Happy Farmers," *American*

Ransom could not envision an end to the scramble for markets among the nations of Western Europe. Europeans had gone too far in the wrong direction. "Let those nations whose populations must live by foreign trade," he wrote in 1932, "fight to the death to get it and hold it, as indeed, they will and must."[17] In the United States, not yet as corrupt as Europe, men still had choices to make and options to pursue. Americans did not have to develop an unnatural attachment, a fatal dependence, on foreign trade.

In the midst of the Depression, the greatest economic and social dislocation within recent memory, Ransom invoked a return to agriculture as the solution to the collapse of the market economy. The availability of vast tracts of untrammeled land distinguished the United States from Great Britain, Germany, Italy, and France. A return to the land, the most valuable natural resource that the United States possessed, would stabilize the American economy by instilling national self-confidence, restoring national self-determination, and promoting independence from foreign competition.

Capitalism and the world market may have bestowed an aggregate wealth unimaginable in the past, but capitalism was, in reality, the cause of the present difficulties. Sustained investment, the essential mechanism for the operation of a capitalist economy, eventually exhausted the surplus capital of the entrepreneurial class and drove them to financial ruin.

Ransom's analysis of capitalism made no provision for capital accumulation stimulated by the profit motive. He developed no conception of the distinctions between "use-value," the consumption of a commodity to satisfy human need; "exchange-value," the value of one commodity relative to another; and "surplus-value," the value that accrued to the capitalist as profit beyond the costs of production.[18] Ransom's economic model operated on the assumption of limited capital available

---

Review, I (1933), 513–35; "Regionalism in the South," *New Mexico Quarterly,* IV (May, 1934), 108–13; "The South Is a Bulwark," *Scribner's Magazine,* XCIX (May, 1936), 299–303. See also Kelsie B. Harder, "John Crowe Ransom as Economist," *Modern Age,* II (1958), 389–93.

17. Ransom, "The State and the Land," 8.

18. Karl Marx, *Capital: A Critical Analysis of Capitalist Production, Volume I: The Process of Capitalist Production,* ed. Friedrich Engels, trans. Samuel Moore and Edward Averling (New York, 1967).

for investment, and thus he argued that economic growth would eventually cease as capitalists exhausted their resources.

Despite the severe economic reversals they experienced, entrepreneurs did not suffer most or suffer longest. In capitalist economies, especially susceptible to periodic disruption and stagnation as they were, the workers endured a chronic threat of unemployment and destitution. This menace not only surfaced in times of industrial failure and commercial instability but attended regularly upon capitalism even as it moved toward higher levels of efficiency, productivity, and prosperity. Technological unemployment, corporate reorganization, and economic consolidation repeatedly evicted workers, managers, and merchants from factories, offices, and shops and threatened them and their families with misery and starvation. Although Ransom did not know it, his analysis of the social consequences of capitalism paralleled those of numerous antebellum southern political economists, notably George Tucker and Thomas Roderick Dew. Tucker and Dew observed that under the so-called system of free labor, the working class was fated to live not only with brutal exploitation but also with unremitting poverty.[19]

Those unfortunate persons displaced by capitalism, Ransom suggested, should go back to the land and take up the lives of their frontier ancestors. They should cease trying to extract a meager livelihood from a capitalist economy that preyed upon their strength and dignity and instead take their living directly from the bounty of nature.

To assist the unemployed industrial workers and the beleaguered commercial farmers, as well as black and white tenant farmers and sharecroppers who had been turned off the land by their impoverished landlords, Ransom insisted that the agrarian economy have as little contact as possible with the commercial economy of capitalism. The land was not another factory in which exploited workers produced goods exclusively for sale. For true agrarians, the land was not a source of profit. Farmers ought first to make a living for themselves and their families, he averred, and only then to think of making money.

Ransom understood that complete self-sufficiency was impractical. Not since the earliest days of settlement, if then, had American farmers practiced it. They had always exchanged some of their produce for the

19. See Eugene D. Genovese, *The Slaveholders' Dilemma: Freedom and Progress in Southern Conservative Thought, 1820–1860* (Columbia, S.C., 1992), 10–45.

goods and services necessary to supplement their own labor. But they had also always fed themselves and their families, and the surplus that they produced fed the populations in the neighboring villages and towns. American farmers might still make a little money from the sale of their crops, yet that preoccupation must remain secondary, Ransom argued. Their primary objective was to work the land, to support themselves and their families in dignified independence, and to relish the material and aesthetic satisfaction attendant upon such accomplishments.

The miserable plight that had befallen southern farmers in the 1930s genuinely dismayed Ransom. To relieve their distress, he formulated a program that gratified his humanitarian instincts but that he hoped would also prove economically viable. He began from a premise that assumed the imminent demise of commercial agriculture in the United States. "American commercial agriculture is doomed," he announced. "Its great day is past beyond recall."[20] Since the end of World War I, the profits generated from commercial agriculture had steadily declined. By 1933, with the country in the throes of a deep depression, Ransom could begin his death watch.

He traced the history of commercial agriculture in the United States to demonstrate his thesis. Although they produced enough to feed their own countrymen and most of Europe, American farmers throughout the nineteenth century did not realize their maximum productive capacity. They still concentrated predominantly on meeting their own needs and producing for local markets. They had not yet adopted agricultural technology or applied modern techniques of crop rotation, soil preservation, and fertilization to enhance their yields. They relied primarily on horsepower, their own wits, and the benevolence of nature to harvest a crop. This situation persisted until near the end of the first decade of the twentieth century.

World War I created an artificial boom for American agriculture and American manufacturing in Europe. European belligerents invited the importation of foodstuffs and industrial merchandise to aid in their prosecution of and recovery from war. American farmers and manufacturers invaded foreign markets previously closed to them. The affluence that wartime production generated was tremendous: in the space of a few short years, it transformed the United States from a debtor nation into

---

20. Ransom, "Happy Farmers," 514.

the greatest creditor nation in the world. Unfortunately, such boisterous prosperity could not endure.

In the postwar years, Ransom pointed out, the American economy faltered not because of its deficiencies but paradoxically because of its vitality. The output of American farms and factories far exceeded the capacity of an already glutted market. Industrialists could, of course, adjust more easily to market conditions than could farmers. They could get trade barriers erected, tariffs enacted, and embargoes imposed that at least assured them of preserving a domestic market for their wares.

Commercial restrictions injured farmers in two important ways. First, in order to undersell foreign competitors, industrialists had to cut costs. They demanded lower food prices so that they could implement lower wages and thus lobbied for the greater importation of foodstuffs. American industrialists thereby deprived American farmers of their domestic market. Second, the efforts of the federal government to protect and buttress American industry by limiting or prohibiting the importation of foreign manufactured goods either caused foreign governments to institute similar policies against American agricultural produce shipped abroad or prevented European nations, short of currency, from purchasing that produce even if they so desired. Ransom concluded that American farmers had been crucified not upon a cross of gold but rather upon the cross of foreign trade. "They built up a scale of production far beyond domestic needs," he wrote, "and their present pains are somewhat proportionate to the collapse of the foreign markets."[21] The flight of American farmers from the agrarian economy constituted the worst catastrophe in American history.

Ransom saw little prospect of recovering the foreign markets for American agriculture, so he sounded a general retreat from commercial farming. Only a duplicitous and misguided revolution could have induced American farmers to believe that they might purchase a better life from Woolworth's department store or from the Sears, Roebuck catalog than they could make with their own hands. To deliver the United States from its gross economic miscalculations, Ransom hoped to agitate a counterrevolution that would reinstate a traditional agrarian way of life, freed from the burdens of international commerce. The national, and ideally even the international, economy must again become subordinate

21. *Ibid.*, 516.

to the agrarian community in which men relied mainly on their own homemade items. If Americans would put the "agrarian economy above their money economy," Ransom promised, they "may have about all the money they are now making and most of their own living besides."[22]

Any permanent solution to the economic crisis had not only to find men work to do but to find them work that was productive, meaningful, and rewarding. Honest and able men would not permit themselves to accept charity. Philanthropic campaigns organized and funded by agencies of the federal government or by big business might temporarily ease their suffering. But these efforts, however noble and generous, could never develop and sustain lasting opportunities that would render such munificence unnecessary. Neither government nor business could satisfy their obligations by furnishing the needy with some wretched allotment or subsidy that was little better than a bribe. Not only would that solution have been flagrantly and crassly immoral; it would have constituted irresponsible social and economic policy.

To maintain their identity and their self-respect, men had to work. The federal government had to establish economic self-sufficiency as the main goal of its national policy, making it possible for men once again to assimilate themselves into an agrarian community that would care for them and enable them to care for themselves. "The chief consideration of any political economy at this moment," Ransom concluded, "is to assign a really economic function to every member of economic society."[23] Subjected to the impersonal demands of the corporation and the inhumane fluctuations of the market, ordinary citizens in capitalist society had lost control over their economic lives. To recover their individuality and their independence, Ransom counseled, Americans should look to the land, enduring, inexhaustible, fecund.

The blessings of the agrarian way of life were abundant. American farmers raised corn, wheat, and cotton aplenty. Additionally, the agrarian way of life produced superior human beings. If agriculture represented a commercial liability within the expanding money economy, it remained the finest material asset the United States had for establishing homes, preserving families, implanting patriotism, and preparing men to face the vicissitudes of life.

22. Ransom, "The State and the Land," 9.
23. Ransom, "Land! An Answer to the Unemployment Problem," 216.

Politically terrified and spiritually desperate Americans could find solace on the land. Subsistence farming, unlike commercial farming, would excite a simple joy in living and laboring. Agricultural work would remedy the routinized monotony of machine labor and soothe the anxious nerves of overwrought businessmen, shopkeepers, and factory workers. The leisurely rhythm of the agrarian life, which Ransom thought was practiced with more devotion by black than by white farmers, offered a sure antidote to the hectic pace of the modern world.[24]

Reverting to a predominantly agrarian economy, Ransom was convinced, would also cultivate responsibility and pride in the hearts of the American people. The specialization of labor that industrialism required deprived men of their intelligence, individuality, and independence. They learned to obey orders, not to make decisions. They were neither blamed for shoddy workmanship nor credited for a job well done. Industrial laborers were reduced to hirelings who did as they were told, without question or consideration. Such a malleable work force might have comprised an efficient army of industrial automatons, but it hardly composed a republican citizenry of independent and virtuous human beings.

Agrarians were the last free men in America. The farmers designed and executed each of the tasks that they performed. They controlled the whole job and answered to no one save themselves and their God. Without complaint or regret, they accepted responsibility for the consequences of their actions. They owned, administered, and worked their private enterprises, the very model of propertied citizens.

Agrarian farming also enabled men to experience the full spectrum of the human condition. They were "the most whole," Ransom wrote, and "therefore the most wholesome" of men.[25] The social relations of an agrarian community were personal, moral, and neighborly, not perfunctory, juridical, and economic. Unlike industrial work, farm labor of the agrarian sort was not intent on enslaving men to a system that demanded their perfect adherence in order to obtain absolute efficiency and maximum output. The old-fashioned agrarian economy was, by nature, inefficient, its proprietors savoring the privileged liberty to work

---

24. See Ransom, "Happy Farmers," 527–32, and John Crowe Ransom, "Sociology in the Black Belt," *American Review*, IV (1934), 147–54.

25. Ransom, "The South Is a Bulwark," 302.

or not and in their ample spare time to read or doze, to hunt, to fish, or to contemplate the splendor of creation.[26]

Nostalgia shines through Ransom's vision of agrarian life. More revealing is his insistence that agricultural labor resisted specialization. Behind Ransom's assertion that the agrarian order subverted the division of labor lay a conviction, to which he adhered faithfully if temporarily throughout the 1930s, that agrarianism could resolve the conflict between the individual and society. Ransom conjectured that if the farmer "is his own carpenter, painter, roadmaker, forester, meat packer, woodcutter, gardener, nurseryman, dairyman, poulterer, and handy man— then he has a fair-sized man's job on his hands which will occupy him sufficiently at all seasons." He continued describing the farmer's life: "His hard work will come in the spring and summer, but if his work slackens after that, no confirmed lover of nature will begrudge him a little leisure time for hunting, fishing, and plain country meditation." Given his animosity toward Marxism, it is astonishing how similar Ransom's sentiments were to those reflected in *The German Ideology* of Karl Marx. Marx wrote:

> For as soon as the division of labour comes into being, each man has a particular, exclusive sphere of activity, which is forced upon him and from which he cannot escape. He is a hunter, a fisherman, a shepherd, or a critical critic, and must remain so if he does not want to lose his means of livelihood; while in communist society, where nobody has one exclusive sphere of activity but each can become accomplished in any branch he wishes, society regulates the general production and thus makes it possible for me to do one thing today and another tomorrow, to hunt in the morning, fish in the afternoon, rear cattle in the evening, criticise after dinner, just as I have a mind, without ever becoming hunter, fisherman, shepherd, or critic.[27]

In the agrarian society that Ransom imagined, the antagonism between mental and physical labor would vanish, and men would work willingly and joyfully, without compulsion. Unlike Marx, Ransom did

26. See Ransom, "Land! An Answer to the Unemployment Problem," 219, 223, and Ransom, "Happy Farmers," 531–32.

27. Ransom, "Land! An Answer to the Unemployment Problem," 223; Karl Marx, *The German Ideology,* in *The Marx-Engels Reader,* ed. Robert C. Tucker (2nd ed.; New York, 1978), 160.

not contemplate or countenance the sustained development of the forces of production and the continued expansion of material prosperity. It was not that Ransom predicated his agrarian social order on material scarcity and deprivation. Instead, he depended on the bounty that men, with a minimum of effort, could coax from nature to satisfy all human needs. He hoped that agrarian civilization would at last enable men to accept the limitations that nature imposed on them and halt their incessant struggle to extend their dominion over it. Perhaps the greatest advantage of the agrarian way of life was the restraint it imposed on human ambition.

Ransom, for a time, even advocated arresting technological innovation and eliminating the division of labor as the only sensible means of releasing men from the bondage of industrial capitalism. Only a subsistence economy could support a free, humane, cooperative, communal life. And the United States could afford the luxury of freedom. Americans were already well on their way to securing a more opulent economic future than was historically allotted to the other peoples of the earth. "The per capita natural wealth of this country," Ransom declared, "is all but beyond comparison greater than that of other nations, and it is astonishing to find economists concluding that its development can proceed only by tactics which are harsh and sacrificial of human rights."[28] Great Britain, for example, plagued by a shortage of arable land, would find an agrarian economy impracticable, if not intolerable. In England, farmers could engage in only commercial farming and thereby make the most of what little they had.

Nature had favored, or cursed, the United States with too much land. Without the formation of an agrarian movement to enforce subsistence farming, Americans would find it difficult to overcome this potentially disabling endowment. If commercial farming continued unabated, the agricultural sector of the economy would eventually succumb to a crisis of overproduction, as the industrial sector already had. Under those circumstances, Ransom argued, only the surrender of the traditional American commitment to liberty and independence, the acceptance of a planned economy, and the state ownership of property would avert disaster. To Ransom, the communists alone, among all the political parties

28. Ransom, "The South Is a Bulwark," 301.

operating in the United States, understood this possibility, but they, of course, welcomed, and even worked to hasten, its coming.

If Americans did not ratify the agrarian solution to the current predicament, then they would perforce begin to take their orders from a Supreme Soviet. Industrial capitalism, with its commercial base, would likely collapse, which would, in turn, precipitate massive unemployment, labor violence, and class warfare and would culminate in socialist revolution in the United States. Amid the anarchy ensuing in the wake of revolution, bedeviled citizens would clamor for the reimposition of order and would listen to anyone who promised to deliver.

The Communist party, fully prepared to take advantage of this situation, would recommence where its capitalist enemies had left off. Having wrested control of property from private hands, the communists would place it under the control of the state. They would collectivize, or "sovietize," industry and agriculture, setting production quotas, allocating resources, and assigning personnel without regard to individual preference, traditional prerogative, or natural propriety. The American people, already obedient and disciplined through long familiarity with the industrial regime, would surrender their integrity, responsibility, and independence in exchange for assurances of economic prosperity and social peace.

The backward, agrarian South thus stood as the last bulwark against socialist revolution, postponing indefinitely the communist millennium. "Farmers," Ransom rejoiced, "are bad medicine for Marxians."[29] Communism naturally proceeded from corporate capitalism, and both threatened the agrarian South.[30] Southern civilization rested on a tradition of local independence, and southerners defied the concentrated power of the corporation and the state, whether dominated by capitalists or communists. Nor were southerners temperamentally or culturally suited to the rigors of industrial civilization. "There are many instances that show that . . . the Southern tempo is not too hospitable to the civilization of the machine."[31]

---

29. *Ibid.,* 302.

30. I have found no evidence that Ransom read Lenin, but the idea that communism proceeded from corporate capitalism was the thesis of V. I. Lenin's *Imperialism: The Highest Stage of Capitalism* (New York, 1979).

31. Ransom, "Regionalism in the South," 111.

Southerners were devoted to leisure, and leisure was the prerequisite for aesthetic experience. The addiction to machines, on the contrary, purged the aesthetic sensibility. The elimination of the aesthetic component from life, Ransom feared, would finally and irrevocably destroy the South. Southerners had long ago settled in a place between the rocks and the trees and made their peace with nature and man. Were machines to come to the South, not only would they disrupt the harmony of southern civilization, which had persisted for centuries, but they would also defile the beauty of the southern countryside, which had existed since God gathered the waters into the sea and separated the earth from the sky.

Ransom despaired that so many of his neighbors seemed eager to exchange their rich inheritance for the paltry rewards of the machine age. He insisted that the level of civilization could not be measured out by the miles of paved road or by the number of homes wired for electricity or by the amount of money in the bank. The South may have been impoverished, but the region and its people possessed a secret spiritual wealth that empowered them to take their stand against the machine. If the South had to endure a partial economic reconstruction to survive in the modern world, Ransom implored, then southerners themselves should undertake and direct the process. Only southerners who knew and loved the land could save the South from becoming yet another victim of blind industrial progress.

As a political and economic strategy, Ransom's agrarian proposals would no doubt have condemned countless southerners to lives of grinding poverty and acute deprivation at the level of minimal subsistence. The legacy of slavery, the decline of the cotton economy, and the failure to distribute land to those who needed it most left twentieth-century southern agriculture backward and inefficient, groaning under the double burden of tenant farming and debt peonage. Ransom's advocacy of a general movement back to the land and a nearly universal resumption of subsistence farming exposed his ignorance of the economic and political realities that rural southerners faced during the 1930s.

THE RETREAT FROM AGRARIANISM

Whether Ransom recognized the implications of his views, by the mid-1930s there was a decided change in the tenor of his essays. He began to advocate innovations that would "improve" the traditional farm economy and soften the hardships of agrarian life.

The state, he now argued, should provide its rural population with a good general education to accompany instruction in applying the latest agricultural techniques of selecting the finest seeds, breeding the healthiest livestock, and choosing the best fertilizers. There should also be additional amenities. Farmers should have paved roads. Electricity should be delivered inexpensively to their homes. Ransom even confessed, albeit reluctantly, that the prosperity of the urban-industrial sector of the economy benefited farmers by assuring them of a domestic market for their produce and by supplying them with the goods that they could not make for themselves.[32] By 1936, Ransom had qualified his opposition to industrialism as well as his commitment to agrarianism.

As Ransom's questions mounted about the feasibility and the desirability of implementing the Agrarian program, he began to weary of the cause. "I'm signing off but a little by degrees," he advised Tate in April, 1937 (*SL, 222*). In June, he wrote to Edwin Mims that he no longer intended to concern himself much with issues of regionalism or agrarianism. Ransom sensed that, for him, the political defense of the southern tradition had unduly circumscribed the range of his thought.

There were deeper reasons for Ransom's retreat from Agrarianism. A subtle irony troubled his Agrarian vision. He had long maintained that the agrarian way of life did homage to the land, dictating the concessions that men ought reasonably to make to nature. Yet the Agrarian philosophy also enabled men to use nature. For all that it complicated men's relations to nature, the Agrarian philosophy offered no guarantee against nature's eventual exploitation. The land did not transform men; men transformed the land.

Even in the limited sense that Ransom approved, the use of nature involved rational planning and scientific calculation. Such actions may have appeased the material appetite, but they did nothing to satisfy the aesthetic sensibility. In this sense, art was superior to economics and science, which, in distinct but related ways, not only permitted but encouraged the exploitation of nature. Indeed, nature itself possessed a certain utility that poetry did not. Men could use nature; a poem they could merely contemplate. Ransom, unfortunately, never commented on the

32. See Ransom, "The South Is a Bulwark," 302.

political manipulation of art and literature that took place during the 1930s in Germany, Italy, the Soviet Union, the United States, and elsewhere.

Poetry imitated, and thereby acknowledged, the superiority of nature. Science and economics, to the contrary, attempted to master, possess, and manipulate nature for the supposed improvement of mankind. "Art exists for knowledge," Ransom wrote, "but nature is an object both to knowledge and to use; the latter disposition of nature includes that knowledge of it which is peculiarly scientific, and sometimes it is so imperious as to pre-empt all possibility of the former" (*WB*, 197).

Men had repeatedly coerced nature to fit scientific categories that assumed a monopoly on truth. Armed with formulas and equations, scientists limited the world to identifiable patterns, manageable classifications, and definable categories. They established the typical relation: the formal hypothesis, the abstract precept, the universal law. Phenomena in their complex multiplicity neither captured the interest nor commanded the attention of the scientific mind. Instrumental, pragmatic, and relentless, scientists dissociated the intricately related facets of experience and attempted to extract from nature its material utility or its exchange value. The scientific method thus accommodated comfortably to the requirements and aspirations of modern economics.[33]

For Ransom, Agrarianism did not in the end offer an alternative to the scientific and economic exploitation of nature. His gradual abandonment of Agrarianism brought him back to his first loves, poetry and criticism, which he believed he had neglected. Whatever concessions men of letters had to make to live in the modern scientific-industrial world, Ransom was certain that poetry and criticism offered an alternate vision of order for those daring few who could acknowledge and accept it. Thus, by the mid-1930s, he had turned aside from politics and economics and took up once more the philosophical inquiry into the nature and meaning of poetry that he had temporarily forsaken.

33. See *WB*, 29–75, 111–42, 193–232.

2

Ransom and the Republic of Letters: A Faraway Time of Gentleness

> O hear the maiden pageant ever sing
> Of that far away time of gentleness
> —John Crowe Ransom, "Of Margaret"

ART AND THE HUMAN ECONOMY

Urbane, erudite, and reserved, John Crowe Ransom was an unlikely leader of a political crusade. His temperament and his intellect were unsuited to partisan enthusiasm. He approached problems from multiple perspectives and saw issues in all their complexity. Inevitably, he uncovered the logical inconsistencies that plagued even his favorite arguments and positions. He was forever rethinking, reappraising, and revising, as he did even with his poetry late in life. For Ransom, no work was ever complete, no idea ever final. All earlier formulations, judgments, and conclusions were subject to amendment. These characteristics are hardly the mark of the committed ideologue devoted to his exclusive vision of the truth.

Indeed, Ransom refused to view himself as the leader of the Agrarian movement, much as he had earlier refused to view himself as the leader of the Fugitive poets. Nevertheless, he became the foremost spokesman for Southern Agrarianism. He wrote the "Statement of Principles" that prefaced *I'll Take My Stand*. His "Reconstructed but Unregenerate," a compilation of two earlier pieces, was the first essay in the collection.

After publication of *I'll Take My Stand,* Ransom urged his fellow Agrarians to join him in formulating practical strategies to transform American political, social, and economic life. He proposed the acquisition of small-town newspapers across Tennessee to introduce and popularize Agrarian doctrine among the masses.[1] He debated the relative merits of "the Agrarian way of life versus the industrial or American way," twice with Stringfellow Barr, professor of history at the University of Virginia and editor of the *Virginia Quarterly Review*, and once with William S. Knickerbocker, editor of the *Sewanee Review*.[2]

During the 1930s, Ransom wrote a series of essays that offered a detailed, if at times superficial, analysis of the Depression. He outlined political and economic alternatives to Franklin D. Roosevelt's New Deal agricultural policies and public works programs and to the more sinister projects of the socialists and the fascists.[3] Ransom, already an accomplished poet and essayist and a blossoming literary critic, tried throughout the 1930s to make himself into a political economist and a social activist. When John Crowe Ransom took his stand, he meant it.

But by 1937, when he left Vanderbilt University for Kenyon College, Ransom had abandoned the Agrarian movement, even as he sought to realize similar ideals by other means. In a letter to Edwin Mims, Ransom announced that he had just about given up writing on regionalism and agrarianism and planned to devote himself fully to literary criticism. Ransom wrote of the scholarship he would pursue at Kenyon: "It is true that if this kind of writing were on regionalism or agrarianism, I would be going to foreign parts. But I have about contributed all I have to those movements, and I have of late gone almost entirely into pure literary work. My group does not need me" (*SL*, 223).[4]

Even before he left Vanderbilt and the South, Ransom had begun to edge away from Agrarianism. He warned Tate, writing on September 17, 1936, that politics and poetry did not mix. The Agrarians could not be both patriots and poets, unless they were content to write bad poetry.

1. See *SL*, 188–99.
2. See Donald Davidson, "3,500 Pack Hall as Ransom, Barr Debate Southern Problems," Richmond *Times-Dispatch*, November 15, 1930; "Whither Dixie?—Mr. Barr and Mr. Ransom," Chattanooga *News*, November 22, 1930. George Fort Milton, editor of the Chattanooga *News*, first suggested and then arranged the debate.
3. See *ITMS*, xxxvii–xlviii, 1–27, and the following articles by John Crowe Ransom: "Shall We Complete the Trade?," *Sewanee Review*, XLI (1933), 182–90; "A Capital for the New Deal," *American Review*, II (1933), 129–42; "Heads and Hearts," *American Review*, II (1934), 554–71; "Modern with the Southern Accent," *Virginia Quarterly Review*, XI (April, 1935), 184–200.
4. See *SL*, 224–25. See also Paul K. Conkin, *The Southern Agrarians* (Knoxville, 1988), 127–34.

Their political defense of the South, however admirable, had compelled them to accept certain limitations as poets. Politics had hedged them in. Initially, Agrarianism had seemed, as Donald Davidson said nearly twenty years later, "as much a defense of poetry as of the South." By 1937, however, Ransom had concluded that for him Agrarianism was an impediment to poetry. Having to choose between a defense of hearth and rooftree and a defense of poetry, he left no doubt about where his sympathies lay. "*Patriotism* is eating at *lyricism,*" he told Tate. "What is true in part for you (though a part that is ominously increasing) is true nearly in full for me: *patriotism* has nearly eaten me up, and I've got to get out of it" (*SL,* 217).[5]

To diminish the influence of the "Agrarian-Distributist Movement in our minds," Ransom suggested to Tate, they should formulate an "objective literary standard" (*SL,* 217) and found an American Academy of Letters. In his letter of September 17, Ransom outlined to Tate specific guidelines for election to his proposed academy and offered specific recommendations about eligibility.[6] Ransom's American Academy of Letters bore little resemblance to the academy of "Southern positive reactionaries" that Tate had proposed eight years earlier.

The qualifications for membership were literary dignity, productivity, scope, "positive traditionalism" (by which Ransom hoped to eliminate all those who employed novel or revolutionary literary devices and refused to assimilate their work to a recognized literary tradition), and style, which enabled individual writers to operate distinctively within an established literary tradition. Ransom supplied Tate with an alphabetical list of acceptable members. This list contained twenty-five names, including John Gould Fletcher, John Donald Wade, Stark Young, and Tate himself, whose name, Ransom wrote, "leads all the rest." Beside his own name, Ransom, who maintained that perhaps he should take no part in founding such an organization since he was "diffident as to whether [his] public position would justify [his] part in it," placed a question mark (*SL,* 217).

---

5. See also *SL,* 220–22. For the Agrarians' use of "rooftree," see, for example, Allen Tate's "Sonnets of the Blood": "Think too the rooftree crackles and will fall / On us, who saw the sacred fury's height" (*The Collected Poems of Allen Tate, 1919–1976* [Baton Rouge, 1989], 52).

6. See *LC,* 229–33.

Ransom also included such notable writers as Willa Cather, Theodore Dreiser ("with reluctance"), Robert Frost ("we're almost obliged"), Ellen Glasgow, Joseph Wood Krutch, Archibald MacLeish, Marianne Moore, Paul Elmer More, Ezra Pound, George Santayana, Edith Wharton, and Yvor Winters. On the list of the "*nearly* qualified" were Robert Penn Warren, Frank Owsley, Andrew Lytle, Caroline Gordon, and Donald Davidson (*SL,* 218). Conspicuous by his absence, whether by design or possibly by oversight, was William Faulkner.[7]

Tate intended his program not only to conceive a distinctly southern literary and intellectual tradition but to articulate a complete world view that would form the basis of a southern conservative movement. Ransom, instead, eschewed politics and economics and subordinated history, tradition, and religion to pure fiction, pure poetry, and pure criticism. "Our intentions would be two," he wrote Tate subsequently, "and they would look contradictory; to have our literature created by persons of philosophical capacity; to have its pure forms without taint of explicit philosophy" (*SL,* 220).

More important, Ransom insisted that his academy was the "American Academy of Letters," not the "Southern Academy of Letters." He told Tate that membership would have to be "pretty catholic"; literature, like politics, necessarily made "strange bedfellows." Ransom's would be a national academy of letters in the service of American, not southern, literature and thought. To confuse an American Academy of Letters with a Fugitive or an Agrarian organization, or with an academy of "Southern positive reactionaries," was to court disaster. To establish such a southern academy would bring the Agrarians, at least those who composed poetry, into dangerous proximity to the patriotic fervor that threatened to dissolve their poetic sensibilities. "It wouldn't do us any good," Ransom concluded. "We can whip out our Southern writers too easily" (*SL,* 219).

Eight years after Ransom left Vanderbilt and wrote to Tate to suggest the creation of an American Academy of Letters, he publicly announced his break with the Agrarian movement. In "Art and the Human Economy," which appeared in the *Kenyon Review* in 1945, Ransom de-

---

7. Ransom frequently praised Faulkner's work. However, in a review of Faulkner's novel *Pylon* published in the Nashville *Banner* on March 24, 1935, Ransom wrote, "I think it is time to conclude: William Faulkner is spent."

clared that the Agrarians suffered a nostalgia for a southern past that never existed. He now adopted a position similar to that of William Knickerbocker, one of the earliest critics of the Agrarian movement. In an essay entitled "Mr. Ransom and the Old South," published in 1931, Knickerbocker had written of Ransom's impassioned defense of the South:

> Undoubtedly he knows the immense power of the existing nostalgia in the South for "the good old days," for the seductiveness of his appeal lies largely in his subtle employment of sentiment. Therefore, since he makes a sentimental appeal to the Old South I shall limit myself to the discussion of the reasonableness of that appeal. I shall be blunt: I dispute it. I shall make every effort to demonstrate that a rounded economic life for the South was a major effort made by some of the best known and most inspiring leaders of the Old South. Those statesmen and publicists were aware of the dangers of an agrarian monopoly which excluded the possibilities of a fully-orbed economic, or indeed, cultural life. In making this criticism, therefore, of the Nashville agrarians and particularly of Mr. Ransom, I am convinced that I am merely defending the increasing industrialism of the South today, I am only demonstrating how that order is the fruition of their most ardent hopes.[8]

By 1945, Ransom had come to agree with the substance of Knickerbocker's critique. He concluded that the Agrarians, himself included, had been little more than dreamy romantics of the sort that they had always despised. They had been young then, but time had now remedied that deficiency. The perspective that accompanied age enabled Ransom to see Agrarianism for what it was: a penalty inflicted on a defeated people.

The immediate context of Ransom's reassessment of the Agrarian movement was the Declaration of Potsdam, which, he argued, imposed an agrarian economy on a defeated Germany. A way of life that Ransom once thought would provide "no greater happiness for a people" now became an "inhuman punishment" for a people who "in the natural course of things have left the garden far behind."[9]

Ransom doubtless had in mind a different context for his remarks, one more distant and historical yet at the same time more immediate and contemporary: the fate of the antebellum South and the Agrarian defense

8. John Crowe Ransom, "Art and the Human Economy," *Kenyon Review*, VII (1945), 683–88; William S. Knickerbocker, "Mr. Ransom and the Old South," *Sewanee Review*, XXXIX (1931), 222–39.
9. Ransom, "Art and the Human Economy," 687.

of the southern tradition. Adherence to an agrarian economy, he was now convinced, had retarded the development of the antebellum South and effected its collapse before the progressive forces of modernity. The Agrarians, vindicating the South and its traditions even in defeat, believed that they had discovered a way of life in which the original innocence of humanity might be recovered.

Although they struggled to revitalize that world, the Agrarians never practiced what they preached. They did not, Ransom noted, return to the farm or to the plantation, save "with the exceptions which . . . were not thoroughgoing."[10] He applauded the youthful enthusiasm of the Agrarians in celebrating agriculture, which remained a valuable component of any properly balanced economy. Yet in time, he declared, conscience would not permit them to require of others what they could not themselves do: become practicing agrarians.

The mistaken quest to reestablish an agricultural economy and an agrarian way of life was futile from the start. For Ransom, by 1945, and even as early as 1937, the only practical strategy became realistic surrender to industrialism and capitalism. He consoled himself with the thought that industrialism and capitalism, subjected to exacting regulation and shorn of their worst abuses, would become at least tolerable and might, in fact, yield unforeseen benefits.

The new economy that southerners had already begun to embrace would in time bring them wealth and power, which Ransom hoped they would learn to use judiciously. Mass production and mass consumption would improve the standard of living and the quality of life in the South for whites and blacks alike. The solution to the problem of race relations, for example, would come, Ransom thought, primarily not through coercion, confrontation, or moral suasion but through the recognition that the benefits of industrial capitalism had to be extended to all. "Otherwise," he concluded, "it will be the worse for the prosperity of captains of industry, bankers, farmers, and storekeepers alike."[11] Mass production and mass consumption offered a powerful economic incentive to eradicate the most historically delicate of southern problems.

Of course, Ransom found industrial capitalism far from perfect. Its great potential for the alienation, exploitation, and destruction of man

10. *Ibid.,* 686. See also Conkin, *The Southern Agrarians,* 131.
11. "A Symposium: The Agrarians Today," *Shenandoah,* III (Summer, 1952), 15.

and nature remained. He believed, though, that the New Deal had "humanized" the industrial-capitalist economy, not only by making its blessings more universally accessible, but by according perceptive and articulate critics, like Ransom himself, the license to analyze, expose, and censure its deficiencies.

Artists and writers who had accommodated themselves to industrial capitalism could retreat from the rough world of economics and politics into the isolated enclave of the liberal arts college, where art, literature, and criticism flourished. Although these delicate souls lived economically and politically in the world of mass production and mass consumption, they could somehow live intellectually and spiritually according to the ancient Western tradition of letters, which, Ransom declared, "was founded upon the life of the land." [12] They could still enjoy and produce art, poetry, and criticism, for they did not have to conform to the economic determinism of modern life.

In a curious, perhaps ironic, way, the essential component of the modern economy, the division of labor, even enhanced the possibilities for the flowering of art. The division of labor, in Ransom's analysis, made human action more effective and efficient by limiting the materials with which a laborer worked. Although a productive society had eventually to confront the whole of nature, each individual worker knew nature only as the stubborn set of materials that he had to subject to the transformative power of his labor. The labor of a single worker was no longer sufficient to sustain himself or his family. Consequently, he, like his counterparts, grew ever more dependent on his fellow workers.

His relations with other workers, however necessary for survival, were not spontaneous, individual, and deep as had been the relations between men in an agrarian society, in which everyone performed most of the necessary tasks of life for himself. Instead, industrial capitalism, Ransom argued, induced merely functional relations between men, as if the laborers in field or factory who supplied food and clothing for other workers and their families had only an economic existence. Ransom, however distressed at this development, nevertheless concluded that it was now impractical and undesirable for modern men to abandon the division of labor in favor of some primitive form of organization, no matter how attractive it might appear. Modern men would not wish to resume the

12. *Ibid.*, 16.

estate of "good animals" opposing nature without the benefit of reason and science. Indeed, the division of labor had become so ingrained in human nature that it was inescapable. "We are far gone in our habit of specialized labor, whether we work with our heads or our hands; it has become our second nature and nearly the only human nature that we can have, in a responsible public sense."[13]

To live thus, however, was to acknowledge human sinfulness. Human beings lived in a fallen world of their own making. They could not pretend to an innocent harmony with nature and the rest of humanity; they had to recognize that their very survival depended on the use and even the exploitation of men and nature. A condition properly called "decadent" was the human portion, and guilt characterized the human condition. Men in modern society could not return to the original state of human purity, simplicity, and innocence, but they could seek salvation from their fallen state by adopting the means of repentance at hand.

Art returned modern men to their original innocence. This vicarious and formal transformation compensated human beings for their sense of alienation from nature, from each other, from themselves, and from God without requiring them to abandon what Ransom called the "forward economy." He hoped that modern men would not be foolish enough to sacrifice the division of labor in exchange for some more primitive and inferior economic and social order. If men foreswore the division of labor, even with its heavy costs, catastrophe would result. For such division liberated them from drudgery and hardship through technological innovation, from scarcity and deprivation through mass production, from degradation and poverty through the mass market. No one, Ransom confessed, himself included, could now afford to give up the material prosperity and comfort that science, technology, and the division of labor made possible.

Specialization of labor also enhanced the freedom to pursue artistic projects. No longer constrained to produce for themselves the essentials of life, men possessed of literary and artistic genius could devote their time to the contemplation and creation of beauty. Without the specialization of labor, Ransom feared, these aspirations would have been immeasurably stunted, if not utterly repressed. With the disappearance of art, modern men would lose the one means of renewal, revitalization,

13. Ransom, "Art and the Human Economy," 685.

and redemption available to them, the one means of defying the worst ravages of an industrialized world.

Upon the division of labor, therefore, rested not only the production of goods but the creation of art. By freeing writers and artists, the division of labor directly supported their vocation. Independence awaited those courageous and honest few who, "engaged upon the progressive division of labor yet given to hideous lapses of zeal and faith," embraced the salvific power of art, however isolating, alienating, and painful that embrace might be. For the artist or writer, the pursuit of his vocation was worth any adversity or affliction. Ransom clarified his argument in "Art and The Human Economy":

> Without consenting to division of labor, and hence modern society, we should have not only no effective science, invention, and scholarship, but nothing to speak of in art, e.g., Reviews and contributions to Reviews, fine poems and their exegesis. . . . The pure though always divided knowledges, and the physical gadgets and commodities, constitute our science, and are the guilty fruits; but the former are triumphs of muscular intellect, and the latter at best are clean and wholly at our service. The arts are the expiations, but they are beautiful. Together they comprise the detail of human history. They seem worth the vile welter through which homeless spirits must wade between times, with sensibilities subject to ravage as they are. On these terms the generic human economy can operate, and they are the only terms practicable now.[14]

Ransom identified the division of labor as a historical phenomenon that, if not specific to capitalism, was certainly sanctified by the capitalist system. In the "Statement of Principles" that prefaced I'll Take My Stand, Ransom had once condemned the division of labor for facilitating the organized, systematic exploitation of the many by the few, of the weak by the strong. The division of labor, for him and the other Agrarians, unnecessarily and unnaturally fragmented the human community, separated physical from intellectual work, and reduced individual men to economic abstractions from which to extract labor power. Like earlier political economists from Adam Smith to Karl Marx, Ransom, in the "Statement of Principles," deplored the indignity and degradation to

14. *Ibid.*, 685, 686.

which capitalism subjected human beings, enslaving them with the instruments of their own creativity and imagination.

Like Marx, too, the Agrarians posited a historical and political solution to the alienation that arose from the division of labor. For Marx, that solution was the revolution of the proletariat, which would eradicate the exploitative ruling class and free men to enjoy the full bounty of their labor. Marx, who consistently acclaimed both the productive efficiency of capitalism and the revolutionary potential of the bourgeoisie, would have repudiated the Agrarians' call to reestablish the predominance of an agricultural economy. He dealt mercilessly with advocates of precapitalist social relations and would have viewed the agrarian alternative to industrial capitalism as hopelessly reactionary.

Unlike Marx, Ransom eventually gave up trying to reconcile the individual with society. He came to accept conflict, tension, and alienation as inherent aspects of human nature and the human condition—aspects that could not be eradicated by any political, social, or economic arrangements. The effects of these phenomena, however, could be softened by art. Hence, as Ransom lost interest in the politics and economics of Agrarianism, he turned exclusively to aesthetics and literary criticism. Yet despite his withdrawal from "regionalism and agrarianism," he by no means abandoned the underlying goal of the Agrarian movement: the attempt to fashion a humane way of life in the modern world. For Ransom, the principal tools of that work now became poetry and criticism rather than politics and economics.

THE MAN OF LETTERS IN THE MODERN WORLD

Ransom's metamorphosis exposed how strikingly different were his conceptions of poetry and of the role of the man of letters in the modern world from those that his friends and colleagues, Tate and Davidson, had developed. As Tate edged closer to Roman Catholicism, converting in 1950, he became less sanguine about the redemptive power of art and less inclined to envision the artist as a high priest or cult deity. Art could not provide a religious faith or a unifying myth; it could only reflect and illuminate what already existed. In Tate's view, art and culture could not flourish or even survive without Revelation.

The value of art, Tate believed, thus lay in illuminating the contradictory nature of the human condition. Men were finite creatures who aspired to transcend their finitude. They stood firmly rooted in nature and history yet found ultimate meaning for their lives beyond the natural and temporal world. This divided consciousness was the source of the social and psychic tension that characterized the human condition and from which salvation through grace promised a release. Attempts to exalt human beings beyond their proper station and to establish a heaven on earth were at once sinful and disastrous. Although Tate conceded that willful pride was an ancient transgression, its manifestations in the twentieth century were especially disturbing.

The horror of the twentieth century demanded explanation from the modern man of letters. The proper role for writers, Tate thought, was not to incite political revolution, excite religious revival, or inspire social reform but to explain the consequences of ignoring the conditions under which God permitted life on earth. Tate devoted his entire career as a poet and an essayist to challenging the one-dimensional view of man that rejected the transcendent dimension of human existence and suggested that all human problems were subject to human, *i.e.,* political, scientific, or technological, solutions. The modern man of letters, if faithful to his vocation, could not propose alternatives or provide solutions. To Tate's way of thinking, the writer could not construct a social, political, or spiritual order that would hold chaos at bay.

The special contribution of the modern man of letters derived in Tate's analysis from his unique awareness of "Gnostic arrogance" and the pressing need for "Augustinian humility." The modern man of letters, according to Tate, had the responsibility to report the spiritual condition of modern man. In the twentieth century, the scientist, industrialist, entrepreneur, and statesman, bent on secular conquest, had forgotten that hell existed, at least for themselves, because they had lost the language to describe it.

Hence, the principal duty of the man of letters was to revitalize and protect a language that depicted the complexity and mystery, the joy and agony, of the human condition. If men of letters did not call attention to sin and its wages, Tate feared, modern men would confidently deny them, for men lived under the barbarous disability of believing that the evils they could not name did not exist. The poet had to identify and define those aspects of the human condition that others could not discern. He must detail not his enemies' hell but his own.

The modern man of letters, Tate wrote, had an obligation:

[He has] to render the image of man as he is in his time, which without the man of letters, would not otherwise be known. What modern literature has taught us is not merely that the man of letters has not participated fully in the action of society; it has taught us that nobody else has either. It is a fearful lesson. The roll-call of the noble and sinister characters, our ancestors and our brothers, who exemplify the lesson, must end in a shudder: Julian Sorel, Emma Bovary, Captain Ahab, Hepzibah Pyncheon, Roderick Usher, Lambert Strether, Baron de Charlus, Stephen Dedalus, Joe Christmas. . . . Have men of letters perversely invented these horrors? They are rather the inevitable creations of a secularized society, the society of means without ends, in which nobody participates in the full substance of his humanity.[15]

Tate deplored the emergence of a "new provincialism" among modern men in general and among modern writers in particular. He condemned the cult of the alienated, independent man of letters. Shorn of historical allegiance, social commitment, spiritual identity, and moral discipline, the modern man of letters decried the world as irredeemably corrupt, abdicated his responsibility, and retreated to some safe haven where, with followers gathered at his feet, he indulged his private fantasies in a contrived language accessible only to the initiate. Such men, Tate declared, must cease disseminating novelty and distraction and worshiping at the altars of the parvenu gods of modernity, who taught that the "unchanging source of knowledge" was inscribed not in the mind of God but in the minds of men, specifically in the minds of literary men.

Like Tate, but more insistently, Donald Davidson rejected mind as the sole origin of knowledge and meaning. He desired to return mind to the service of a society of myth and tradition. To that end, he attempted to reconstitute the ancient community of the pagan tribe and to resurrect it in the modern South. Davidson scorned the modern products of mind—science, technology, and industry—and declared that the best way to end the crisis of modernity was to cultivate piety for the southern tradition. He discovered his image of the modern man of letters not, like Tate, in the besieged figure of the medieval clerk who depicted the sources of tension in, and the hope for redemption from, the human condition but in the heroic figure of the bard who sang the glories of

15. Allen Tate, "The Man of Letters in the Modern World," in *Collected Essays* (Denver, 1959), 384–85.

his people and who recalled for them their origins, their identity, and their destiny.

Genuine knowledge was neither scientific nor poetic but organic and experiential, arising from the unified, collective consciousness of a people. Davidson yearned to achieve this "spiritualization of the secular" by transforming the South not only through the symbolic but through the actual recovery of a society of myth and tradition. Southern society, he asserted, could replace the fragmented modern world of despair and alienation and resume its character as a redemptive community that could save men from themselves. The authority of the man of letters as bard became, for Davidson, the instrument through which the South would assert its redemptive power.

Hence, Davidson was understandably outraged by what he perceived as Ransom's betrayal of the Agrarian cause. From his perspective, Ransom had joined the liberals and the progressives in renouncing the efficacy and sanctity of traditional society, while Davidson almost alone steadfastly kept the southern faith. As early as 1935, with the planning and publication of the joint Agrarian-Distributist manifesto *Who Owns America? A New Declaration of Independence,* Davidson began to feel estranged from his friends and no longer seemed to enjoy the relaxed sociability that had characterized the group since their days as Fugitive poets. Ransom attributed Davidson's detachment and isolation in part to personality and in part to ideology. Davidson's inflexible southern patriotism, Ransom confessed to Tate, had arrested Davidson's growth not only as a poet but as the crusader that he professed to be:

> Don is a real problem to me. I haven't been able yet to write him about his book of selected poems, and I simply couldn't touch them in a published review; nor do I dare send them out to any good reviewer. Don just stopped growing before the rest of us did. . . . Don's case is partly private but partly, I'm afraid, the effect of ideology; his peculiar patriotism, consciously or unconsciously, is one that calls for no action, just speeches and poems; and I'm sure many Southerners are in the same way their own worst enemies. (*SL,* 257)[16]

Until "Art and the Human Economy" appeared in the autumn of 1945, Davidson and Ransom, though distant, remained cordial. But just

16. The volume of poetry to which Ransom referred is Davidson's *"Lee in the Mountains" and Other Poems* (Boston, 1939).

as Ransom criticized Davidson's apparent limitations as a poet, so Davidson had already come to suspect that Ransom had begun, bit by bit, to shed his old Agrarian allegiances. Two days after Ransom had written Tate, Davidson also confided to Tate, who found himself uncomfortably in the middle of the widening dispute between his two friends, that he had long surmised Ransom was moving away from Agrarianism. Ransom's surrender puzzled and aggrieved Davidson, who admitted that he never fully understood Ransom's gyrations or irresponsibility but attributed them to a lack of a historical sense. When confronted with a program of reform, like the New Deal, Ransom was overwhelmed and lacked the wherewithal to resist. He therefore seized the most expedient political alternative and capitulated to his former adversaries. Davidson wrote to Tate:

> John's view of American affairs, I believe, is economic & aesthetic, not political-historical; he doesn't read history—I really wonder if he has ever read much American history. And so, he is psychologically unprepared for New Dealism when other things seem hopeless. I don't reproach him for this. I am merely trying to fathom a mystery—a kind of cycle of mystery, for these changes come over John at intervals. I don't think it would make any real difference to him what my notion of the matter would be; but if he does haul down the old flag, or, so to speak, alter its design, I'll have very queer feelings—especially when I'm called upon to say whether those are my views. (*LC*, 301)

Ransom corroborated Davidson's mounting suspicions of treason when he not only published "Art and the Human Economy" but pointedly sent a copy of the essay to Davidson. Upon receiving it, Davidson wrote sardonically to Tate: "I have just received, supposedly from John Ransom, a copy of the Autumn *Kenyon Review*—the only copy I have ever received from John since he began editing it, except for one copy I earned for my one and only review contributed. I wondered why he sent me this large new number. Then I looked through it and found out. It contains John's first open & public recantation of his agrarian principles" (*LC*, 344). What Ransom may have regarded as an act of generosity and collegiality only added to Davidson's sense of insult and injury. Two years earlier, in January, 1943, Davidson was already suggesting to Tate that, though Ransom had not publicly disavowed his Agrarian principles, his "narrow aesthetics" effectively signaled his renunciation of them.[17] When confirmation finally arrived in "Art and the Human Economy," Davidson was saddened, indignant, and angry but hardly surprised.

In a poignant and revealing letter to Tate, he did not question Ransom's prerogative to change his mind and to do so publicly if he desired. On other questions, Ransom often had "swung an axe wildly, not much regarding his friends." Who could stop him this time? He was his own man and master. He had already implicitly severed relations with his fellow Agrarians through his silence on all but purely aesthetic questions.

Davidson could not understand, however, why Ransom, in recanting his Agrarian principles, had approved the most loathsome caricature of them proffered by such scoundrels as George Fort Milton and H. L. Mencken. Why would John Ransom, who once stood shoulder to shoulder with other dauntless critics of this urban, industrial, scientific, secular age, now reverse his course and declare Agrarianism a "childish & unworthy belief" that in his maturity he had sensibly discarded? To Davidson's chagrin, Ransom even accepted the charge that the Agrarians were nostalgic for the plantation with its demure southern belles, its julep-sipping colonels, and its happy slaves. Ransom's sole justification for his temporary dalliance with Agrarianism was, according to Davidson, that it enabled him to produce some valuable poetry. When the artistic well dried up, the time had arrived to pull up stakes and move on. In the end, Davidson could only plead with Tate to tell him "what devil has got into John Ransom?" (*LC*, 344).

Ransom's apostasy, Davidson believed, exposed the other Agrarians to insult, derision, and embarrassment, which would no doubt injure each of them personally and might possibly damage their cause. Someone, preferably an ally from outside the group, ought to issue a trenchant and uncompromising rejoinder that corrected Ransom's more egregious errors. After all, Davidson asserted, the Agrarians were not "proposing to create any utopian & simple agrarian community"; they were "defending the one that existed in the South, such as it was" (*LC*, 344).

Davidson urged Tate not to permit the "Ransom of the North," who spoke so differently from the "Ransom of the South," to misrepresent the meaning of Agrarianism, but Davidson himself could not respond. "I don't feel inclined to write John at all, even a personal letter," he told

17. See *LC*, 329–32.

Tate. "I wonder if I shall ever be able to again"(*LC,* 345). If he did for the moment answer Ransom only with silence, five years later, in 1950, still angry at what he could only view as Ransom's defection, Davidson at last expressed some of the bitterness he felt in a letter to his friend and fellow Agrarian John Gould Fletcher:

> Things have been rather soft and easy for him at Kenyon. In effect, when he went there, he left the field of battle to sit in an Episcopalian, quasi-Oxfordian parlor, where, over the tea-cups, he could refine his aesthetic refinements, pretend that he had never heard of a Southern Agrarian, and study the beauties of the Middle Ohio landscape. He may—and certainly should—realize now that his present position, even his aesthetic position, would be sounder and stronger if he had not in 1937–8 very pointedly begun to eschew all mention, all possible implication, of his former philosophical-religious-political-economic-historical-poetical position as a member—and leader—of the Agrarian movement.[18]

Davidson initially opted for silence in part because he believed that he and Ransom no longer had anything to say to one another on important questions. As far as he was concerned, Ransom had turned irrevocably away from the mythic South that Davidson cherished and had formulated a theory of poetry that Davidson found suspect.

Davidson perhaps never understood the subtlety and complexity of his old friend's aesthetic vision of order. Ransom had substituted poetry and criticism for Agrarianism because he came to believe that they, not politics or economics, were better able to sustain a humane way of life in the modern world. He summarized his evolving perspective in his urgent call for an "ontological criticism."

For a time, the South provided Ransom, as it had Davidson, with an image of culture that resisted the raw power of conquest and domination. Southern culture taught moderation, humility, and restraint. Southerners possessed none of the zeal and arrogance of their northern counterparts. For Ransom, the historical South had represented a world that kept at

18. Donald Davidson to John Gould Fletcher, January 23, 1950, in Donald Davidson Papers, Special Collections, Jean and Alexander Heard Library, Vanderbilt University. Davidson and Ransom eventually reconciled during the Fugitive Reunion in 1956 and Ransom's year at Vanderbilt in 1960.

bay the brutal, predatory impulses inherent in human nature.[19] But the defense of the southern way of life grew wearisome for him. Ransom recognized that southerners themselves had their own dreams of conquest, and he found that patriotism unduly and unnaturally constrained his poetic sensibilities and his critical intelligence. A commitment that had initially excited creativity now became burdensome and deadening. He had to break free.

In abandoning the Agrarian movement, Ransom did not believe he was joining the enemy or capitulating to the ravenous chaos of modernity. Instead, he was merely and immediately seeking other means of resisting the violence and degradation of the modern world. Such means he had already discovered in poetry and criticism, and he sensed that his patriotic commitments had prevented the development of his insights to their full magnitude and significance.

THE COMMUNITY OF LETTERS

Ransom continued to extol the restraining influence of humane culture against the rapacious onslaught of modernity. Once he left Agrarianism behind, though, he mounted a philosophical and aesthetic, rather than an economic, political, and historical, defense of that culture. Ransom transformed his defense by grounding it in aesthetics and metaphysics, explicitly dissociating it from the defense of any extant or historical culture. Order and truth no longer resided in or emerged from fidelity to a defined political economy and social order or from allegiance to a particular place, people, and history.

Ransom envisioned, instead, the emergence of an independent community of letters as the source of order, meaning, and identity in the modern world. For him, letters, not politics or economics, was of paramount importance. The independent men of letters who inhabited this realm were not bound by tradition or devoted to any social order. They were faithful only to art, not, as among the fin-de-siècle aesthetes, for its own sake, but for the vision of humane order that it furnished. Absolute, eternal truth, for Ransom, emerged as the singular domain not

19. See Louise Cowan, "Innocent Doves: Ransom's Feminine Myth of the South," in *American Letters and the Historical Consciousness: Essays in Honor of Lewis P. Simpson,* ed. J. Gerald Kennedy and Daniel Mark Fogel (Baton Rouge, 1987), 191–215.

of the scientist, political economist, historian, or theologian but of the poet and his critical exegete.

Ransom intended his poetic theory to be neither prescientific nor antiscientific but postscientific.[20] His epistemology and ontology advanced poetic knowledge and a poetic vision of order as alternatives to scientific knowledge and a scientific order. Nonetheless, he attempted to take full notice of the contributions of science. Modern men, even poets, schooled in the "pure intellectual disciplines" of science and mathematics could not feign ignorance about the accomplishments of science without feeling foolish. Ransom did not view writing poetry, at least any poetry that the adult could accept, as the act of a naïve and childish mind. He regarded as anathema the "Romantic pathology" that identified the inspiration of poetry as the escape from the privations and humiliations of the real world into some idealized dream world.

Modern men, hard and practical, had to face facts. They toiled and bled to remake the earth in their image and were now not likely to pluck out their eyes because they could not bear to look upon their handiwork. They were the "scarred veterans" of many campaigns who no longer desired "to receive the fragrance of the roses on the world's first morning." They had attained their "heart's desires," and more often than not, they found the struggle and the anticipation more satisfying and worthwhile than the possession of the object. Modern poetry had to compensate these kinds of men. Men became poets or read poetry, Ransom maintained, to expiate their sins, to atone "for having been hard practical men and hard theoretical scientists" (*WB,* xi).[21]

In former times, poets had been men of great public eminence. They served their people as patriots, prophets, and priests; in return, their people, following the custom of the ancient Greeks, crowned them with a wreath of laurel to acknowledge their accomplishments. The poet was a bard, much as Donald Davidson had imagined him, who sang the glories of his race and who, in venerating his people, exalted his craft.

If the poet laureate had survived in places as different as England and Oklahoma, his persona remained, in Ransom's opinion, inappropriate for the modern man of letters to assume. Modern poets were another breed. They were not prudent, pious, or patriotic. They had ceased to

20. See *WB, passim.*
21. See also *BB,* 128–35.

tell enticing tales with simple morals that too frequently gave way to lecturing and pontificating. "Sometimes the so-called poet," Ransom wrote, "has only been a moralist with a poetic manner" (*WB*, 57). Such poets had confounded morality with aesthetics. Statesmen, recognizing the advantages of linking virtue and beauty, called upon the poets to effect the union, and the poets, Ransom lamented, had graciously obliged. Poetry was thus unnaturally wed to patriotism.

Modern poets had asserted their independence and had attempted to divorce aesthetics from morality, the beautiful from the good. Modern poetry was, Ransom declared, "pure poetry" (*WB*, 63). Modern poets had abandoned the constraints that bound their work to morality, piety, and patriotism. They no longer offered pleasing allegorical statements on sacred themes. They no longer celebrated popes and kings, Church and State. They no longer composed remembrances of battles won or lost. The subjects of modern poetry often seemed trivial or meaningless to a confused laity: a seascape, a bowl of fruit, a blackbird, a cocktail party, a jar placed on a hill. Indeed, according to former standards, the subjects explored in much modern poetry were trivial and meaningless, and even when they were not, the poet declined to impose an explicit moral upon the material.

Modern poets more and more flagrantly distinguished themselves and their work from the public interest, whether political or moral. They set up in business for themselves and pursued matters of technical interest to those who found poetry itself sufficient. Consequently, they renounced public acclaim and, in return, engendered not only public indifference but frequently public hostility. They were "poets without laurels."

Ransom did not care to speculate on whether the retreat of the poet from society had a beneficial or an unfortunate effect on his art. He noted only that such action was unavoidable, whatever the consequences. In *The World's Body* he explained the poets' dilemma: "Apostate, illaureate, and doomed to outlawry the modern poets may be. I have the feeling that modernism is an unfortunate road for them to have taken. But it was an inevitable one. It is not hard to defend them, from imputations against their honor and their logic. . . . But let us approach the matter from a slightly different angle. Poets have had to become modern because the age is modern. Its modernism envelops them like a sea, or an air. Nothing in their thought can escape it" (*WB*, 62–63).

Ransom insisted that poetic theory constituted a "new science" that offered a new way of looking at and thinking about the world, a new epistemology and ontology. Poetry and criticism stood in opposition to science and, as he proposed to demonstrate, wrested from science its exclusive claims to truth.[22] Poetry and criticism in themselves perhaps even constituted a new kind of truth. Every poem, separate from its content, had its own structure and integrity. Poetic form and technique, like the scientific method, imposed order on experience.

Science engaged men's cognitive faculties and taught them the analytical skills necessary to render the world subject to human understanding and control. Applied science had been especially successful in securing a rich material existence for much of modern society. What science broke into useful components, poetry then recovered and restored in its indefeasible wholeness. The critic's special task was to illuminate the form and technique of the poem, to disclose the way in which the poet conceived and ordered his material, and thus also to reveal the complex and hidden structure of reality itself.

In some of his most celebrated essays, Ransom called for an "ontological criticism" carried on by an "ontological critic."[23] For poetry was not the exclamation of the pure joy of existence, the bedlam and riot of unmediated experience. A poem was rather the result of a deliberate and considered act of imagination tempered by reflection. Writing to Tate on December 17, 1922, Ransom had outlined the ideas that he would later incorporate into his fully developed theory of poetry:

> The art-thing sounds like the first immediate transcript of reality, but it isn't; it's a long way from the event. It isn't the raw stuff of experience. The passion in it has mellowed down—emotion recollected in TRANQUILITY, etc., etc. Above all things else, the core of experience in the record has been taken up into the sum total of things and its relations there discovered are given in the work of art. That is why the marginal meanings, the associations, the interlinear element of a poem are all-important. The most delicate piece of work that a poet has to do is to avoid a misleading connection in his phrasing. There must not be a trace of the expository philosophical method, but nevertheless the substance of the philosophical conclusion must be there

22. See SL, 282–83.
23. See WB, 111–42; BB, 80–92; and John Crowe Ransom, The New Criticism (Norfolk, Conn., 1941), 279–336.

for the intelligent reader. The artist can't stay off this necessity—can't hold aloof, be the impartial spectator, the colorless medium of information, the carrier of a perfectly undirected passion, the Know-Nothing from Missouri. I can't help believing more and more . . . that the work of art must be perfectly serious, ripe, rational, mature—full of heart, but with enough head there to govern the heart. (*SL,* 115)

In "Poetry: A Note on Ontology," published sixteen years later as part of *The World's Body,* Ransom clarified his mature argument:

> It is the dream, the recollection, which compels us to poetry, and to deliberate aesthetic experience. It can hardly be argued, I think, that the arts are constituted automatically out of original images, and arise in some early age of innocence. . . . Art is based on second love, not first love. In it we make a return to something which we had wilfully alienated. The child is occupied mostly with things, but it is because he is still unfurnished with systematic ideas, not because he is a ripe citizen by nature and comes along already trailing clouds of glory. (*WB,* 116)

Poetry was thus a cultural, not a natural, phenomenon; an ordering, not an undisciplined expression, of experience. The ontological critic would furnish the "systematic ideas" necessary to make it comprehensible.

A poem did not carry the strict and precise logic of an expository essay or a scientific treatise, though it contained a distinctive structure and logic of its own. Poetry, as Ransom characterized it, represented a revolutionary departure from the formal conventions of logical discourse. The poet incorporated into the body of his poem apparently irrelevant and extraneous material that did not advance but instead complicated his "argument."

Any work of art conveyed a hypothesis about nature and man. To the extent that art made a statement about the nature of things, it became subject to judgment from scientific and technical standards of value and utility. "Apologists do their art no service," Ransom intoned, "in seeking to exempt it of moral and scientific responsibility, and to have it out of the category of useful human behavior" (*BB,* 83).

Art, especially poetry, venerated the recalcitrance, enchantment, and mystery of the human and the natural, whereas science proposed to enlist the human and the natural in its service. Poetry, Ransom declared, encompassed the particular and the unique. Science moved inexorably toward the abstract, the general, and the universal in an effort to shake itself free of "irrelevant circumstance in order to be ready for further and professional business": the organization of the world for human subjugation and use. The scientist "denatured experience," Ransom wrote, anticipating the future utility of his formulas and hypotheses, his classes and categories. The poet, by contrast, reveled in the particularity of that "situational matrix" out of which he created, without giving much thought to the future utility of the product of his actions.[24]

Ransom's "ontological criticism" revealed that poetry put forth a vision of reality different from what science showed. The poet worked by indirection, innuendo, and implication, employing symbol, metaphor, trope, meter, and rhyme to convey his meaning. He avoided the precise language and the propositional logic of science, favoring instead an expressive language and an associative logic. Taken together, the cumulative effect of these poetic devices intentionally restricted the logic of the scientific process and obscured the analytical precision of scientific prose.

Poetry also challenged the cognitive objectives of science. The structure of poetry constituted its own special logic. Every poem had some identifiable content; every poem was about something. Additionally, poetry related the ineffable complexity of experience, the local, particular, concrete details that, Ransom thought, served no purpose in scientific writing. Neither the critic nor the poet himself could abstract the narrative from the details and analyze one aspect in isolation from the other.

Poems, in Ransom's language, contained two elements: structure and texture. Structure constituted the objective, logical content of a poem; texture, the indeterminate, indefinable detail that restored the substance of experience. These elements proved inseparable but contentious. Ransom accentuated the tension, the duality at the heart of poetry and thus at the heart of reality itself. The literary critic had to comment on both the structure and the texture, for to emphasize the former at the expense of the latter diverted criticism into moral judgment or scientific analysis.[25]

Poetry thus captured a reality that science ignored. Individual, particular, contingent, and unpredictable, poetry defied the restrictive logic of science that insisted on abstraction, analysis, and universality. Poetry reconstituted the "world's body" by acknowledging the fullness and com-

24. See *NC*, 279–336, and *BB*, 80–92.
25. See *SE*, 128–46, 277–305.

plexity (what Ransom called "the qualitative density") of the world of actual things—a fullness and complexity that remained concealed from the scientific understanding. Although Ransom insisted that poetry was neither instrumental nor analytical, the "New Criticism" demonstrated that poetry offered epistemological and ontological insights into reality as it was experienced: "We live in a world that must be distinguished from the world, or the worlds, for there are many, which we treat in our scientific discourse. They are its reduced, emasculated, and docile versions. Poetry intends to recover the denser and more refractory original world which we know loosely through our perceptions and memories. By this supposition it is a kind of knowledge which is radically or ontologically distinct" (*NC,* 281). The poet and the literary critic imagined a world less vulnerable to rational scrutiny and technological manipulation than the scientist, to say nothing of the industrialist, would have contemplated. To Ransom's satisfaction, poetry confirmed that the world was not merely logical or functional, not utterly subject to the preoccupations of human intellect and will.

Aesthetic concerns predominated throughout John Crowe Ransom's long career, from his days as a Fugitive poet to his days as an Agrarian to his days as a "New Critic." In his view, poetry tendered the fullest image of the human experience. As his commitment to poetry grew, however, his interest in the Agrarian movement declined. The defense of poetry was not for Ransom, as it was for Davidson, also the defense of the South. For him, poetry flourished only when liberated from the constrictions of politics and patriotism. "The heavy hand of politics is upon us in these times," he wrote in 1952. "Like Milton's meager Shadow, Death, we can sniff where we sit, where we live, 'the smell of mortal change on the Earth' " (*PE,* 109).

Davidson thought that Ransom had given up Agrarianism for aestheticism. In Davidson's view, the New Criticism became a substitute for, not an elaboration or defense of, the southern tradition.[26] But these tendencies had been present almost from the beginning of Ransom's intellectual odyssey. His aesthetic sustained the critique of rationalism, empiricism, pragmatism, instrumentalism, and science that characterized the Agrarian movement, with the important caveat that poetry, not politics, economics, history, religion, or tradition (all too infused already with

26. See *SWMW,* 63–76.

the scientific ethos) offered the best alternative to scientific-industrial civilization. Poetry had the advantage of being apolitical, of remaining untainted by the half-truths of ideology. The truth of poetry was the truth of life.

Ransom's aesthetic remains tantalizing. He challenged the predominant epistemological and ontological assumptions of modernity—empiricism, positivism, pragmatism, and rationalism—and offered a poetic alternative. He argued that modern epistemologies and ontologies simplified complex relations and realities into binary dichotomies of cause and effect, truth and falsity, good and evil. One of the few genuine philosophical pluralists in the history of Western thought, Ransom attacked the supposition that truth emerged from only one source: rational, scientific processes. His reproach of science inferred the existence of a multiplicity of truths, reflecting the different ways in which men imagined, perceived, and organized their worlds.

Poetic knowledge derived not from a unitary source as did scientific knowledge but from a conglomeration of sources: logical reflection, flights of fancy, dreams, emotional conflicts, unconscious yearnings. The bland, mechanical singularity of truth that science achieved denied the interplay of variation and divergence that occurred in experience as Ransom understood it. He could not accept what he took to be the principal tenet of modernity, which presumed that all reasonable men desired teleological order and harmony based on the immutable laws of science. The scientific quest for regularity, uniformity, and constancy, far from illuminating reality, actually distorted it. Ransom instead posited an infinitely diverse reality in which the poet unified all aspects of experience in an ensemble of reciprocity that was accessible not to the scientific mind but only to the aesthetic sensibility.

In his new poetic order, Ransom privileged the status of the independent man of letters. His description of John Milton could easily have applied to himself: Milton was "content to assert the superiority of the poet to other men" (WB, 49). Ransom's plunge into Agrarianism came about because, by the late 1920s, he found it impossible to separate the composition and criticism of poetry from the social and historical context in which the poet-critic resided. He defined the "good society" as that society which fostered the act of poetry and criticism. For almost a decade, the celebration of poetry seemed possible in the traditional, agrarian South as it did not elsewhere in the modern world.

Ransom's militant Agrarianism represented a way to develop his aesthetic theory and to nurture, politically and economically, a society devoted to manners, custom, ritual, tradition, romance, leisure, and art. Upon reexamining his political and economic assumptions, though, Ransom confronted the unsettling reality that even an agrarian society could not prevent the exploitation of nature. He concluded by the late 1930s that his conception of the agrarian South had been nothing more than a land of his heart's desire. The twentieth-century South, in which he and his colleagues lived and wrote, proved incapable of fully nourishing the aesthetic sentiments.

But if men of letters could not reside in the South, they had to live somewhere. How were they to survive scattered over the bleak landscape of modern scientific-industrial society? Ransom's answer came in 1952 when he published "The Communities of Letters."[27] Poetry, he began, tendered "the freest and fullest and most sympathetic" image of human experience. To cultivate and preserve aesthetic knowledge of the world—a knowledge without desire—men of letters had to declare their independence from the public realm. The poet must assert his freedom and make art his individual commitment and accomplishment.

Thus liberated, modern men of letters could articulate the terms of a higher order of civilization to which a few noble souls aspired. As independent citizens, writers could tell the truth about the human condition, for they were under no obligation to defend a particular national policy, advocate a particular religious doctrine, or honor a particular social order. Gathered around the presiding genius of the author were those persons who had witnessed, deplored, and mourned the disintegration of the old order. From their common interests and sympathies, a writer and his readers could form a new, independent community that would reconstitute something of "that far away time of gentleness."[28]

Ransom maintained that independent men of letters should no longer feel constrained to focus on the rules and conventions of formal society. Poets needed to be free to explore and to communicate the most intimate

27. See *PE*, 109–17. The essay originally appeared as "The Social Role of Art and Philosophy" in *Confluence*, I (December, 1952), 86–92. See also Louis D. Rubin, Jr., "A Critic Almost Anonymous: John Crowe Ransom Goes North," in *The New Criticism and After*, ed. Thomas Daniel Young (Charlottesville, 1976), 1–21, esp. 15–19.

28. John Crowe Ransom, "Of Margaret," in *Selected Poems* (New York, 1969), 143.

aspects of experience rarely exposed to public scrutiny, not overtly or confessionally to be sure, but fictively or poetically. The "choicer spirits" among men, those bold enough to comprehend and accept this aesthetic responsibility, would thus legislate a new order of civilization spiritually set apart from society.

This community of enlightened, but truculent, alienation constituted for Ransom an independent polity of mind, a Republic of Letters. Such a republic, according to Ransom, had no set regional or national boundaries, no codified laws, and no revolutionary programs. Ransom asserted the autonomy of this Republic of Letters and proclaimed the ability of poets to transcend the existing social order and establish a sense of common humanity. He exclaimed: "How much more tolerant and humane, is this community, than the formal society! . . . How could a gentle civilization do without this community? The oversensitive among us would be solitary and miserable, full of guilt and fears, in our dark privacy, if there were not the generous imagination of the artists to release us" (*PE*, 116). The Republic of Letters was, for him, an intellectually cohesive and morally superior alternative to the modern world of science and industry.

The Republic of Letters as Ransom conceived it was also a long way from the Agrarians' vision of the traditional southern community. Although Ransom the man may have cared deeply about the politics, economics, religion, history, or tradition of his native land, Ransom the man of letters did not permit them to intrude on his contemplation of literature. He reserved his primary, and perhaps his only, allegiance for the domain of secular letters that marked the ascendance of mind as the authoritative model of history and consciousness.

Ironically, Ransom accepted the dominion of mind even while he lamented the form in which it had manifested itself. For if poetry had displaced patriotism and piety, then science had surely displaced poetry. Ransom knew his enemy. His struggle to assert the legitimacy and the efficacy of poetic knowledge represented a dramatic attempt to oppose the scientific interpretation of history and consciousness that threatened to overwhelm the Republic of Letters. Ransom sought to reinstate the poetic vision of order embodied in the community of letters so as to counter the enactment of an actual scientific-industrial order in history. The intellectual freedom and the spiritual autonomy of modern men of letters would enable them to mend together the fragments of civilization and experience. Only the aesthetic appreciation of the splendor and diversity of the "world's body" would permit men to recover a sense of individual and communal identity that would enable them to survive and even prosper under the rigors of modernity.

But Ransom's veneration of the aesthetic sensibility separated him from the Agrarian movement in its original intent and helps to explain his gradually waning interest in the movement. When the Southern Agrarians published *I'll Take My Stand* in 1930, they agreed that a return to a society of myth and tradition, located in the South, was imperative to controlling the advance of science and industry. By 1945, when he published "Art and the Human Economy," Ransom had explicitly rejected this conclusion, arguing instead that the realm of science should fall under the sovereignty of art. Poetry would replace science but would itself have no master. Ransom exchanged one product of mind, science, for another, poetry.

In so doing, Ransom distanced himself not only from modern society but also from the society of myth and tradition, which the Agrarians had long identified as existing in the South. He replaced both with the independent Republic of Letters. His retreat from Agrarianism brought with it, almost as a matter of course, an acceptance of the bourgeois conception of the self, which southern conservative thinkers had long and fiercely resisted. Ransom's conception of the literary vocation in the end rested squarely on the bourgeois assertion of the freedom and autonomy of the self. This conception of radical and systematic individualism made possible and sustained the assertion of freedom and autonomy for the man of letters, whose very alienation Ransom transformed into a kind of privileged citizenship.

The sanctification of the individual that took place in bourgeois culture coincided with and supported the radical independence that Ransom appropriated for the members of the Republic of Letters. The aesthetic order of existence, over which the community of letters presided, thus assumed in Ransom's thought a reality and a dignity superior to the realms of politics, economics, and science and history, tradition, and religion as these were historically constituted and institutionalized in State, Society, and Church.

No longer would men of letters, even those born and raised in the

South, be bound and hedged in by patriotism or piety. Free to revel in their private, subjective experience, modern writers could, at the same time, affirm the universal validity of that experience recast and refined as fiction and poetry. Solitary and apostate, "illaureate" (to use Ransom's word), modern, independent men of letters could place themselves at the center of the universe and take as their province the whole world.

3

Tate's Agrarian Faith: Knowledge Carried to the Heart

> What shall we say who have knowledge
> Carried to the heart?
> —Allen Tate, "Ode to the Confederate Dead"

THE MODERN CRISIS

In contrast to John Crowe Ransom, Allen Tate took as his model of history and consciousness not mind but society. Tate attempted to free history and consciousness from the dominion of mind and to subordinate mind to a social order predicated on myth, tradition, and faith—a stunning attempt to reverse the course of Western history that began with the Renaissance, culminated in the Enlightenment, and received political sanction in the French Revolution. In rejecting the view that history was a willful process controlled by reason, he resisted the transfer of everything—man, society, history, consciousness, and God—into mind. In so doing, he also rejected the foundations upon which the universal polity of mind, the independent Republic of Letters, rested. For Tate, mind had to resume its former awareness of the unifying order of a myth, tradition, and faith in which men remained forever submissive to God.

Ransom and Tate never took occasion to discuss their differences fully, but as early as 1927 Ransom articulated the important divergence in their thought that had already emerged. He accused Tate of attaching too great an importance to the sense of community between poets and their readers. "Poetry is individual first," Ransom wrote. "It is social second." For him it was "not so important that Dante's public believed in the Trinity; more important that Dante did." Poets created out of their own experience. They were not stewards, clerks, or bards who served first a people, a history, a country, or a faith.

Tate also placed undue emphasis on the recovery of myth to suit Ransom. Let poets write their poems with or without adhering to an overarching myth or religious doctrine, he declared. The poetry itself was of primary importance. "It is in this sense . . . that I seem to myself to be much more radical than yourself," Ransom told his friend. "I simply renounce Cosmologies and Magic." Ransom did not mean that he was more "radical" as a poet than Tate but that he was a more radical thinker. Ransom himself noted the distinction when he wrote: "When I said I seemed more radical than you, I was certainly referring to my critical or philosophical views, not to my poetical practises [sic]."[1] Ransom had distanced himself not only from modern society but also from the society of myth and tradition that the Agrarians had long identified as existing in the South. He had replaced both with the independent Republic of Letters.

Tate, too, saw himself as a cosmopolitan man of letters, but he lamented, even as he joined, the exodus from the *res publica Christiana* to the *res publica litteraria,* which marked the unprecedented separation of the spiritual from the secular realm. Tate mounted a determined effort to replace mind as the model for history, consciousness, and society. His motives arose from the desire to re-create a unified culture in the West based not on independent mind but on a common understanding and experience of man's "supratemporal," Christian destiny.[2]

In a letter to Robert Fitzgerald written on March 1, 1952, Tate explained his convictions about the position that men of letters should

1. See *SL,* 160–67.
2. See *FD,* 1–17. Readers familiar with his work will recognize the enormous debt that I owe to Lewis P. Simpson here and throughout this book. See especially the following by Simpson: *The Man of Letters in New England and the South: Essays on the History of the Literary Vocation in America* (Baton Rouge, 1973), 201–55; "The South's Reaction to Modernism: A Problem in the Study of Southern Letters," in *Southern Literary Studies: Problems and Possibilities,* ed. Louis D. Rubin, Jr., and C. Hugh Holman (Chapel Hill, 1975), 48–68; "The Southern Republic of Letters and *I'll Take My Stand,*" in *A Band of Prophets: The Vanderbilt Agrarians After Fifty Years,* ed. William C. Havard and Walter Sullivan (Baton Rouge, 1982), 65–91; *The Dispossessed Garden: Pastoral and History in Southern Literature* (Baton Rouge, 1983), 65–100. The best critical assessment of Simpson's singular contributions to southern cultural and literary history is Elizabeth Fox-Genovese and Eugene D. Genovese, "The Cultural History of Southern Slave Society: Reflections on the Work of Lewis P. Simpson," in *American Letters and the Historical Consciousness: Essays in Honor of Lewis P. Simpson,* ed. J. Gerald Kennedy and Daniel Mark Fogel (Baton Rouge, 1987), 15–41.

occupy in the modern world. Any attempt to revitalize, advance, or extend the "humanistic culture" of the West, he declared, must take place not under the auspices of the independent Republic of Letters but under those of the Roman Catholic Church. Tate was not interested in writing Catholic propaganda. Instead, he called for the creation of a literature that revealed the human condition as it manifested itself in the modern world and that justified the ways of God to man. Such cultural work, he thought, must be guided by the Holy Spirit and be carried out not for the aggrandizement of the individual writer but for the veneration of God. He wrote:

> Our aim should be the advancement of humanistic culture within the Church herself for the greater glory of God. For the glory of God will be advanced by the deepest culture of the social order of which the Members of the Mystical Body are capable. As such a program develops, its influence would inevitably extend beyond the Catholic community. But this extrinsic result cannot be achieved as a conscious aim. A great Catholic culture as an end in itself—that should be, as I see it, the aim, simple and ambitious, of an association of Catholic men of letters. . . . The internal purpose of our association should be the comfort and inspiration of a common ideal in letters; the external purpose, the supervision and the propagation of literary standards: in the end a single purpose that shall be guided by the counsel of the Holy Ghost.[3]

Only in the context of his Catholicism is Tate's status as a cosmopolitan man of letters intelligible.

There was nothing new in the statement of principle and faith contained in Tate's letter to Fitzgerald. Tate had long believed that "a philosophy of literature had . . . no validity without religious authority to sustain it" (MO, xi). The day after Tate had written to Fitzgerald, March 2, 1952, he wrote to his friend the French philosopher Jacques Maritain. Tate told Maritain that they should form "a Catholic literary academy" that would challenge not only the dominance but the very premises of the modern, secular world view. This act Tate regarded as a return to what he originally believed:

> For I have long opposed, publicly and privately, the overt action of American men of letters in immediate political issues; and I see no

3. *Exiles and Fugitives: The Letters of Jacques and Raïssa Maritain, Allen Tate, and Caroline Gordon,* ed. John M. Dunaway (Baton Rouge, 1992), 102–103.

reason to change my mind now that I am a Catholic. Since the early 1930's American men of letters, Catholic and non-Catholic, have frittered away the advantages of a generally traditional position in a series of skirmishes fought on the ground, and with the weapons, of the "liberal" opposition. Similarly, at the present time, Catholic writers are likely to meet the same frustration *vis-à-vis* the uninformed Philistinism in the Church. I agree with you that the only way to make works of imagination and sensibility a part of Catholic life is to produce enough of them, of sufficient power and distinction, [to] affect the education of the Catholic community as a whole, clergy as well as laity. This is a platitude in the history of literature which we should be very imprudent to neglect.[4]

Tate found a spiritual home in the Roman Catholic Church and drew both solace and power from the Judeo-Christian tradition that the Church embodied. But what of Tate's other commitment, his allegiance to the southern tradition? Did his conversion to Roman Catholicism in 1950 alter the stand that he had taken in 1930? The simple answer to this question is yes. From his perspective as a Roman Catholic, Tate could more fully appreciate the deficiencies of the southern tradition. In fundamental ways, though, Tate's conversion marked not a break with but the culmination of his Agrarianism, enabling him to elaborate his beliefs both within the context of a specific history and tradition and within the context of a universal faith and divine revelation.

During the same year in which he had written to Fitzgerald and Maritain about the proper demeanor and responsibilities of Catholic men of letters, Tate declared that he had not changed his mind about Agrarianism.[5] In 1952, twenty-two years after the publication of *I'll Take My Stand,* Tate still espoused the ideals and principles put forth in that southern manifesto.

He feared, perhaps more deeply in the 1950s than in the 1930s, that the world was not so much governed by men and women as it was dominated by abstractions, ideologies, and things. Modern men and

4. *Ibid.,* 41–43. The controversy that prompted this exchange of letters arose over the film *The Miracle.* Many Catholics, including Francis Cardinal Spellman, believed this film blasphemous and insulting. Others disagreed, and an enormous row ensued. Dunaway presents a succinct discussion in his fine introduction.

5. See "A Symposium: The Agrarians Today," *Shenandoah,* III (Summer, 1952), 28–29.

women had lost the sense of joy and torment that distinguished the human condition. Without a transcendent reference, an acute self-consciousness was all that remained to them. Isolated from God, in whom they no longer believed, and cut off from their fellow human beings, modern men and women could only express their private psychic anguish over and over again in a tiresome repetition of eccentricities intended to liberate them. "In an age of abstract experience," Tate wrote, "fornication is self-expression, adjunct to Christian euphoria."[6]

The weak, who could not face loneliness with equanimity, or the timid, who were reluctant to engage in any sort of "self-expression," could either retreat into unreflective, frantic, almost hysterical sensation or put their faith in some juggernaut that would surely create an earthly paradise in the near future. From Tate's point of view, membership in the local chamber of commerce or in the Third International would serve equally well in this regard.[7]

Significantly, Tate's reaffirmation of Agrarianism came two years after he joined the Roman Catholic Church. Following his conversion, Tate advocated a Christian vision of reality and in some sense hoped to re-establish a socially and spiritually unified culture in the West. His conversion shifted the focus, but not the substance, of his thought. Tate's version of Agrarianism had a powerful religious component from the beginning. Far from compelling him to give up his earlier beliefs and commitments, Catholicism deepened his conviction of their rectitude, propriety, and beneficence. Catholicism did not supersede, much less negate, Agrarianism. It represented the logical conclusion toward which Tate's thought had been moving since the late 1920s.

On February 18, 1929, he wrote from Paris to his friend and soon-to-be fellow Agrarian Donald Davidson of his growing sympathy for Roman Catholicism. Tate insisted that he and Davidson were "doomed to live a harrowing life" because they sought some "ultimate discipline of the soul" (LC, 223). All men in all times and all places who engaged in the same quest suffered as they now did. In that respect, life in the

6. Allen Tate, "Causerie," in *The Collected Poems of Allen Tate, 1919–1976* (Baton Rouge, 1989), 13–16.

7. See M. E. Bradford, *Rumors of Mortality: An Introduction to Allen Tate* (Dallas, 1969), 3–17, and Monroe K. Spears, "The Criticism of Allen Tate," *Sewanee Review*, LVII (Spring, 1949), 317–34.

twentieth century was not unique. Men and women found it no easier to attain salvation in the twentieth century than they had in the thirteenth.

The chief difference between the thirteenth century and the twentieth, Tate suggested, was that during the former, salvation was available to all who lived under the Christian dispensation. Whether one was literate or illiterate, wealthy or impoverished, male or female, lord or serf did not matter. The meaning of salvation arose from a shared culture and from knowledge of one's place within it. The "idea" of salvation, if not the reality, was thus equally accessible to everyone. In the twentieth century, Tate told Davidson, salvation, whether in idea or actuality, had become merely a personal affair. There was no shared, unified, Christian culture to sustain it. This observation brought Tate to his main point:

> I am more and more heading towards Catholicism. We have reached a condition of the spirit where no further compromise is possible. That is the lesson taught us by the Victorians who failed to unite naturalism and the religious spirit; we've got to do away with one or the other; and I can never capitulate to naturalism. . . . There is no dualism without religion, and there is no religion without a Church; nor can there be a Church without dogma. Protestantism is virtually naturalism; when morality lacks the authority of dogma, it becomes private, irresponsible, and from this is only a step to naturalism. . . . Without the external authority good conduct cannot last, it becomes . . . merely "gentlemanly feeling" which is not enough to keep control of those who lack it. (LC, 224)[8]

Skeptical of the good effects that "gentlemanly feeling" alone could generate and maintain, Tate, in seeking an "ultimate discipline of the soul," also sought a social order that could counter the disorder of the modern world. Inevitably, this search prompted him to try to revitalize the transcendent order that he believed characterized Western Christen-

---

8. For an assertion that Tate's conversion to Catholicism was a repudiation of Agrarianism, see Daniel Joseph Singal, *The War Within: From Victorian to Modernist Thought in the South, 1919–1945* (Chapel Hill, 1982), 254–60. For views closer to my own, see Cleanth Brooks, "Allen Tate and the Nature of Modernism," *Southern Review,* n.s., XII (1976), 685–97, and Donald Davidson, "Allen Tate: The Traditionalist as Modern," MS in Donald Davidson Papers, Special Collections, Jean and Alexander Heard Library, Vanderbilt University.

dom before the Renaissance, the Reformation, the Enlightenment, and the Industrial and French Revolutions.

Individualism, positivism, and materialism and rationalism, narcissism, and solipsism were only a few in the long litany of agonies that beset the modern world. The modern mind, Tate argued, was governed by aimless, abstract intellectuality; the modern world, by violence, disorder, and perversion. Yet, as he pointed out, modern men paradoxically saw the world as ultimately fathomable, manageable, and rational. Confident that science and technology had solved most of the riddles that puzzled their ancestors, moderns succumbed to the ancient but always fatal temptation that men could alter life on earth to produce, through human agency, a perfect world.

Tate rejected the view of human nature fostered by social scientists. He did not accept their conclusion that human beings were simple creatures whose deepest motives could be analyzed, whose behavior could be predicted, and whose personalities could be modified. He argued instead that human beings were complex, mysterious, stubborn, enigmatic, and imperfectable.

As Tate saw it, since the Renaissance the vision of human nature as infinitely malleable and ultimately perfectible had gradually emerged and steadily gained currency. Renaissance humanism, he thought, sparked a cultural revolution by freeing the mind from the strictures of myth, tradition, and faith. This new emphasis on the power of reason, combined with the Protestant doctrine of the "priesthood of all believers" that gave rise to the pernicious notion of the right of private judgment in matters of faith and morals, directly challenged the authority of the Roman Catholic Church in both spiritual and secular affairs. The decline of ecclesiastical Latin, the rise of vernacular literatures, and the subordination of Christian revelation to natural philosophy signaled the end of the cultural unity of Western civilization. Francis Bacon summarized the new attitude, rather too gleefully Tate imagined, in his trenchant aphorism: "Knowledge is power."[9]

Certain that Bacon's words anticipated the modern world view, Tate remained unenthusiastic about the consequences. He acknowledged that

9. See Simpson, "The Southern Republic of Letters and *I'll Take My Stand*," 71–72, and Christopher Dawson, *Religion and the Rise of Western Culture* (New York, 1950). On Renaissance humanism, see William J. Bouwsma, "The Culture of Renaissance Humanism," American Historical Association Pamphlets (Washington, D.C., 1973), 401.

freeing the mind from the rigid and reactionary authority of the medieval Church encouraged the burst of literary, artistic, and scientific creativity from which the modern world benefited tremendously. At the same time, he concluded that the power of reason, unleashed from any form of discipline and authority, was virtually unlimited in its destructive capacity. In an essay published in 1953 but written at least three years earlier, about the time that Tate became a Roman Catholic, he made explicit his misgivings: "The Renaissance doctrine of the freedom of unlimited enquiry [*sic*] has had consequences for good and evil in the modern world. This doctrine has created our world; in so far as we are able to enjoy it we must credit unlimited enquiry with its material benefits. But its dangers are too notorious to need pointing out. An elusive *mystique* supports the general doctrine, which may be stated as follows: We must keep up the enquiry come hell or high water" (*FD*, 22).

Twentieth-century thinkers blamed Catholicism for its historic conservatism in refusing to sanction, indeed, in attempting to suppress, scientific advances. But Tate observed in "To Whom Is the Poet Responsible?" that even before the advent of Christianity, the professors of "special knowledge" limited access to it lest it be put to irresponsible uses. Hippocrates, the practitioner of the one science that affected the daily lives of men and women in the ancient world, concealed his secrets to prevent their abuse or perversion. The idea of the publicly responsible application of knowledge was old—older even than Christianity. The skepticism that contemporary thinkers identified with Christianity in general and with Catholicism in particular Tate traced to the beliefs and practices of the Arabs and the Greeks. No doubt, he conceded, modern men would regard these insidious customs as illiberal suppressions of knowledge and truth. Writing shortly after the world entered the atomic age, he added a single caveat. "Is it a suppression of truth," he inquired, "to withhold from general use the means of exploiting a technique of slaughter?" Tate did not think so.

He could not explain why past civilizations had withheld certain bodies of knowledge, carefully guarding their secrets and mysteries from all but the initiated. He could not even say whether such tactics were now possible or desirable, but he knew that something had to be done. The Greek world had lasted nine hundred years. The Christian world had survived the collapse of the two great ancient civilizations by more than a millennium. Tate argued that the modern world could hardly hope for such longevity, for modern men did not possess the proper relations to nature and to God.

The ancient Greeks, like the medieval Christians, understood that the pursuit of knowledge must never interfere with the delicate foundation upon which civilization rested. They investigated nature, but they never forgot that nature, in itself, was incomplete and that their knowledge of it was imperfect. Before undertaking their study they already knew and accepted the relation of nature to the transcendent order that alone gave it meaning.

Since the sixteenth century the proper relation of nature to the transcendent had steadily eroded. Modern men had almost completely lost sight of their proper relation to nature. They no longer believed that they, too, were part of nature, subject to its vicissitudes, driven by its necessities, and compelled by its impulses. Instead, they projected their own image onto nature and presumptuously identified themselves with the divine and the eternal. All the world was but an undifferentiated extension of the self and the will. For modern men, nature thus gradually but inexorably lost its majesty and mystery and became something to be conquered, possessed, analyzed, and exploited. Ambitious, restless, and insatiable, modern men waged a savage war against nature and, inevitably, against each other. Murder had become the defining act of humanity.

To restore a sense of proportion to human life, to honor God and nature, and to revitalize a dying civilization, Tate insisted that modern men had to return to direct and full participation in the "metaphysical dimension" of life. Like the ancient Greeks and the medieval Christians, they had to recognize that they could not escape the human condition; they could not master nature or control the destiny of man. They had to endure suffering, loss, and death. At its most elemental level, Tate insisted, human life was a tragedy.

Tate believed in the innate sinfulness of man. Under the conditions of modern life, human depravity prospered as never before. There was "a deep sickness of the modern mind," he wrote in the Preface to *Reason in Madness*. The modern inclination to restrict the problem to the narrow scope of politics would prove disastrous, for it brought out the most destructive aspects of human nature. Modern men suffered from a spiritual disorder, of which the political crisis was only a superficial manifestation. Political measures could not comprehend, let alone resolve, it.

Following Oswald Spengler, whose *Decline of the West* and *Hour of Decision* he admired, Tate asserted that liberal politics had moved in a straight line from Jacobinism to Bolshevism and in the process had reduced human spirituality to either the rational pursuit of economic self-interest or the abject obedience to the state. Careful to distance himself from Spengler's bellicose German nationalism, which he dismissed even in the early 1930s as "Teutonic jingoism," Tate accepted Spengler's diagnosis of the pathology infecting modern political life even while he rejected his antidote: a call of the Teutonic peoples to arms and a call for Germany to produce a new Caesar.

Tate recoiled from such rhetoric but, writing in 1934, acknowledged that "it will be difficult . . . to disentangle the truth of Spengler's diagnosis of the needs of modern civilization from the bellicose pro-Germanism of his point of view."[10] Despite his reticence about Spengler's proposals, which, incidentally, offered precisely the kind of political solution that he had repudiated, Tate did think Spengler correct in asserting that the two great ideologies of the modern world, capitalism and socialism, had become simply different names for the same phenomenon. Both attacked private property, the sole ground in which the humane values of traditional society might take root and flourish. The political economies of capitalism and of socialism, however superficially at variance, brought the same results. Far from realizing the promised material prosperity and spiritual liberation, men unfortunate enough to live under the tyranny of either capitalism or socialism suffered deprivation and enslavement.

The confident intervention of science and politics into the spiritual realm, Tate concluded, had certainly augmented, if not actually created, the modern crisis. The blithe assumption that all experience could be ordered scientifically and all problems solved politically brought the modern world to the threshold of destruction. This assumption led logically to the reduction of man's spiritual existence to "irresponsible emotion, to what the positivists of our time see as irrelevant feeling" (*RM*, 4). But Tate argued that this "feeling" was "irrelevant" only because it could not be reduced to scientific analysis or subjected to diverse forms of political manipulation and violence.

10. See Allen Tate, "Spengler's Tract Against Liberalism," *American Review*, III (1934), 41–47. Tate missed, or let pass, an opportunity to challenge Spengler's prediction that engineers would be the last heroes before the decline of the West, about which he certainly disagreed with Spengler.

The politicians and the social scientists, the Herbert Hoovers and the John Deweys with their strategies and their theorems, taught the present generation that the defining aspect of humanity was not intelligence but adaptability, not freedom but obedience. Together they schooled men in the importance of adjustment to society, not in the importance of striving to attain some approximation of the "good society." This was so, Tate believed, because neither Hoover nor Dewey nor any of their like-minded contemporaries in the United States and around the world had a conception of the "good society." Planning led not in that direction but only toward a mechanical society in which men were conditioned to realize a "bourgeois paradise of gadgets and of commodities" (RM, 6). To this degradation and indignity had the myth of omnipotent reason brought the modern world.

Tate foresaw in the rise of the scientific world view, the advent of the social sciences, and the conjunction of both with politics a powerful impetus to creating a slave society. Operating under the illusion of omnipotent reason, social scientists accumulated vast amounts of data on social trends, social behavior, and social dynamics. They, in turn, offered their information to the politicians, who intended to use it as a means of social control, a way to construct a "pseudo-mystical" and "pseudo-democratic" utopia. Theirs, however, was a vision of mindless perfection.

To put it bluntly, Tate maintained that the emphasis on manipulation, adjustment, and control would end in confusion, degradation, and anarchy. The politicians and the social scientists, on the one hand, had ignored a crucial element in their analysis: people were willful, recalcitrant, and difficult to manage. No matter how perfectly conceived a social order might be, men in any age would find some way of subverting and perhaps of destroying it. That was a lesson of history that the politicians and social scientists preferred to overlook. Tate, on the other hand, insisted on facing the reality that men lived in a fallen world requiring the grace of God for its salvation. Men could not solve their problems without God. Tate contended that the modern effort to do so through the rational application of social science, social adjustment, and social control would only make matters worse. "If you get a society made up of persons who have surrendered their humanity to the predatory impulses," he concluded, "the quickest way to improve matters is to call in a dictator; for when you lose the moral and religious authority, the military authority stands ready to supervene" (RM, 8).

Sinful by nature, men were thus in need of God's grace. Although imperfect and dependent, men also possessed immortal souls and had to find the ultimate meaning for their lives in the transcendent mystery of the birth, death, and resurrection of Christ. In the modern world, Tate was convinced, men needed to formulate a religious myth that would enable them to acknowledge the existence of evil and to account for human misery and sorrow. They needed somehow to offset their naïvely optimistic faith in reason, which predicted only repeated success and continued happiness. Without a world view that embraced the whole of human existence and recognized the true source of Being as God and not man, human beings were condemned to accept the dictatorship proffered by the social scientists simply to keep from killing each other.

The most systematic statement of Tate's extensive reflections on the crisis of Western civilization came in two essays written between the late 1920s and the mid-1930s: "Humanism and Naturalism" and "Liberalism and Tradition." First appearing as "The Fallacy of Humanism" in T. S. Eliot's *Criterion* in July, 1929, and shortly thereafter in *Hound and Horn,* "Humanism and Naturalism" ranks among Tate's most vitriolic and impassioned criticism.[11] This essay, ironically, is not a diatribe against liberals or Marxists but a critique of fellow conservatives: the New Humanists Irving Babbitt, Norman Foerster, and Paul Elmer More, toward whom Tate felt a certain kinship.

Family fights are often bloodiest, and Tate was neither cowardly nor squeamish. He could wield his analytical knife with deadly skill when circumstances called for it. In a letter to John Crowe Ransom written in 1929, Tate offered his opinion of the three principal members of the New Humanist group whose thought he had probed: "More is thoroughly honest, and Babbitt is as honest as his sense of reality (which isn't strong) will permit him to be. The others are mainly politicians who are not interested in fundamental problems, but think that the issues of philosophy may be settled by a committee vote of the M. L. A. [Modern Language Association]. Foerster is a perfect example of this."[12]

---

11. Tate republished the article twice with minor revisions. It appeared as "Humanism and Naturalism" in *RE,* 113–44, and in *MO,* 170–94.

12. Allen Tate to John Crowe Ransom, July 27, 1929, in Davidson Papers. See also Allen Tate to Bernard Bandler II, February 7, 1930, in Allen Tate File, *Hound and Horn* Papers, Beinecke Rare Book and Manuscript Library, Yale University.

Tate conceded from the start that the New Humanists issued a damning indictment of modernity. They decried the vulgarity, licentiousness, malevolence, perversion, violence, and chaos that pervaded the modern world and called for a revival of the classical virtues of old: moderation, restraint, courtesy, magnanimity, generosity, and modesty. But who, Tate asked, would not favor these things? It was not that Babbitt, Foerster, and More espoused the wrong values. Quite the contrary. They espoused the right values for the wrong reasons, or, more accurately, for no reason at all. They pursued their values as ends in themselves rather than as means to some higher end. For instance, Tate argued, they practiced restraint because restraint was good, modesty because modesty was a virtue, courtesy because it was better than vulgarity. Certainly this was true. But what motive might they have for behaving virtuously instead of viciously? According to Tate, the New Humanists could not answer this question because the authority on which they based their judgments was vague or nonexistent.

In none of their writings did the New Humanists appeal to the idea of cultural unity, based on a common religious faith, to resolve the spiritual and moral crisis of the modern world. They relied, instead, on abstract and external methods of social control, just as did the social scientists whom they despised. They attempted to impose good conduct and social order through compulsion, by a sort of moral fiat. Tate's comments on Babbitt's moral philosophy illuminate the weaknesses that he detected in the Humanists' position as a whole: "Professor Babbitt's moral man deliberately undertakes to do, say, four good deeds a day to *offset* his evil impulses, which thus are counterbalanced but not transformed—just as the late Henry Clay Frick collected pictures to offset his transactions in steel. . . . Professor Babbitt's explicit morality is the finger of the Dutch boy in the dyke, or the main [*sic*] sitting gingerly on the keg of dynamite lest it explode. The modern problem is desperate, and Professor Babbitt recommends the police force" (*MO,* 178).

The Humanists' doctrines had no philosophical, moral, or spiritual core. Their thought was not bound to any center of judgment, conviction, or action. They could not find a ground for their values in any specific time and place and consequently could oppose the modern crisis with nothing more than an eclectic appeal to the established "wisdom of the ages." For Babbitt, Foerster, and More, there were no specific problems that needed to be solved, only abstract principles that had to be defended. Far from countering naturalism, by which Tate meant the predominant rational and scientific world view, the New Humanism accommodated to it.

Humanism, Tate declared to Davidson, merely derived from "the main faith of the age." Clearly, he thought that the "main faith" of the modern age was naturalism. He drew the logical conclusion: "Humanism must be naturalistic also." Babbitt, Foerster, and More had embarked on an impossible quest. They put their faith in reason and science and then sought to establish a spiritual discipline and authority on the basis of a scientific naturalism that implicitly denied the efficacy of spirituality.

Naturalism, as Tate defined it, translated into mechanism, process, change, an endless logical sequence that viewed human life in the aggregate but never could provide the religious foundation on which to build a unified culture. Naturalism offered an incomplete and therefore irresponsible vision of human experience. It provided no stopping place, no fixed doctrine or belief through which men could contemplate the transcendent order of existence that alone gave earthly life whatever meaning it possessed. As Tate explained to Davidson, the New Humanists did not understand the internal contradictions inherent in their thought and had, without knowing it, cut their own throats: "The modern humanists, however they try, cannot, without religion, get rid of the monistic assumptions of naturalism; without a clean break between the natural and supernatural humanism commits suicide. It can't be both monistic and dualistic, and unless it espouses a religion (which it refuses to do) it must cling to science which is monistic" (*LC,* 224).

Humanism was not enough. For the Humanists' values to amount to more than nice sentiment or special pleading required an "objective religion," a universal and transcendent referent that permitted men to judge life in the modern world not only against the past but against some higher authority—a referent that would, in effect, render all human judgments provisional and incomplete. The union of intellect and emotion, of reason and sensibility, provided the only circumstances in which the Humanists could make coherent and intelligible the values that they long advocated. Such a union, Tate maintained, could be effected only under the auspices of religion.

A religious outlook enabled men to acknowledge the reality of evil in its numerous manifestations and to distinguish it from merely disagreeable conduct. This distinction Babbitt, Foerster, and More could not make. Although they knew when someone was behaving disagreeably—behavior that, without religion, was nothing more, Tate said, than conduct of which they personally disapproved—they could not determine when someone was acting perversely or immorally. They had neither doctrine nor faith and, therefore, had no means of confronting the challenge of evil. Along with the optimistic social scientists, whom they ridiculed, the Humanists could proclaim categorically that all the unpleasantness attendant upon modern life would disappear if men and women learned to behave with moderation and to conduct their affairs according to the principles of reason.

Tate disagreed. The Humanists' program was ambitious and erudite, but it lacked an essential ingredient that would have grounded its precepts and strengthened its appeal: the religious imagination. For Tate, it was not so much that the Humanists' judgments were wrong as that they were beside the point. The Humanists wished to cultivate nature, including "natural human nature," and, at the same time, to subject nature to the dictates of reason in order to establish some objective point of reference beyond both nature and reason.

They assumed a dualism between man and nature, positing the human world as "qualitative" and the natural world as "quantitative." Tate charged that the proposed opposition between "quantity" and "quality" was spurious because the Humanists had never set the meaning of the terms. They used "quality," Tate argued, to mean that one thing was better than something else, on "the philosophic level at which the fashionable tailor uses it." The distinction between "quality" and "quantity" was only semantic; in effect, the real distinction for the New Humanists was between one quantity and another.

What, Tate asked, was the source of "qualitative" experience? The Humanists could not say, for they had made nature a "closed system" susceptible only to rational analysis, *i.e.,* to quantification. If there was even the hint of a genuine dualism in the Humanists' thought, it arose from the tension between the belief in scientific naturalism and the belief in the existence of some "higher reality." But this dualism, too, proved false. Babbitt, Foerster, and More, each in his own way, affirmed faith in scientific naturalism and rejected as an illusion the notion that there was a reality beyond the comprehension of rational, scientific analysis. For them, the religious imagination was an aberration of the intellect. As

Tate pointed out repeatedly in his essay, rationalism, scientism, and naturalism could not be overcome by an "illusion" or an "aberration."

The New Humanists, in his estimation, had capitulated to the demands of naturalism. In their formulation, humanism and naturalism had become inseparable. The situation was different during the Renaissance; humanism had not yet given itself over to naturalism "because it was still energized by the Church." Tate was unwilling to grant the validity of the Humanists' assumption that certain timeless values could be adapted and applied effortlessly and felicitously to the unique historical circumstances of the modern world. He thought that there was no such thing as "pure value," and he steadfastly believed that no values could exist apart from the historical means by which and the historical conditions under which men had created and preserved them.

Tate was no moral relativist. He did not believe all things good in their time and place. He believed in absolutes, but he considered absolutes imperatives not of belief but of intellectual and moral reference by which men lived in the world of time and change. He objected to the Humanists' efforts to transfer certain values and beliefs from the past and impose them wholesale on the present, in which they could not possibly carry the same significance. Comprehending the means and conditions through which values were historically established and sustained was far more difficult, Tate declared, than convincing ourselves that we needed to have values of some sort. He would not accept what he took to be the Humanists' position: having discovered the need for values, they flattered themselves that they already possessed them.

Tate knew that philosophizing did not make men good. Philosophy did not enable men to create the historical traditions and the unified culture that had both to form the background of their lives in the present and to provide a solid, fertile ground for their values and beliefs. Such traditions and cultures either existed or they did not. The religious imagination, in Tate's view, afforded the only viable source of tradition and culture. The respect that the religious imagination displayed for the power of God and nature lay in its skepticism toward the rational effort to understand nature completely.

The religious imagination contented itself with contemplating the mysteries of nature, satisfied that all attempts to uncover nature's secrets, and thus to alter the terms of human life and history, would end in disaster. Redemption from this evil came only through the mysterious intercession of God's grace. Faith enabled men to accept nature and history as they found them, in all their concreteness, complexity, particularity, and intractability. It was the indispensable office of the religious imagination to restrain men's insatiable desire to impose intellect and will on nature and history in an effort to refashion them to suit men's own purposes and ambitions. The scientific naturalism of the New Humanists, devoid of religious imagination and consequently lacking any sense of historical tradition or unified culture, could hardly hope to discourage this tendency, which was growing ever more fierce and insistent as genuine challenges to the predominance and power of scientific naturalism grew weaker and fewer.

In his essay "Liberalism and Tradition," Tate mounted such a challenge to scientific naturalism and explored the possibilities of reestablishing in the modern world the kind of cultural unity that he believed existed in Europe during the Middle Ages. Tate did not wish to return to the thirteenth century. That much is clear. Such an endeavor, he thought, would be foolish and undesirable; it would amount to romantic nostalgia for a way of life that probably never existed as he envisioned it. He did not share the world view of the men of the thirteenth century. If that were the prerequisite for being a traditionalist, as liberal critics declared, then, Tate countered, he could not qualify. He was attempting to do something else—something far more reactionary than impersonating a chivalrous knight-errant, an anachronistic Saint George battling the dragon of modernity with a rusty sword.

Tate may seem to contradict himself by glorifying a society that he admitted might never have existed. That, however, is not the case. In this sense his reverence for the Middle Ages is similar to his reverence for the antebellum South, for he did not worship either society in itself. Tate revered only those values and sentiments manifest in the Middle Ages and in the Old South upon which modern men could build. He wanted to create—not to re-create—another way of understanding and organizing knowledge and experience than that which positivism, rationalism, naturalism, and science provided.

Liberal pragmatists from William James to Walter Lippmann maintained, in Tate's view, that they could believe only in what was "real" and "possible." Relying on the principles and assumptions of positivism, naturalism, rationalism, and science, they defined the "real" and the "possible" as what already existed or what they could predict would exist.[13] The "Liberal Positivists," as Tate now called his opponents, could not accept the assertion of the "modern Traditionalists" that the real problem of belief in the modern world had nothing to do with the ability to restore the Middle Ages but had everything to do with finding a way to reunify the fragments of Western civilization. Tate depicted the liberal positivists' skepticism toward the traditionalist argument in a hypothetical conversation between representatives of the two points of view. During the course of this conversation, the Liberal tells the Traditionalist:

> Based upon your assumptions are many beliefs that I find interesting and even desirable, but I cannot go all the way with you because not only will the ground of my beliefs hinder me; the very fact that nine out of ten today share my view makes your program extremely doubtful of success. We are committed to a view in which your beliefs have little or no efficacy; we are committed to a program of our own that, in spite of its defects, has dominated the modern world. For good or ill we must make the best of it. (*RM,* 198)

Tate wondered what good could come from a program that emphasized only the practicable, demonstrable, and workable as legitimate objects of belief. For the modern traditionalist and the liberal positivist, Tate pointed out, the historical foundations of belief were the same. Both employed the same "historical method" to recover and understand the past, and, Tate conceded, this method was based on the principles of scientific naturalism. The historical method itself was neutral, however; it embodied no truth. The information it yielded could be arranged to accommodate any pattern of belief. Taken in the strictest sense, the historical method was only a technique for studying the past.

In the minds of liberal and traditionalist thinkers, the historical method assumed distinct and contradictory meanings. Using the historical method, both liberals and traditionalists constructed a point of reference from which to view the past. Although, on the one hand, the liberal might be well disposed toward "Tradition," he could not believe in it. The traditionalist, on the other hand, discovered in the past a unified culture and a spiritual life, the reality of which he accepted on the basis of empirical evidence, the same authority to which the liberal appealed in denying their existence.

13. See *RM,* 198–99.

To the liberal thinker, Tate contended, the idea of "unity" seemed invalid, if not patently absurd. Liberals who lived in an age of cultural disunity and spiritual isolation could not believe that men and women in the past had at least tried to construct a unified culture based on common beliefs, values, and faith. The traditionalist, who was unavoidably a modernist and thus a historical, but not a moral, relativist, included in his account of the past the possibility that men and women had once enjoyed cultural unity and shared a collective world view, even though they no longer did so. The modern traditionalist was convinced by the evidence of history, Tate concluded, that men and women have always needed a more or less unified civilization organized around a set of common values to realize their full humanity.

Tate's assessment of liberal thinking about history was hardly justified and often excessively polemical. Liberal thinkers and historians, the sins that Tate properly attributed to them notwithstanding, were not the only ones guilty of misreading the historical record. Tate himself took liberties with the past when it suited him: he was never especially interested in historical accuracy. Although he probably knew that he overstated his case, his exaggeration did not diminish the importance of his argument. He had a larger point to make, and if his means of making it were not exactly fair or precise, his observations remained critical.

A world that had rejected absolute values and repudiated traditional forms of authority, most notably, the Roman Catholic Church, was left with only the independent, autonomous self isolated in history. This emphasis on self, Tate concluded, was the logical outcome of liberal thought. Liberalism destroyed all criteria for determining the qualities of collective human experience that were worth preserving, and it also negated any possibility of creating a living, unified culture that could be handed on from generation to generation.

Although Tate was quick to point out that the "perfect" traditional society had never existed, could never exist, and was, in fact, an illusion, he maintained that such a society had always existed as a point of reference by which to judge historical reality, as an ideal toward which to strive. Liberal historians and philosophers could not envision the traditional society as either subject to scientific analysis or fit for mechanical perfection. They could therefore discredit it or dismiss it as fictitious and fantastic. The traditionalist was less ambitious. He did not aim at achieving perfection, only at approximating some image of it. "The traditionalist," Tate wrote, "attempts only what the sculptor attempts to do with his stone—to bring his experience to form and order" (*RM,* 215).

Liberals distorted and obscured traditionalists' intentions. Traditionalists had no desire to recover or to restore the past. Tate attributed that impulse to the peculiar "psychosis" of modern, "anti-traditional" men. Traditionalists, rather, created something new, and though they drew on the past, they adapted it to their own moral problems and spiritual needs and thus assimilated past and present into an organic whole.

Formulating a tradition and transmitting it to future generations was, Tate knew, no easy task. Believing that a morally and spiritually unified culture was desirable was not the same as believing that it could readily be attained. The traditionalist had to work hard to secure his inheritance, and no group of American writers worked harder at "inheriting their inheritance" than the Southern Agrarians. Of their number none worked harder than Tate himself.[14]

Yet the traditionalist could not transform himself into a seer and predict the ultimate success of his venture. To enjoin him to do so constituted the fallacy of liberalism. For the liberal positivist, according to Tate, the validity of the traditional way of life lay in the sheer accident of its future success. Tate understood that no such guarantees were possible and that to require them was utter folly. Tradition never transferred from one generation to the next whole and solid. Inheritance was fragile and had to be delicately nurtured: "The traditionalist has never had tradition lying about him in lumps, nor hanging luxuriantly from the trees. Tradition is not the object of belief. It is a quality of judgment and of conduct, rooted in a concrete way of life, that demands constant rediscovery; and it must be maintained with the hardest vigilance" (*RM,* 207).

Tate's Agrarianism was nothing less than an attempt to establish on a solid and particular ground—the ground of the South—the unified culture that he believed once characterized the aspirations of Christendom before the Renaissance, the Reformation, the Enlightenment, and the Industrial and French Revolutions. Only a culture that provided a total and coherent view of human nature by accounting for both the reality of evil and the possibility of redemption could present a viable alternative to the chaos and disorder of life in the modern, scientific, industrial

14. Simpson makes this point admirably in *The Man of Letters in New England and the South,* 248.

world. For Tate, this endeavor took the form of an inquiry into the meaning of southern history and into the possibility that the South was the sole remaining ground on which to create, nurture, and sustain a traditional culture. For him, Agrarianism was thus not primarily a venture into political agitation, economic change, and social reform. Although he was certainly concerned with questions of politics, economics, and society, he never reconciled himself to the modern view that a transformation of the political, economic, and social venues could bring about a spiritual revival.

To be worthwhile, Agrarianism did not have to generate practical or political results, such as nurturing a mass return to the land or persuading a majority of citizens to support an agrarian platform at the polls. Tate differed in this respect from some of his fellow Agrarians who hoped that they could develop a program of political action and perhaps form a political party. Tate saw the potential danger, and perhaps the futility, of this strategy from the beginning. He recognized that if Agrarianism failed as a political movement, its doctrines would automatically be discredited in the public mind. Alternately, he looked to Agrarianism, much as he later looked to Catholicism, to provide the moral principles and the spiritual discipline that would empower and encourage men to see their world through new eyes. The rest would naturally follow.

THE REBIRTH OF NEW ENGLAND

When Samuel Slater circumvented the British prohibition on exporting industrial technology to the United States by memorizing the design of textile machinery and building a cotton-spinning mill in Pawtucket, Rhode Island, he set in motion more than spindles. Transforming raw cotton fiber into finished yarn, the spindles seemed to Tate to symbolize the unraveling of the old world while they simultaneously spun out the new. Slater's factory, in Tate's analysis, marked the beginning of the industrial phase of capitalism in the United States. At the same time, it signaled the beginning of the end of the older values and culture that had enabled Americans to maintain their allegiance to premodern Europe. The change occurred earliest in New England. From the late seventeenth century, the New England theocracy, which gave final, definitive form and meaning to the lives of all New Englanders, pious and impious, rich and poor, learned and vulgar alike, steadily declined both as an ideal and as a reality. Industrial capitalism, which gave meaning to nothing except the cash nexus, gradually arose to take its place. "The energy that built the meeting house," Tate mused, "ran the factory" (*RE,* 5).

The old order, though rigid and doctrinaire, molded a wide range of personal experience and private behavior into a comprehensible, unified whole. The seventeenth-century Puritans could tolerate individual oddities of conduct and manners because they agreed on a set of fundamental beliefs that ultimately governed all that they did, thought, and felt. No action, however intimate, was ever intensely personal or private. The Puritans were never completely alone in the world.

For their descendants, however, the situation was reversed. No longer enjoying the benefits of cultural unity that the formidable New England theocracy provided, a later generation of New Englanders, decadent and depraved in Tate's eyes, clung to a sterile cultural uniformity that accentuated the personal and idiosyncratic while keeping the growing spiritual disorder tucked safely away just below the surface. The crisis was becoming acute, however, and could not long be ignored.

Ralph Waldo Emerson, whom Tate called the "Lucifer of Concord," did not ignore it. He declared the routine conformity that dominated the New England way of life to be the result of the tyranny of tradition and theology. Emerson's pronouncement, Tate believed, was a huge intellectual blunder. He had administered a fatal blow to the enfeebled New England theocracy and thus hastened the development of a piratical industrial capitalism that robbed men not only of their liberty and their dignity but of their very souls.

For Emerson, Tate declared, man alone was the measure of all things. Man was innately perfect and, in time, would realize his perfection and fulfill his true nature. More than any other thinker, Emerson discredited the Puritan idea that human beings were sinful and were engaged in a fierce, dramatic, and ceaseless struggle against evil. In Emerson's conception of reality there was no struggle in the soul and no drama or tragedy in life, for there was no terrible flaw in the human character, no possibility of failing or of doing evil. Man could redeem himself from the world of time and change through his own efforts. Emerson's thought and career, in Tate's view, embodied the heresy of New England and illustrated the extent to which the New Englanders of the nineteenth century had repudiated their ancestors and their past.

By 1850, New England had become a parasite. Nostalgic, decadent, and dependent, New Englanders lived materially and economically off the South, spiritually and culturally off England. New England had become a European museum. As New Englanders realized how far removed from European culture they were, they became intensely self-conscious about the inadequacy of not being good Europeans and grew eager to imitate European ways. They became provincial.

New Englanders emulated European culture and style because, unlike southerners, they had no indigenous, unified culture available to them. They forfeited it when they rejected John Winthrop and Cotton Mather and embraced Ralph Waldo Emerson. They had not the wherewithal to revitalize their older, homogeneous culture. Only their huge fortunes, amassed from textile manufacturing and the slave trade, remained. With those fortunes they accumulated the moldering symbols of their dead culture to remind themselves of the people they had once been. Tate described in eerie detail the weariness and languor that oppressed New England by the middle of the nineteenth century: "The whatnots groaned under the load of knick-knacks, the fine china dogs and cats, the pieces of Oriental jade, the chips off the leaning tower of Pisa. There were the rare books and the cosmopolitan learning. It was all equally displayed as the evidence of a superior culture. The Gilded Age had already begun. But culture, in the true sense, was disappearing" (*RE,* 6).

Tate had to explain how, at a moment when their culture seemed moribund, New Englanders rallied to challenge and defeat the South in a bloody war and to impose their victorious will upon the nation. Despite the original strength and resilience of the old New England theocracy, it grew weaker and more corrupt and eventually fell to an even more powerful force, industrial capitalism—a force that Tate recognized as the most revolutionary and disruptive force in history.

Tate observed that New England capitalists, like their bourgeois counterparts in France during the French Revolution, contrived an alluring, though false, myth about the origins of capitalism. Like all ruling classes, or aspiring ruling classes, New England capitalists concealed the real source and nature of their power and argued that they were "morally sanctioned" to rule. They were not duplicitous; they hid the truth even from themselves. Such deception was necessary, Tate reasoned, both to maintain the confidence of the ruling class itself and to secure acceptance of its political and economic authority from those least likely to benefit. Obfuscation was a fact of political life in all ages, and it was useless to denounce the tactic.

The myth on which New England capitalists drew to legitimize their power was especially pernicious. Begun at the end of the eighteenth century, the concerted effort to deliver mankind from the scourges of monarchy, aristocracy, and other illicit forms of oppression such as slavery resulted in the creation of an ideology that emphasized liberty, equality, and the rights of man and that formed the basis for a new "rationalization of power" to sustain capitalism.

Throughout its history, Tate argued, the leaders of the United States had never seriously tried to make equality of economic opportunity or condition a reality. The heralded revolution of the common man that accompanied the advent of Jacksonian democracy contented itself with the achievement of an illusory social and political equality not by raising ordinary men to power but by bringing social and political life down to their level. To accede to demands for economic equality would have jeopardized the "plutocratic aims of the middle class."

Holding out the promise of political and social equality, while carefully sanctioning and protecting the reality of economic inequality, American capitalists "discovered" the myth that enabled them to consolidate their power: capitalism was the sworn enemy of the southern slavocracy, the sole means of preserving democracy, and the only hope of saving the Union. Hence, northern capitalists clamored for war against the southern slaveholders, the only class that could effectively oppose them in both the political and economic realms.

Not until the 1850s, when the Republican party appealed to the moral authority of antislavery sentiment, could the New England capitalists wage and win a war. They intended not to ensure liberty and equality for all or even to preserve the Union but to protect their property and enhance their political power. The triumphant northern politicians and capitalists, Tate concluded, illegally confiscated property, systematically plundered the South, and effectively reduced their victims and their own people to wage slaves. Americans deluded themselves into believing that they had fought the war to determine whether four million blacks should remain slaves and did not see that the real fight was between the aristocratic ruling class of the South and the plutocratic ruling class of the

North. The capitalists were thus free to seize power, dictate Reconstruction policy, devastate the South, and write history to suit themselves.[15]

Although often based on scant evidence, Tate's reading of history has merit. Certainly slavery had become abhorrent, or at least politically and morally troublesome, to the bourgeois world long before 1861. A powerful, reactionary slaveholding regime in the South posed a threat to a northern bourgeoisie struggling to exert its influence over the young American nation. Tate was also at least partly correct to point out the important historical and philosophical connections that linked the antebellum South to the European world that had existed before the French Revolution. As a broad statement of a more complex and intricate reality, Tate's judgments and conclusions serve as well as any.

But Tate paid dearly for the unforgivable liberties that he took with the past. He obscured his insights into the nature of the conflict between the southern planters and the northern bourgeoisie by failing, or refusing, to acknowledge the centrality of slavery to southern society. Tate posited a conflict between "agricultural" and "industrial" interests, not a fight over whether the South would remain a slave society or become a capitalist society. He pretended, though he appears to have known better, that the South was the idyllic and enchanting agrarian world that Thomas Jefferson described in "Query XIX" of *Notes on the State of Virginia*: a community in harmony with nature and at peace with man, except, of course, for the Yankees, in which slavery was an insignificant and unfortunate aberration.

The war destroyed this traditional way of life and opened the South to the corrosive influences of northern industrialism, world capitalism, and bourgeois culture. Through their common experience of defeat and desolation, however, southerners became conscious of the tragedy inherent in history. Losing the Civil War and suffering the humiliation and oppression that accompanied defeat, southerners gained a superior wisdom about human prospects and limitations. They came to understand, in a way that their naïve conquerors never could, the pretension and folly that blinded men to their own weaknesses and that frequently brought them to unanticipated ruin.

From the late 1920s until the mid-1930s, when the Agrarians were most militant and active as a group, Tate refined the interpretation that

15. See Allen Tate, "Where Are the People?" *American Review*, II (1933), 231–37, *RM*, 196–230, and *ITMS*, 155–75.

the "New England way," culminating in the political-military-industrial machine that had so ruthlessly prosecuted the Civil War, was the harbinger of the modern world. By conflating the "New England way" with the rise of the modern world, Tate attempted to push his argument beyond a mere defense of the South and to initiate a discussion about the nature of the good society, the crisis of modernity, and the perils of history for both the vanquished and the victorious.

THE PERILS OF HISTORY

On July 29, 1929, Donald Davidson wrote to Tate that he and John Crowe Ransom had for some time been contemplating the possibility of publishing a collection of "openly partisan" essays that would discuss southern history and culture, as well as southern politics, art, literature, and religion. Davidson urged that he, Ransom, and Tate recruit other southerners who shared their views about the South, "a small, coherent, highly selected group," to undertake a resolute defense of the southern way of life. The apology, Davidson hoped, would not be limited to a mere assertion of principles. He wanted to call the faithful to arms to fight for home and kin.

Tate's response is memorable and revealing. Writing from Concarneau, Finistere, France, on August 10, 1929, Tate declared his allegiance to the "Southern movement" that Davidson proposed. Tate's letter was, as Lewis P. Simpson has shown, a "key document" not only in the history of Agrarianism or even in the history of American letters but in the history of modern Western letters.[16] As Tate's letter makes clear, he was not committed to restoring the social order of the antebellum South. Instead, he outlined a strategic program designed to organize a disciplined and militant "academy of Southern *positive* reactionaries" who would create "*an intellectual situation interior to the South.*"[17]

Tate's proposed southern academy would initially consist only of persons intimately associated with the Agrarian movement but would be expanded in a few years to include fifteen active members and ten inactive members. The active members would be men of letters or scholars: poets, critics, historians, and economists. The inactive members would

16. See Simpson, "The Southern Republic of Letters and *I'll Take My Stand,*" 66–67.
17. See *LC,* 229–33, esp. 229, 230.

be professional men or public servants: lawyers and statesmen. Together the members of this southern academy would compose a "philosophical constitution" in which they would articulate a "complete social, philosophical, literary, economic, and religious system," in other words, a world view.

Although the intellectual situation that Tate wished to establish would inevitably draw upon southern history, it would seek to remedy what he regarded as the principal defect of that history: the failure of the antebellum South to correspond to its social prototype, medieval Europe. He explained to Davidson that they and their compatriots should value their Southern heritage "not in what it actually performed, but in its possible perfection." He continued with his plan: "Philosophically we must go the whole hog of reaction, and base our movement less upon the actual old South than upon its prototype—the historical social and religious scheme of Europe. We must be the last Europeans—there being no Europeans in Europe at present" (*LC*, 230).

It bears repeating that Tate did not want to restore anything but wanted to create something new. About three weeks before he wrote to Davidson, he had written to John Crowe Ransom: "As the years pass and a certain sourness of spirit comes over me, I lose sympathy with all designs merely to restore the ruins. The Southernism that I am more and more concerned with would probably issue, if successful, in something superficially very dissimilar to the order our fathers swayed in 1850. The truth is one, yet its garments change with fashion. It makes little difference to me what clothes the truth wears."[18] The cultural unity that characterized medieval Christendom had fallen to the combined onslaught of the Protestant Reformation and the French Revolution. The authority of Church and Crown succumbed to the rationalism of the Renaissance, the scientific revolution, and the Enlightenment. But Tate suggested in his letters to Davidson and Ransom that such a unified culture might again be coaxed into existence, removed from its original European setting and relocated in the South.

In such a world men would no longer live wholly by the dictates of reason and science but under the auspices of a social and spiritual order shaped and bounded by myth and tradition. Ritual, custom, and manners would govern everyday life and simply mark every important episode

18. Tate to Ransom, July 27, 1929, in Davidson Papers.

with a special ceremony. Sensing their proper relation to both the timeless and the temporal, the eternal and the historical, men would once more be content to remain faithfully submissive to the will and sovereignty of God.

Tate admitted that the antebellum South had never been this kind of traditional society, but it was the closest approximation possible in the bourgeois world of the nineteenth century. The antebellum South was a traditional society insofar as the material basis of life, the way men made their living, did not require men to lay aside their moral natures. Men in a traditional society had achieved, however imperfectly, a unity between their "way of life" and their means of "making a living." Tate explained: "They are never quite making their living, and they never quite cease to make it. . . . They are making their living all the time, and affirming their humanity all the time" (*RM,* 210, 229).[19]

If such a society had come into being during the 1930s and had no past whatsoever, Tate asserted, it would have been a traditional society because it could pass on to future generations a moral conception of man in relation to material life. In a traditional society, material life was not hostile to the preservation of a unified moral code; it was, in fact, the basis for it. Property was the medium through which men living in a traditional society expressed their moral natures and handed on their customs, beliefs, traditions, and code of conduct to their descendants. For Tate, having property implied not only ownership but control. Property carried with it economic, social, and political privileges as well as moral obligations, an appreciation of rights as well as an acceptance of duties. One of the Southern Agrarians' primary objectives, Tate suggested, should be to restore private property or to find its equivalent.[20]

Modern finance-capitalism destroyed private property. By removing men from responsible control over the material conditions of life, it also inhibited the development of man's moral nature. Under this system, "moral nature" reduced to "economic purpose," and "Economic Man" substituted for "Moral Man." Economic Man was a living abstraction (if

19. See also Richard Gray, *The Literature of Memory: Modern Writers of the American South* (Baltimore, 1977), 80–82.

20. See *RM,* 208–10, 229–30, and *Who Owns America? A New Declaration of Independence,* ed. Herbert Agar and Allen Tate (New York, 1936), 80–93. See also Louis D. Rubin, Jr., *The Wary Fugitives: Four Poets and the South* (Baton Rouge, 1978), 254–55, and Gray, *The Literature of Memory,* 80–82.

such were not a contradiction in terms) wholly subservient to a system of production and utilizing reason, science, and technology only to subdue and master nature and turn it to his profit.

For a society dominated by economics and composed of economic men, whether workers or capitalists, there existed a vast separation between the means of "making a living" and the "way of life," between the means of production and the code of morality. Both workers and capitalists, Tate declared, operated the means of production without controlling them. As moral life lost its hold on material life, men's conduct became irresponsible and society dissolved in the anarchy of the market. Tate concluded: "The further the modern system develops in the direction that it has taken for two generations, the more antitraditional our society will become, and the more difficult it will be to pass on the fragments of the traditions we inherit" (*RM, 230*).

Since its founding, the history of property in the United States was the story of the struggle between small, local ownership, typified by agriculture, and big, dispersed ownership, epitomized by the giant industrial corporation. Tate believed that holding the stock certificates of a huge corporation like United States Steel or Standard Oil was not equivalent to owning a tract of land in Kentucky or Tennessee, no matter how small. J. P. Morgan and John D. Rockefeller had little in common with the subsistence farmer. But the poor farmer, who thought himself less successful than Mr. Morgan or Mr. Rockefeller, actually owned genuine property, while his wealthy and prestigious counterparts owned only worthless pieces of paper.

Tate was quick to point out the irony. Thousands of small investors owned U.S. Steel and Standard Oil, but they had little or no voice in the operation of those companies. Morgan, Rockefeller, and the boards of directors made all the important decisions. They effectively controlled property they did not really own. From Tate's perspective, the joint stock company was as much an enemy of private property as the Soviet or the Comintern. Indeed, the very logic of corporate ownership pointed toward political centralization and economic collectivization. As Tate put it in one of his more flamboyant passages, "corporate structure strives toward the condition of Moscow."[21]

21. *Who Owns America?* ed. Agar and Tate, 83.

Directors of huge corporations felt no inclination to assume the responsibilities of property ownership. They could be as careless and indifferent, as callous and corrupt, as suited their moods or designs. They were literally irresponsible. Although Tate thought that effective control of property alone made responsibility possible, he also knew that such control did not make responsibility inevitable. A stock certificate represented a certain amount of investment capital at work somewhere to produce a certain amount of exchange value from which someone hoped to derive a certain amount of profit. The process was vague, complex, abstract, and far removed from ordinary life, but it was no less real, powerful, or insidious for that. The chairmen of the boards of huge corporations had only legal relations with the stockholders, who actually owned the companies. An unscrupulous, ambitious, and clever man could use the property of unsuspecting men and women in ways they neither imagined nor approved.[22]

The real choice, Tate was convinced, had always been a moral, not merely an economic and political, choice. By the 1930s, it had become imperative that the American people choose either morality and tradition or immorality and chaos. The modern capitalist system operated efficiently regardless of the moral stature of the men who ran it or the moral implications of their economic pursuits. If that situation were ever to be rectified, however, Americans would have to accept a political economy that somehow rejoined the ownership and control of property and that thus imposed moral constraints on the use of property. For ownership without control amounted to enslavement, and control without ownership masked tyranny.

Tate called on American citizens to revitalize their political life and to reassert the rights of effective ownership. Politics and economics should be concerned with the well-being of each member of the community—a concern that ran counter to the impulse to reduce men to economic integers and to calculate their productive capacity. Tate understood what was required: "We have been merely economists, and now we have got to be political economists as well. Economics is the study of wealth. But political economy is the study of human welfare."[23] Tate never deluded

22. Tate's understanding of modern economic trends was largely shaped by two books: John R. Commons, *The Legal Foundations of Capitalism* (New York, 1924), and Adolf A. Berle, Jr., and Gardiner C. Means, *The Modern Corporation and Private Property* (New York, 1933).

23. *Who Owns America?* ed. Agar and Tate, 90–93.

himself. He knew that the odds were long against the success of a political movement based on the redefinition and revitalization of private property. If he was pessimistic about Agrarianism as a political movement, he was nevertheless determined to articulate a set of principles that represented an alternative to the progressive ethos that dominated the modern age.

The antebellum South offered Tate both a history and a series of concrete images around which to structure this program. But how, Tate wondered, could he defend the southern tradition and, at the same time, make it intelligible to modern men not likely to be well disposed toward it? How could he simultaneously "take hold" of the southern tradition and transform it to meet the exigencies of the moment? "We need a stable order," he wrote to Ransom in 1929.[24] The question was how and on what basis to establish it.

Tate appealed to the past, not to southern or American history alone, but to the history of Western civilization since the Middle Ages. He wrote to Davidson in 1927 that he was trying to develop a perspective that would enable him always to comprehend the present in relation to the past. Without such a perspective, he declared, neither past nor present made any sense, and persons were constantly forced to recreate what had gone before and to confront all problems as if they had never heard of them. "My attempt is to see the present from the past, yet remain immersed in the present and committed to it," he wrote. "I think it is suicide to do anything else" (*LC,* 189).[25]

In Tate's interpretation of Western history, the antebellum South represented the final flowering of medieval Europe. Southerners had rooted their society in a native soil and, unlike New Englanders, did not need to define themselves as a people or investigate their place in history because their collective identity was self-evident to them. In contrast to New Englanders' obsession with Europe, southerners could live their own lives and let Europe alone. They cultivated their own manners, customs, and values just as they cultivated the soil. They lived by humane principles and saw in the great European civilizations of the past an image and anticipation of their own society. "The South could be ignorant of

24. Tate to Ransom, July 27, 1929, in Davidson Papers.
25. See also Brooks, "Allen Tate and the Nature of Modernism," 691–92.

Europe," Tate wrote in the essay he contributed to *I'll Take My Stand,* "because it *was* Europe" (*ITMS,* 171).[26]

Antebellum southerners were unwilling to base their judgments, actions, or values merely on how well or how poorly something worked or on whether it enhanced or hindered their pursuit of the main chance. They were only interested in the work that needed to be done and the joy they derived from doing it. Southerners hated everything that was unnatural or extraneous, everything that was ornamental or superfluous. They did nothing, Tate wrote, that was not essential or beneficial to sustaining their way of life: "They planted no corn that they could not enjoy; they grew no cotton that did not directly contribute to the upkeep of a rich private life; and they knew no history for the sake of knowing it, but simply for the sake of contemplating it and seeing in it an image of themselves" (*ITMS,* 172).

Tate knew that this vision of the antebellum South was at best partial and at worst false. His correspondence with his fellow Agrarians and his magnificent essays on southern literature and history reveal as much.[27] Tate had to explain, however, why southerners had failed when their way of life had so much to recommend it. Tate concluded that antebellum southerners suffered not a failure of nerve but a breakdown of ideas and belief. Theirs was an intellectual and, more serious, a religious and spiritual failure. Southerners' religious impulses remained inarticulate because they attempted to define themselves and their destiny as a people in the terms set forth by Protestantism. But Protestantism could not encompass all that the antebellum South was.

The South was a feudal society without a feudal religion, Tate wrote in "Remarks on the Southern Religion." To force the South to conform to Protestantism was a tragic and fatal error, for Protestantism was a "non-agrarian and trading religion, hardly a religion at all, but a result of secular ambition" (*ITMS,* 168). It more nearly suited New England, "one of those abstract-minded, sharp-witted trading societies" (*ITMS,* 170).[28]

26. See also Michael O'Brien, *The Idea of the American South, 1920–1941* (Baltimore, 1979), 18–19, 144–50; Rubin, *The Wary Fugitives,* 224–26; Brooks, "Allen Tate and the Nature of Modernism," 688; Singal, *The War Within,* 246–49.

27. See *ITMS,* 155–75, Allen Tate, "Last Days of a Charming Lady," *Nation,* October 28, 1925, pp. 485–87, and Allen Tate, *Essays of Four Decades* (Chicago, 1968), 519–34, 577–92. See also George Core, "Allen Tate and the South," *Southern Review,* n.s., XII (1976), 767–75, esp. 772–73.

28. See *ITMS,* 166–70.

The colonists who settled in the South carried within themselves a sense of community, a sense that the only proper social order was hierarchical, a sense that authority and obedience were essential to the creation of a stable, civilized way of life. These imperatives were incompatible with the ideals of individualism and equality inherent in Protestant doctrine.

Consequently, southerners had no body of religious doctrine on which to draw to sustain themselves and their society during and especially after the Civil War. Southern defeat was the more complete, permanent, and irreversible because southerners lacked the proper religious sentiment and theology. In Tate's view, religion formed the crux of the Agrarians' critique of modernity. He had little doubt that the southern way of life, if not the southern nation itself, would have survived for centuries if southerners' religious beliefs had been more in accord with southern political, social, and economic life.

In his letters to Davidson and Ransom, Tate stated his meaning more explicitly than he did in his published essays. The antebellum South, he thought, should have become a Roman Catholic nation. He wrote to Ransom in 1929 that he believed the remote origin of the old southern mind, notwithstanding the evangelical zeal of Methodists, Baptists, and Presbyterians, was to be found in Catholicism, or at least in High Church Anglicanism. He proposed that the Agrarians take this insight as their starting point, the "master-idea," for the southern movement. He told Ransom that the best way for them to begin to reassess the meaning of southern history was to show that "the old Southerners were historically Catholics all the time."[29]

Southerners also inherited an unsatisfactory history. Southern politicians could defend their cause and their nation only in a political language drawn from the eighteenth century. The appeal to liberty, individualism, and the rights of man did not serve well an aristocratic, hierarchical society. The Republican party, if not Abraham Lincoln himself, was determined to dominate the South. The radical secessionists, such as Robert Barnwell Rhett of South Carolina, Robert Toombs and Howell Cobb of Georgia, and William Lowndes Yancey of Alabama, were equally determined to secede from the Union before it was too late to save the southern way of life.

29. Tate to Ransom, July 27, 1929, in Davidson Papers. See also *LC,* 222–29.

The Republicans and the fire-eaters, Tate asserted, were the only two parties in the United States during the 1850s who knew their own minds and each other's minds. But the men who came to power in the Confederacy did not want secession. Jefferson Davis, Alexander H. Stephens, and most of the delegates to the Montgomery Convention who brought the Confederacy into existence as a political nation were reluctant to part from the Union. They desired only compromise with the North. Devoted to the Constitution, they believed that it provided the legal, political, and moral basis on which they could argue their right to independence. They were sadly mistaken.

"The Montgomery Convention lost us the war," Tate lamented to Davidson. Living in the political world of the eighteenth century, southern politicians and thinkers, save for a few notable exceptions, could not see that the future of the South lay outside the Union to which they had developed an unfortunate emotional and sentimental attachment. Tate seems instinctively to have grasped, and to have despised, the attitude of T. R. R. Cobb and many others who believed that secession would force northerners to welcome the southern states back into the Union on terms favorable to the South. Cobb and like-minded southerners held out the hope, even after secession, that they had engaged in a political ploy rather than a rebellion.

Tate also recognized that when they were outside the political forms and language of the eighteenth century, just as when they were outside the doctrine and theology of Protestantism, southerners fell silent. No southern thinker, not even the redoubtable Thomas Roderick Dew of Virginia or the eloquent William Harper, chancellor of South Carolina, could present an original vision of their society. No southern thinker or statesman, Tate concluded, was half so original as the society that produced him.

Southern thinkers had a genius only for politics, and in the end that genius proved their undoing. The year 1861 was no time for tired political rhetoric that recalled the former benefits of union now lost or that presumed the government in Washington, D.C., remained in the hands of high-minded gentlemen eager to debate constitutional principles. The South needed a fearless man who could act without precedent and who could envision and articulate what should have been the real destiny of the South: to become an agrarian society based on the ownership of land

and slaves and ruled by a conservative aristocracy who had embraced the teachings of the Roman Catholic Church.[30]

The Montgomery Convention supplied no such leader. Quite the contrary. The delegates to the convention, much to Tate's dismay, took care to repudiate, discredit, or nullify the influence of the men who were the prophets of southern nationalism. Had Rhett, Toombs, or Yancey been elected to the presidency instead of Davis, Tate believed, the South would have won the war in a year—or lost it. He depicted these men, the heroes of his biography of Jefferson Davis, as the most thoughtful, determined, and aggressive proponents of the southern cause, the only persons capable of sensing the desperate nature of the crisis facing the South.

Tate especially admired Robert Barnwell Rhett. He once wrote that "Rhett was not so great a writer or philosopher of the state as [John C.] Calhoun, but he was the greatest practical statesman the South ever produced." He found valuable Rhett's "belief in statesmanship, as opposed to economic drift, and his fundamnetal [sic] belief that the social aim is definable and achievable, and that the economic structure of a society is the tool to that end." Finally, however, Tate had to concede that his story had no heroes, for these men never got an opportunity to behave heroically. The Montgomery Convention saw to that.[31]

Tate warned Davidson that the Agrarians must avoid the errors of their ancestors. Although the Agrarians were not founding a nation, they were trying to create a new society, or at least a new way of thinking about the world. They must not employ the language of their enemies, compromise their principles, or accommodate to any world view to which they were opposed. "We must take logic to the most extreme ends," Tate urged his friend, "and then perform the best we can." The delegates to the Montgomery Convention did not have the example of their own conduct to guide them: "Those men *felt,* but they would not *think* through habits and political inertia. . . . There was no one to tell them the logical consequences of their position" (*LC,* 231). Tate's final judgment of them was bittersweet: "As a collection of portraits their like will not be seen again in American history; for had they but known it, they were there to enact their own extinction, to write the obituary of their race" (*JD,* 17).

30. See *JD,* 3–115. See also *LC,* 231.
31. Tate to Bandler, February 24, 1932, in Tate File, *Hound and Horn* Papers.

If the delegates to the Montgomery Convention wrote the obituary of the South, Tate did not want the Agrarians to deliver the eulogy. He conceived of Agrarianism not as some palliative administered to convince remorseful southerners that their civilization had once been glorious and to alleviate the anguish they felt at its passing. Nor did he think of the movement as merely a challenge or rebuke to the present. Rather, he envisioned Agrarianism as an alternative to modernism, proposing a distinct tradition and a set of cogent ideas, beliefs, and values around which to organize life in the modern world.

Confounded by their adherence to Protestantism and beguiled by their acceptance of the political language of eighteenth-century liberalism, antebellum southern thinkers did not bring their world view to maturity. Tate intended the Agrarian movement to redress this failure. He suggested that had antebellum southern thinkers dispensed with the doctrines of the Protestant Reformation and the Enlightenment and come to see themselves as the legitimate heirs of an older Catholic tradition, they would have broken decisively with the North and established a society that was at once completely novel and thoroughly reactionary. "Reaction is the most radical of programs," he wrote, for "it aims at cutting away the overgrowth and getting back to the roots." In contrast, "a forward-looking radicalism is a contradiction; it aims at rearranging the foliage" (*ITMS*, 175).

From its inception Tate believed that for Agrarianism to succeed, not as a political movement, but as an "intellectual situation interior to the South," he and his compatriots would somehow have to assimilate southern history to European history. They would have to redefine the South as a traditional society hostile to the authority of rationalism and science, industrialism and capitalism. It was a catastrophe when Europeans liberated reason from a defense of myth and religion. Myth and religion, institutionalized in the medieval Church, restrained men from exploring nature too deeply. The Church taught that such exploration was dangerous and better avoided, for Nature was temporal and contingent and, as such, offered only echoes of Being. The true source of Being lay in the timeless realm of the supernatural. By using reason to endorse and protect the supernatural, the Church performed an extraordinary feat of cultural and spiritual unification. Reason, once freed from the strictures of myth and religion, destroyed that unity by proving it to be a fiction that could be fitted into no logical system tolerable to the rational mind.[32]

For Tate, Agrarianism was a religious quest to revitalize the society of myth, tradition, and faith, modern man's most precious historical legacy and the only means of preserving Western civilization and the humane life that it engendered. If *I'll Take My Stand* had been the book that Tate wanted it to be, it would have been one of the great religious documents of the twentieth century. Critics and scholars have justly recognized Tate as a fine poet and a talented essayist. With the exception of Cleanth Brooks, however, few have acknowledged him as one of the most important religious thinkers of his time, a rarity in any age but even more exceptional in a day when educated persons can ignore religion with impunity.[33]

But because of the deficiencies in southern religion, Tate judged that he had to defend a society of myth, tradition, and faith with the only means at hand: reason. By using reason, he realized that he had violated the essence of myth, tradition, and faith. This was what Tate meant when he wrote in "Remarks on the Southern Religion" that southerners must take hold of their tradition "by violence." For myth, tradition, and faith to operate, they had necessarily to remain tacit, spontaneous, and unconscious. Tate believed that under present circumstances, southerners had to become self-conscious about the myths, traditions, and faith by which they had always lived. They could no longer accept anything on faith, for their religious convictions were inchoate and their myths and traditions confused and disparaged.

Modern southerners could not simply will history to reverse its course to make the South once again a society of myth, tradition, and faith. Had that been possible, the crisis of modernity would have been easy to solve. At times, Tate hoped for such a reversal of fortune, though he never deluded himself into believing that this fiat of will had any chance of success. He knew better and understood, too, that such an aggressive act of will would bring only disaster in its wake. Describing the melancholy predicament of the modern southerner, which, of course, he took as his own, Tate lamented that he could almost wish for his consolation

32. See *ITMS,* 163–66.
33. Brooks, "Allen Tate and the Nature of Modernism," 685–97, and Cleanth Brooks, *Modern Poetry and the Tradition* (New York, 1965), 151–62.

and peace of mind "to believe that history is not a vast body of concrete fact to which he must be loyal, but only a source of mechanical formulas; for then he might hope to do what the Northern industrialist has just about succeeded in doing—making a society out of abstractions." Were he able to do that, however, he would enmesh himself in the contradiction of achieving what he wanted through means he decried: "The Southerner would conjure up some magic abstraction to spirit back to him his very concrete way of life. He would, in short, in his plight, apply the formula by his inheritance—that the ends of man may be established by political means" (*ITMS,* 174).

Politics, like reason, was not the proper instrument to use in reestablishing the "private, self-contained, and essentially spiritual life" that Tate desired (*ITMS,* 175). Yet what else but politics and reason were at hand? Tate did not want Agrarianism to become chiefly a political movement organized to pursue definite and limited objectives. To restrict Agrarianism to political agitation, Tate thought, was to play into the hands of his opponents. As a political movement, Agrarianism would rise or fall on the basis of its success in winning elections and in getting its proposals enacted into law. If the Agrarians failed in this regard, Tate supposed, "the people" would ignore their principles because they would mistakenly believe that Agrarianism had been rejected at the polls or spurned in the legislature. Tate admonished his fellow Agrarians not to create a situation in which their program would be evaluated on the basis of its practicality or workability. To do so would be to give away the cause to their enemies without a fight.

Tate also feared that the Agrarians would fall victim to a still more enticing and treacherous evil if they insisted on envisioning the South as the transcendent, redemptive community that could save the modern world from itself through political action. Neither the South, the southern tradition, nor the Agrarian political economy, Tate declared, was an appropriate object of belief. They might provide an image, a symbol, or a method, but they could never be ends in themselves. They could not substitute for faith because, as he wrote to Ransom, they "may ripen our minds with partial insights (i.e. cultivate us)," but "only God can give the affair a genuine purpose."[34]

---

34. Tate to Ransom, July 27, 1927, in Davidson Papers.

Tate feared that southerners' assertions of the unique advantages of their history represented another instance of the desire to impose human will on history that he deplored. It was an example of the sinful impulse to divinize secular history that, in his letters to Davidson, he called "mystical secularism."[35] Possibly by the time *I'll Take My Stand* was published and certainly by the time he converted to Roman Catholicism, Tate concluded that he and his fellow Agrarians had confused secular and sacred history in an attempt not only to redefine the past but to outwit the future.

With this insight, Tate identified the irony of southern history that afflicted not only the Montgomery Convention but also the Agrarian movement. He recognized that southerners had the same idolatrous and heretical vision of their society as the salvation of mankind as did New Englanders, whose ancestors had built "a city upon a hill" in the wilderness of the New World.

35. See *LC,* 328–29.

4

TATE AND SOUTHERN REDEMPTION:
ALL ARE BORN YANKEES

> Soldiers, march! we shall not fight again
> The Yankees with our guns well-aimed and rammed—
> All are born Yankees of the race of men
> And this, too, now the country of the damned
> —Allen Tate, "To the Lacedemonians"

THE HISTORY OF FAILURE AND THE FAILURE
OF HISTORY

The history of the South, Allen Tate declared, was the history of failure and defeat. Appomattox had been but one of many such moments throughout southern history and perhaps not the most serious or devastating. More important, Tate thought, was the almost complete spiritual failure of the southern people, demonstrated by the eagerness with which they made a religion of the "lost cause." They had little else to sustain them.

Southerners had put their faith in history, and in 1865, history disappointed them. Defeated in war, they could not certify their vision of the past or of the future. The victorious northerners could write history to suit themselves and could make of the future what they wanted. In the northern interpretation of events, southerners naturally became the villains responsible for all the evils that afflicted the nation. Consequently, after the war, southerners remained on the defensive, retreating into a self-willed isolation—a "moral secession," Tate called it—that was more thoroughgoing after 1865 than it had been before. They convinced themselves that if only "those people over there" had let them alone, the vast southern paradise would have endured forever.

Antebellum southerners had been virtually indifferent to time and change. Unlike northerners, for whom time and change were almost sensuous facts of experience, southerners could contemplate only a static and permanent existence. In another kind of civilization, such as the settled, stable, harmonious world of the Middle Ages or even of eighteenth-century Virginia, this quality of permanence would have been a virtue. In modern civilization, which thrived on time and change, however, southerners operated at a distinct disadvantage. Haughty and complacent, they could not imagine the death of their world. When the end came, Tate wrote, they were only "shocked by events into a sort of dumb resistance."[1]

The theme of failure and defeat captivated Tate, who identified intimately with the collapse of southern civilization. He took the failure of the South personally, equating the meaning of his life with the defeat, humiliation, and subjugation of his ancestors. Tate was most frustrated by his inability as a man of letters to formulate for the defeated South an authoritative moral and spiritual order through the disciplined use of language. Why had the South not realized its historical destiny and carried out a spiritual, not merely a political, secession from the North and become at last a redemptive community that would save mankind? How could the values that Tate associated with the southern way of life be preserved in defeat? Were they worth preserving at all? How could he discover any meaning in southern history beyond failure and defeat? What significance could he, as a man of letters, find in the only image available to him: the cursed and benighted South? There were no easy answers to these questions. Tate wrote of his distress to his friend John Peale Bishop:

> The older I get the more I realize that I set out about ten years ago to live a life of failure, to imitate, in my own life, the history of my people. For it was only in this fashion, considering the circumstances, that I could completely identify myself with them. We all have an instinct—if we are artists particularly—to live at the center of some way of life and to be borne up by its innermost significance. The significance of the Southern way of life, in my time, is failure. . . . What else is there for me but a complete acceptance of the idea of failure? There is no other "culture" that I can enter into, even if I had the desire. (*RLA*, 34)

1. See *RLA*, 33–34. See also Allen Tate, *Collected Essays* (Denver, 1959), 554–68, and *MO*, 35–38, 144–54.

Tate's vision of the antebellum South as a traditional, agrarian community that provided an alternative to the fragmented world of modernity simply could not bear the scrutiny to which he himself subjected it. Indeed, history, which Tate could not ignore entirely, had already discredited it. The antebellum South had once afforded him a point of reference from which to judge modernity. It offered an image of a unified, stable, hierarchical social order of the kind that prevailed during the Middle Ages and that persisted in modern peasant cultures like those he had encountered in France.

In such a world there was none of the modern "dissociation of sensibility"; intellect and emotion were joined. This imaginative conception of the South represented Tate's attempt to overcome the subjectivity and isolation of modern existence. He knew, or at least he came to know, however, that Virginia was not Provence. The antebellum South resembled medieval Europe only superficially, if at all. On October 9, 1932, Tate wrote to Davidson:

> Have you ever been to Provence? If I were not all resentment at being abroad at all, I should think it the most wonderful foreign country I have seen. This is real, pure agrarianism, and it will outlast the upheavals of Europe, as it outlasted the Roman Empire. These people will never absorb the psychology of capitalism and the machine. After Christmas I intend to make some kind of real study of this region, mostly to find out what it is in the people that has kept them pure of modern contamination. If we can discover this it might be valuable as a lesson to our people.[2]

Tate had to uncover the reasons that "real, pure agrarianism" had failed in the South and left his people open to "modern contamination." He began with a familiar premise now commonly associated with the Agrarian movement. Like Ransom and Davidson, he initially saw the epic struggle between good and evil manifested in the historic struggle of the traditional, religious, organic, agrarian South against the modern, secular, dehumanized, industrial North. Almost as soon as Tate accepted this formulation of the problem, though, he began to question it. In

---

2. Allen Tate to Donald Davidson, October 9, 1932, in Donald Davidson Papers, Special Collections, Jean and Alexander Heard Library, Vanderbilt University. See also *LC*, 271–78. Tate apparently never produced the promised study.

time, his criticism of the South became almost as tenacious and one-sided as his defense of it had been.

As early as March, 1927, as Tate began to identify with the South, he wrote to Davidson: "I've attacked the South for the last time, except in so far as it may be necessary to point out that the chief defect the Old South had was that in it which produced, through whatever cause, the New South" (*LC,* 191). Tate's proclamation of undying loyalty to the South suggests that the antebellum South was somehow tragically flawed and that the internal contradictions afflicting the southern way of life brought it down more decisively than did the armies of Mr. Lincoln, Ulysses S. Grant, and William T. Sherman. Despite his love for the South, Tate came to understand that the crisis of Western civilization transcended the dichotomy between North and South and was rooted in the decline of the medieval synthesis, which long antedated the Confederacy. Although he agreed that there remained much of value in the southern way of life and that the South still had much to teach the nation, he could not pretend that the antebellum South was some Edenic paradise violated by demonic Yankees. The struggle between good and evil, previously represented in the struggle between the South and the North, was in reality, Tate concluded, the struggle of the South with itself.

Tate himself never reconciled these conflicting visions of the South as the redemptive community of myth and the contingent community of history. Nor did he derive any satisfaction from the efforts of an earlier generation of southern writers—writers who came of age in the decades immediately after the Civil War—to do so. These authors produced a sentimental literature of romantic illusion, a literature of "narcissism" rather than of introspection. Indeed, the writers of the "Glasgow and Cabell school," in which Tate included the likes of Thomas Nelson Page and Edwin Mims, were singularly incapable of introspection. They tried to define the South "by looking into a glass behind [their] backs: not inward" (*RLA,* 35).[3] They praised the southern gentleman for his grace and courtesy, only to condemn him for not being a cultivated New Englander or a sophisticated European. They advocated a respect for custom and tradition but complained that the South was not progressive and contemporary.

3. See also *MO,* 146, and *LC,* 243–46.

James Branch Cabell, Ellen Glasgow, and the other southern writers of their ilk spoiled their talents, Tate feared, by refusing to judge southerners and the South without appealing to some external referent, whether New England, Europe, or the Idea of Progress. Distracted and confused, they engaged their talents to create instruments of propaganda rather than works of art. Southern writers generally during the years between the Civil War and World War I, with the notable exception of Mark Twain, composed a literature of apology that simultaneously defended the Old South and extolled the New South. Desperate to justify the continued existence of the South, they mounted a nostalgic defense of slavery and, at the same time, showed the benefits that had accrued to the South with the destruction of slavery. Confused, duplicitous, and perhaps hypocritical, most southern writers could weep for the lost cause while they were "whooping it up in boosters' clubs along with the veritablest descendant of carpet-bagger and poor white."[4]

Tate encountered these attitudes not only among writers. In a letter to his Agrarian brethren on June 5, 1930, he described an incident that he and his wife, the novelist Caroline Gordon, had witnessed several days earlier. While attending a memorial ceremony to honor the Confederate dead, they were subjected to an address that they considered an insult to the South and its defenders, past and present, and a perversion of the southern tradition. Tate wrote that the speaker, a Baptist minister, declared the following farrago:

> The old South was a country of slavery and tyranny, but because State Rights [*sic*] had been a principle held both North and South no one need apologize for having an ancestor in the Confederate army. Such was the error of the South, however, that it took a bloody war to show the hand of God—God at the end showed this country the way he intended it to go, which the speaker described in terms of high tariff, the factory system, and prosperity. The South, he said, would soon lead the nation—Northern capital moving here, and soon the blessings of industrial prosperity will be with us. Let us forget[,] he exhorted, the

---

4. Allen Tate, "Last Days of a Charming Lady," *Nation,* October 28, 1925, pp. 485–87, esp. 485. See also Paul M. Gaston, *The New South Creed: A Study in Southern Mythmaking* (New York, 1970), *passim;* Jonathan M. Wiener, *The Social Origins of the New South: Alabama, 1860–1885* (Baton Rouge, 1978), 186–221; C. Vann Woodward, *The Origins of the New South, 1877–1913* (Rev. ed.; Baton Rouge, 1971), 142–74; and Edward L. Ayers, *The Promise of the New South: Life After Reconstruction* (New York, 1992).

South of oppression and slavery (his own words) and build up the South of Henry W. Grady.[5]

Tate castigated both his literary forebears and his Southern contemporaries who espoused the myth of the lost cause and advocated the influx of northern capital and the development of southern industry and commerce. They accepted, even welcomed, the results of Reconstruction. Southerners were getting rich again, and these writers encouraged them to enjoy the benefits of the Union. Blame did not rest entirely with the postbellum southern writers, though, for they had inherited no tradition and no moral or spiritual values to equip them to weather the violent transition from the Old South to the New. The real failure, in Tate's mind, belonged to the writers of the antebellum South and with the literature they produced.

The aristocratic planters who ruled the South had no use for literature. They did not care to support a class of professional men of letters in the South or to cultivate a southern literary tradition. At first glance, this situation seems to have been anomalous. Wealthy, learned, and refined, the southern aristocracy, Tate supposed, exemplified the class most likely to devote its energy and vitality to nurturing the literary arts. But there was a "grave fault" in the intellectual life of the antebellum South: it was "hag-ridden with politics" (*EFD*, 523). Like the members of all aristocracies, the southern planters were obsessed with politics and with protecting their class interests, status, and power.

The "political mania" of the southern aristocracy suppressed most attempts to produce an independent literature or to maintain an independent class of literary men. Gifted writers defended their society against the northern assault that threatened its life. They developed an ideology that stated their point of view and voiced their objections to the northern point of view. Their writing was political and polemical. They did not, perhaps because they could not, create a great literature that examined the human condition, bringing into focus its magnificence and its misery.

5. Allen Tate to Confederates, June 5, 1930, and Allen Tate to Donald Davidson, June 9, 1930, both in Davidson Papers. See also Lewis P. Simpson, *The Man of Letters in New England and the South: Essays on the History of the Literary Vocation in America* (Baton Rouge, 1973), 242–43.

The reasons for this state of affairs were many and complex. In his writing on antebellum southern literature, culture, and history, Tate concentrated on the two that he considered most important: the character of the southern mind and the nature of southern society. The southern mind was not much given to introspection. Unselfconscious and extroverted, it was incapable of self-examination or self-criticism. Southern writers, and, indeed, traditional southern gentlemen, did not take seriously the "life of the mind."

Southern writing, therefore, like southern conversation, was not a dialogue. It was not, as Tate put it, "dialectical," the give and take between two minds, but "rhetorical": someone talked in an effort to persuade while someone else listened. For a New England sage such as Emerson, the "scholar is man thinking." Had antebellum southerners cared to take issue with Emerson's definition, Tate conjectured, they would have replied that "the gentleman is man talking." The literature of the antebellum South, from Tate's perspective, was nothing more than the rhetorical expression of the southern mind.[6]

Wholly committed to the "rhetorical mode" of imagination and expression, southern writers, from before the Civil War until after World War I, cast themselves as southern patriots dedicated to speaking out on behalf of their society. First in defense and then in defeat, they invented a myth that portrayed the South as a peaceful and prosperous land of farms and plantations presided over by the archetypical agrarian heroes: the scholar-statesman Marcus Tullius Cicero, "leaving his rhetorical studies to apply them patriotically to the prosecution of Cataline," and the farmer-warrior Lucius Quinctius Cincinnatus, "dropping his plough for the sword." The embodiment of this mythic hero combination Cicero-Cincinnatus was, of course, General Robert E. Lee, commander of the Army of Northern Virginia.

A man of action, not of letters, Lee nevertheless represented for Tate the rhetorical character of the southern mind. Lee assumed that he owed his very life and, therefore, his deepest allegiance to a particular people, place, and history. He could conceive of no existence apart from the land and the hands that planted, cultivated, and harvested the fruits of the land.

6. See *EFD*, 554–68.

But, Tate insisted, Lee had not fought to defend slavery or to ensure the existence of an independent southern nation. Instead, Lee stood with his neighbors to preserve the local community that constituted the only world he knew. Although Lee hated slavery, he could not renounce his community because some of its members mistreated others. The image of the rooted man, of which Lee was only the most distinguished example, was the basis of the archetypical myth of the South as a community of families presided over by a wise and gentle patriarch. Tate himself, his misgivings notwithstanding, could conceive of no better way to capture the essence of what southern civilization had once been than to conjure up an image of the typical southern patriarch, for whom Lee was the exemplar. Tate described the old gentleman in this way:

> [He] sat every afternoon in his front yard under an old sugar tree reading Cicero's Letters to Atticus. When the hands suckering the tobacco in the adjoining field needed orders, he kept his place in the book with his forefinger, walked out into the field, gave the orders, and then returned to his reading under the shade of the tree. He was also a lawyer, and occasionally he went to his office, which was over the feedstore in the county seat, a village with a population of about 400 people. (*EFD,* 563–64)

According to the southern myth, however, the South was more than simply an aggregate of families under the permissive sway of an indulgent patriarch. Through marriage—and the transfer of property that often accompanied, and sometimes prompted, matrimony—southern families became so interrelated as almost to constitute one family, with black and white members. If left to its own devices, southerners conjectured, this great southern family would have established an inviolate agrarian civilization.

This rhetorical defense of the South, which constituted for Tate the whole of the southern literary tradition, contained an element of truth. For that reason, Tate thought, it was far more dangerous than if it had been completely false. Southern rhetoric made the Yankees responsible for the dreadful fate that had befallen the South. Southerners themselves, the architects of a tranquil world governed by kind masters and peopled by happy slaves, were innocent. Whatever advantages this world view may have had, Tate asserted, they were nullified by its defects. This view excused southerners from examining themselves and their world, an undertaking that, if it were not the beginning of wisdom, at least could have been the beginning of literature.

Events before, during, and after the war so absorbed and preoccupied southern writers that they indefinitely postponed this exercise in self-examination. They consoled themselves with a false image of the South as an arcadian paradise that, had northern fanatics not interfered, would have saved men from all the miseries that plagued them. Tate recognized the limitations of this point of view, for he saw the many imperfections in southern civilization that had so long been overlooked. Southerners, especially southern writers, had to face the reality that the Yankees were not to blame for everything. Southerners, too, had much to answer for.

Tate maintained that to comprehend the meaning of southern history, Southern writers had to abandon "melodramatic rhetoric" and embrace "the dialectic of tragedy." They could no longer conveniently imagine that "the Southern gentleman was the Chevalier Bayard *redivivus,* the Poor White a picturesque buffoon who spoke quaint dialect, and the Negro Rousseau's Natural Man spoiled by having been deprived of the benefits of slavery" (*MO,* 146). The transformation in the southern literary consciousness had begun to take place after World War I, but it was far from complete by the 1930s. Southern writers had to realize that literature began with inner turmoil, not in the quarrel with a wicked enemy to the North or with anybody else. To underscore his argument, Tate quoted William Butler Yeats's aphorism that "Out of the quarrel with others we make rhetoric; out of the quarrel with ourselves, poetry" (*EFD,* 592).[7]

SLAVERY AND THE SOUTHERN IMAGINATION

The quarrel that the South had with itself, in Tate's view, was joined over slavery. Slavery was a curse like original sin, Tate thought, for which no one person was responsible but which afflicted everyone. Although slavery was not, he maintained, demonstrably the worst form of subjugation and exploitation, certainly it was as solid a foundation as any upon which an aristocracy could base its authority and its rise to power.

"Domestic slavery," as antebellum southerners called it, also entailed a definite social and moral responsibility on the part of the master—a responsibility with which the capitalist could dispense. The slaveholder

---

7. See also *MO,* 146.

felt an obligation to his slaves. He welcomed them into the world. He fed and clothed them. He cared for them when they were too young to work, too ill to work, or too old to work. He bade them farewell when they went to their final reward. They were his people—unless, of course, he sold them and made them someone else's people.

Despite these positive aspects of slavery, Tate concluded that the enslavement of blacks had undoubtedly been the worst ground on which to cultivate a unified culture in the South reminiscent of medieval Europe. The white master was irrevocably separated from the black slave in a way that the white landlord and the white serf never could have been, even after the destruction of feudalism. The peasants belonged to the land, and Tate, like Jefferson, believed that all virtue came from the land.

The slaves in the South, however, did not form a peasantry. Too different from their white masters to allow whites to make common cause with them to create a unified culture, the slaves became a frightening, evil presence who threatened to destroy the virtuous, agrarian way of life that prevailed in the South. The master could not see in his slaves an image of himself tied to the land. The slaves, in fact, imposed a barrier between the masters and the soil and, at the same time, bound the masters to the marketplace through the sale of the products of slave labor and through the slave trade itself. Slavery thus condemned the South to accept and to participate in the commercial market economy that opened the way for the penetration of the bourgeois values, such as individualism and equality, that southerners had long professed to abhor.

In Tate's analysis, antebellum southern thinkers had not "realized their genius in time" and had thus failed to attain a detached and critical perspective on their society. They recognized the sinfulness of their enemies but remained blind to their own. Their defense of slavery was misguided, Tate thought, primarily because the ownership of slaves disrupted the historical continuity between the antebellum South and the organic, patriarchal communities of medieval Europe.

Tate sensibly dismissed as romantic nonsense the idea that the master-slave relation was wholly "organic." Such a relation was not based only on feelings of mutual affection, kindness, and obligation but also on the exercise of despotic power, cruelty, domination, and hatred. Owning slaves excited the most pernicious sentiments in the masters and eroded their sense of private morality and public virtue. Black slaves and white masters were not united by organic relations similar to those that had joined lord to peasant. Blacks, slave or free, could never have been integrated into southern society; their presence drove a wedge between slaveholding and nonslaveholding southern whites.

In the antebellum South, Tate argued, slavery thus precluded the development of genuine social classes of the sort that had existed in medieval England and France, each one distinctively contributing to the common culture. The slave, Tate wrote, "had much the same thinning influence upon the class above him as the anonymous city proletariat has had upon the culture of industrial capitalism." Slavery destroyed all hope that a common, unified, and homogeneous culture could have been established in the South.[8]

More than any other twentieth-century southern thinker, Tate advanced and perpetuated the legend that continuity with medieval Europe was the shaping force of southern history. In so doing, he ignored, or at least obscured, the role of slavery in creating the unified culture of the antebellum South. Had Tate studied more carefully the writings of antebellum southern thinkers—not only the novelists and poets, but the political philosophers, social theorists, political economists, and, especially, the theologians—he would have discovered a more complete and better balanced analysis of the southern connection to the Middle Ages. Instead, he emphasized the failure of the antebellum South as a feudal society, maintaining that under the historical circumstances of the antebellum period, the South could not have become a traditional, agrarian community of the sort that flourished in medieval Europe.

Contrary to Tate's interpretation, southern slaveholders were not trying to become feudal lords or to found a society that resembled medieval Europe. As he seems almost to have surmised, southern slave society, along with societies in the rest of the Atlantic world, owed its existence to the collapse of feudalism and to the rise of capitalism. Slavery in the Western Hemisphere did not originate or develop in the context of an agrarian revival but grew in the context of an expanding capitalist world market.

In Tate's estimation, for example, the Virginia aristocracy conducted the American Revolution not to establish an independent republican society composed of happy farmers, each enjoying the benefits of his own freehold and reaping the fruits of his own labor. Rather, the Virginia

8. See *EFD*, 524–25.

aristocrats who led the revolution sought to increase their influence, wealth, and power at home and abroad. As Tate was quick to point out, their authority rested on the ownership of land and slaves. The planters wished to rid themselves of British interference with slavery and to gain free and equal access to the world market for the products of slave labor.[9]

Even this interpretation places slavery at the heart of the southern world view. By 1830, if not earlier, proslavery theorists recognized that the South was not a traditional, agrarian community with precise European antecedents but a slave society unique in world history. Their effort to connect the South with the Middle Ages, of which Tate made so much, was not a cynical manipulation of history. It was a candid, if deeply flawed and ultimately futile, attempt to invent a tradition that linked the organic community of medieval Europe to the slave society of the antebellum South and to provide southerners with a past upon which to construct the future. The literature of the antebellum South—not only the poetry and fiction but also the essays, speeches, sermons, diaries, and letters that constituted southern literary culture—reveals the extent of southerners' commitment to slavery and the intensity of their struggle to create a past.

Southern thinkers needed some precedent to which they could appeal, for they sensed that southern society had been erected on the unequivocal right of some men to hold property in other men. Hence, their respect for and their defense of tradition was never an end in itself. Like Tate, they did not intend to revive the sensibilities of an earlier epoch. The battle, as antebellum southern thinkers understood it, was to be waged not between an established traditionalism and an insurgent modernism but between two antithetical visions of modernity: bourgeois and slave. To put the matter succinctly, they saw in the social order of the slave South the best, if not the only, means of preserving a Christian society in the modern world. Tate had more in common with them than he recognized.[10]

9. See *ibid.,* 524–27.

10. For a comparison of the Southern Agrarians with several antebellum thinkers, see Richard Gray, *Writing the South: Ideas of an American Region* (New York, 1986), 146–58. For a comparison of Tate's and Lytle's ideas about politics and race with those of John C. Calhoun, see Anne Ward Amacher, "Myths and Consequences: Calhoun and Some Nashville Agrarians," *South Atlantic Quarterly,* LIX (Spring, 1960), 251–64.

By affirming the continuity with the European past, antebellum southern thinkers hoped to remedy the horrifying and destructive tendencies of modern life. They stressed the organic and paternalistic side of southern social relations, in contrast to the chaotic and exploitative social relations of bourgeois society, as an antidote to the ills of the modern world. In concentrating on these aspects of the master-slave relation and in de-emphasizing the commercial aspects of slavery, they tendered a vision of a society apparently spared the worst abominations of modernity: poverty, crime, violence, immorality, and alienation.

Southern thinkers did not see themselves, or the slaveholding class that they represented, as failed feudal lords. Rather, they saw themselves as modern men who successfully introduced a progressive, moral, and coherent alternative to the bourgeois social order. Their vision was unmistakably utopian, all protests to the contrary notwithstanding. They believed, as Henry Timrod celebrated in his poem "Ethnogenesis," which sang the glories of the Confederacy, that southern slave society would save the world.

Timrod wrote "Ethnogenesis" during the meeting of the first Confederate Congress, or Montgomery Convention, which took place in Montgomery, Alabama, in February of 1861. In the poem, he not only anticipated southern victory in the coming war but contemplated a unique role for the South in history. The powerful forces of nature and the guiding hand of God would serve the southern cause, enabling southerners to rout their enemies and to establish an enduring civilization that would forever end the torment and distress of the human condition. For Timrod, the South was the New Zion. At the conclusion of "Ethnogenesis," he imagined a vast southern empire from which war, crime, and poverty had been eliminated. This new southern social order would at last bring earthly life to perfection:

> Not only for the glories which the years
> Shall bring us; not for the lands from sea to sea,
> And wealth, and power, and peace, though these shall be;
> But for the distant peoples we shall bless,
> And the hushed murmurs of a world's distress:
> For, to give labor to the poor,
>   The whole sad planet o'er,
> And save from want and crime the humblest door,

Is one among the many ends for which
God makes us great and rich![11]

Although he shared more with his southern ancestors than he realized, Tate never took this view of slavery and, in the end, questioned the redemptive possibilities of southern history. To his mind, slavery was not the essence of the southern social order. Rather, slavery prevented the South from becoming the kind of society it should have been. The southern planters held their land and their slaves in absolute, or, as Tate said, in "unfeudal," ownership. They bore no obligation to their land; they could, and did, wear it out. They granted their slaves only an economic status. Slaves were property that could be bought and sold. They were considered at best inferior human beings. They were denied not only political and social but meaningful moral and spiritual lives.

Consequently, for Tate, the evils of slavery were twofold. Not only did enslavement enable one human being to use another in ways that God had never intended; it also permitted white men to abuse nature itself to enhance their own power and glory. By holding slaves, Tate suggested, southerners were guilty of manipulating and exploiting nature to as great an extent as their New England, or their modern, counterparts. They had, as he wrote, been "too strict with nature" and, as a result, had violated their own best principles by attempting to conquer, possess, exploit, and master not only nature but human nature as well.[12]

To compound their sin, the masters and their spokesmen formulated an ideology (by Tate's definition, a partial view of reality) that declared they acted in accordance with the will of God. They looked forward to the millennium, positing the timeless perfection of their social order as a divinely ordained, redemptive community intended not to fulfill history but to transcend it.[13]

Tate's vision of southern history, on the contrary, is close to being apocalyptic. He tried to cultivate an image of the South as a timeless agrarian community that displaced the modern world of cities and fac-

11. *The Poems of Henry Timrod*, ed. Paul Hamilton Hayne (New York, 1873), 100–104. Interested readers should compare Timrod's "Ode Sung on the Occasion of Decorating the Graves of the Confederate Dead, at Magnolia Cemetery, at Charleston, South Carolina" (1866).

12. See Allen Tate, "Sonnets of the Blood," in *The Collected Poems of Allen Tate, 1919–1976* (Baton Rouge, 1989), 50.

13. See *EFD*, 524–27, and *MO*, 150–52. See also Simpson, *The Man of Letters in New England and the South*, 201–28.

tories, of ceaseless change and fractured sensibilities. He had used the antebellum South as a symbolic alternative to modernity, a new, and better, way of ordering life in the modern world. To Tate, the antebellum South, despite its numerous imperfections, represented the best aspects, the last hope, of Western civilization. He imagined the South as a free and virtuous community, enjoying a peaceful, prosperous, and permanent existence. Slavery subverted that vision.

THE REAL LOST CAUSE

In the end, Tate abandoned the vision of the South as redemptive community and accommodated to the vision of the South as historical community, partially and incompletely realizing many of the values that he espoused but still subject to time and change, evil and decay. The characterization of the South as redemptive community, he conceded, mistook the temporal and the historical for the divine and the eternal. Antebellum southern writers, exemplified by Timrod, were guilty of this misconception in holding up their society as the apotheosis of human life on earth.

But if they were to be condemned, so, too, were Tate and his fellow Agrarians. Tate came to believe that the Agrarians had also failed to distinguish between sacred and profane history. They had instead conflated the two in an effort to discover a religious faith in the secular history of the South. They, too, were idolaters. In a letter to Donald Davidson, Tate reflected on their heresy: "We were trying to find a religion in the secular, historical experience as such, particularly in the Old South. I would now go further . . . and say we were idolaters. But it is better to be an idolater than to worship nothing, and as far as our old religion went I still believe it" (*LC,* 370). As a twentieth-century southern man of letters engaged in his own fierce and dramatic struggle with modernity, Tate still needed to believe his old Agrarian religion, as far as it went. Eventually, though, he reconciled himself to the loss of traditional society, both southern and European. His conversion to Roman Catholicism enabled him to see more clearly the sinful tendency to "spiritualize the secular," to exalt beyond their proper station men and the things that men's minds and hands had made.

Tate did not turn away from the South. He continued to value its rich but troubled past. Yet his conversion subtly but decisively transformed his understanding of southern history. No longer could he accept the

South as a redemptive community embarked on a divinely ordained mission to save mankind. No longer could he envision the epic struggle between good and evil in the concrete terms of the traditional, religious, organic, agrarian South versus the modern, secular, dehumanized, industrial North. Instead, the image of the South as redemptive community gave way to the image of the South as fallen world, which singularly embodied and reflected the sinfulness of the human condition—a world from which redemption nonetheless remained possible.

Tate continued to argue that the historical meaning of the sectional conflict was the effort of "Christianity and Civilization" to withstand the chaos of modernity. Although southern statesmen after John C. Calhoun failed to realize it, they were making a last stand. The antebellum South and the Confederacy represented the final, forlorn hope of a conservative Christian civilization based on agriculture and hierarchy. Europe had already succumbed to the destructive forces of modernity—the forces of individualism, rationalism, science, industrialism, egalitarianism, and capitalism–and by 1850, the South, a "profoundly antiscientific society," was more European than Europe. The principal philosophical issue that underlay the sectional crisis was relatively simple for Tate to define, if virtually impossible to resolve: "Class rule and religion versus democracy and science."[14]

As advocates of "Christianity and Civilization," antebellum southerners saw themselves as superior to northerners, and, Tate thought, in many ways they were, though at first glance they may not have seemed to be. The slaveholders, especially in the Deep South, set out to get rich quickly. Everyone was on the make. So long sentimentalized as the last vestige of chivalry and romance, the Deep South, Tate pointed out, was a society of nouveaux riches. Like nouveaux riches everywhere, however, they gladly shed the trappings of the frontier and assumed the customs, manners, and values of the established aristocracies of tidewater Virginia and South Carolina. The men and women who removed to the Deep South transformed the wildernesses of Georgia, Alabama, Mississippi, Louisiana, and beyond into a stable, hierarchical society that emulated as much as possible the tidewater society characterizing the Upper South.[15]

14. See *JD*, 86–87.

15. See *ibid.*, 32–35. For a more precise formulation of the argument that Tate seems to have been making, see Eugene D. Genovese, *The World the Slaveholders Made: Two Essays in Interpretation* (New York, 1971), 137–50. Also helpful is W. E. B. Du Bois, *Black Reconstruction in America, 1860–1880* (Cleveland, 1935), 32–54, esp. 42–46.

Although only a minority of southerners owned slaves, and most of those who did worked in the fields beside them, slavery was the foundation of the social order of the cotton South.[16] Despite thinking slavery an evil, Tate, like his antebellum forebears, believed that slavery was more humane than the modern system of free labor. Capitalism enabled employers to exploit workers as long as it was profitable to do so and then to dispose of them in the most ruthless fashion imaginable when it was not. Slavery, whatever its deficiencies, bound masters and slaves together in relations of mutual obligation and even affection that exceeded all considerations of economic interest. The advantages for the slaves that arose from this arrangement included the right to demand a certain measure of generous and responsible treatment from their masters. Capitalists, by comparison, obeyed no law save that of the market. They were otherwise subject only to their own whims, desires, and needs of the moment. As a result, wage-laborers were burdened with freedom, which frequently meant the freedom to starve.[17]

In the three or four decades before the Civil War, Tate insisted, southerners steadily retreated from the liberal, democratic ideals of the North and embraced a hierarchical and aristocratic social, political, and economic order. By 1850, southerners had all but abandoned their always tentative and superficial allegiance to democracy. Tate explained: "The new system to which the . . . Southerners owed their prestige and power speedily brought with it a new social attitude, a new philosophy, and a spade was called a spade. Democracy, except in stump speeches, went by the board" (*JD*, 44).

Southerners, in fact, had never really believed in democracy at all. Except for Jefferson's heretical and ludicrous declaration that all men were created equal, southerners consistently disclaimed the doctrines of the rights and equality of man. The final repudiation of this doctrine, Tate concluded, came in 1831 during the Virginia Debates on slavery, when Professor Thomas Roderick Dew, drawing from history, Aristotle, and Scripture, first articulated the "philosophy of inequality," which clarified the meaning and implications of the southern social order.

There is no evidence to suggest that Tate read more of Dew's work than *The Review of the Debate in the Virginia Legislature of 1831–2,* and he

16. See *JD*, 40.
17. See *ibid.*, 35–43.

does not seem always to have read that essay very carefully.[18] His account of Dew's thought in his biography of Jefferson Davis is frequently little more than a caricature. He insists, for example, that Dew maintained slavery was and would forever remain more economically viable than free labor. Even without reference to another word Dew wrote, a careful reading of the *Review of the Debate* suggests otherwise. Dew argued that the productivity and profitability of slavery depended on circumstances, and the circumstances that prevailed in the South at the time favored slavery. He doubted that those circumstances would last forever. Free labor would eventually become cheaper than slave labor and thus extinguish it.

Despite his misunderstanding of Dew's political economy, Tate did recognize that Dew, in defending slavery on historical, philosophical, and religious grounds, made the argument that a stable social order was impossible without relegating some men and women to a permanently inferior status. Civilization was inevitably based on hierarchy and inequality, not on democracy and equality. Recognizing this fact and stating it plainly were Dew's worthy contributions to southern political philosophy and social thought.[19]

Visions of the most advanced and beneficent social order the world had ever known soon persuaded southerners of the moral rectitude of slavery, if they needed any persuasion. In this world, already approaching perfection, every white man would be free, and every person, white and black, male and female, would be content, for they would know their place in the social order and would enjoy a prosperous and comfortable way of life. Poverty, crime, and misery would virtually disappear.[20]

The southern ruling class had already come to associate its power with the sense of social responsibility that its members inherited from their ancestors. This identification of power with responsibility, Tate thought, was the best foundation upon which to erect a stable social order. Antebellum southerners, in his view, discharged their obligations through a "definite physical legacy," land and slaves, that inhibited their desires to

---

18. See Allen Tate to Donald Davidson, July 21, 24, 1930, both in Davidson Papers.
19. See *JD*, 44. See also Thomas Roderick Dew, "Abolition of Negro Slavery," in *The Ideology of Slavery: Proslavery Thought in the Antebellum South, 1830–1860*, ed. Drew Gilpin Faust (Baton Rouge, 1981), 23–77.
20. See *JD*, 44–48.

accumulate inordinate wealth and wield despotic power. Northerners, on the contrary, created a social system that contained no built-in check to their appetites. Consequently, they grew ever more avaricious and insatiable in their attempts to satisfy the acquisitive instinct, often at the expense of the South.

Tate implied, but lacked the sophistication in political economy to specify precisely, a distinction between capital accumulation and economic acquisitiveness. The latter has existed always and everywhere in different degrees and is associated with "use value," *i.e.,* the accumulation of goods to be enjoyed and displayed. The former is historically specific to capitalism and emerged with the development of the "profit motive." The capitalist makes money to invest his profits to make more money in an endless progression. Tate's failure to comprehend the subtleties of political economy notwithstanding, he presented a cogent argument that southern slaveholders withdrew from the Union not primarily to stoke their economic ambitions but to perpetuate an ordered and stable way of life that they feared the North would destroy.

By 1860, Tate contended, the South had become a distinct civilization. To southerners, on the one hand, the war was merely a way to formalize and ratify politically a deep cultural division between North and South that already existed. Northerners, on the other hand, justified the war to preserve the Union by adhering to the fiction that the separate states constituted a single nation. The conflict was irreconcilable. Tate concluded that "when historians are far enough from the event, they will speak of the years 1861–1865 as the period of the dual Presidency," and he pondered their conclusions: "Their vision cleared, they will see the Lower South in its unique quality, and wonder what, if it had been left alone, it might have become" (*JD,* 48).

The War for Southern Independence was thus of remote origin, and Tate thought its causes incomprehensible apart from understanding the history of Europe since at least the fifteenth century. The South represented for Tate the last bulwark of traditional European civilization, a conservative restraint on the restless expansiveness of the North. The war was the final and decisive battle of the "Western spirit" against the "European spirit," or the fitful spirit of aggression and conquest against the peaceful spirit of stability and order. The meaning of European history since the fifteenth century was, for him, dramatically concentrated in the war between the North and the South.

With the defeat of the Confederacy, the only society capable of resisting modernity collapsed. Rationalism triumphed over tradition, secularism over religion, individualism over community, science over sentiment, barbarism over civilization. Indeed, Robert E. Lee's handing his sword to Ulysses S. Grant on April 9, 1865, at Appomattox Court House marked for Tate the end of all that was noble and heroic in the civilization of the West.

THE REDEMPTION OF HISTORY

Tate did not rejoice in southern defeat. That, he thought, was the privilege of fools. In the tragic history of the South he glimpsed the universal plight of humanity. Southerners possessed some special virtues—virtues such as a code of honor, courtly manners, a love of the land, a respect for tradition, piety, and a sense of the innate mystery of life—that set them apart from other men. But southerners had relied on political means to achieve essentially spiritual ends. Using politics to save their world, they did more violence to themselves and all that they loved than they did to their enemies and all that they despised.

Southerners' millennial aspirations paradoxically mired them firmly and absolutely in the material, temporal, and historical world. Only in defeat, Tate declared, could southerners subject their world view to the corrections of the transcendent. If there was some truth that men could derive from southern history, it was to stop deceiving themselves about human nature and the earthly dispensation under which they were privileged and doomed to live. Hardship, suffering, and torment, evil, cruelty, and injustice would not disappear, no matter what humanitarian reforms men pursued or what social and political mechanisms they set in motion. Everyone called to act in the world was destined to err, to sin, and to fail. Blinded and emboldened by the false sense of their own knowledge and power, men repeatedly embarked on the same messianic pursuits, only to falter again and again. Good intentions and noble aspirations were not enough and never had been.

Political reforms designed to improve material welfare and encourage social justice were especially nonsensical in an age when belief in the transcendent no longer prevailed. To devise schemes for the improvement and perfection of humanity and to impose them with procrustean efficiency, even as the historic civilization of the West disintegrated before men's eyes, was to cast humanity adrift in an absurd and faithless world.

In such a world, men lost a sense of moral certainty; they could not tell the difference between right and wrong. They no longer posed the moral question "Is this right?" but asked the pragmatic question "Will this work?" Severed from the past and bereft of the wisdom derived from experience, they assumed the present moment was unique and their present problems unprecedented. They lived by chance, approaching each day as if there had been no yesterday and as if there would be no tomorrow.

The crisis of Western civilization, as Tate understood it, amounted to a war against the institutions (family, church, and society) and beliefs (the omnipotence and omniscience of God and the servitude, imperfection, and mortality of man) that had anchored and sustained the unified culture of Christendom for at least six hundred years. The battle now raged between the "dehumanized society of secularism" and the "eternal society of the communion of the human spirit" (*EFD*, 4–5; *CE*, 381). That "eternal society," Tate feared, had all but vanished. Christian civilization no longer existed in any meaningful sense. For Christians in the modern world, the blessings of faith were privately available but had no power to reestablish an authoritative and transcendent order of existence.[21]

As belief in Christian revelation waned, a belief in history took its place. History was better than nothing; at least men could appeal to the example of their dead ancestors in times of crisis. But history was a poor substitute for faith. In the modern world, history itself had been superseded by science and technology, which had come to exercise a tyranny over the mind of modern man that was intolerable. Men needed more than a mechanized concept of nature, more than a servile routine of meaningless activity, more than a multiplicity of means without ends in which to put their faith. If men could no longer participate in society with the full substance of their humanity, if they could no longer think, feel, or act like men but only play their wearisome roles in a plotless drama, then they would rebel, or die. Sinister, frightening, and monstrous, they would bring civilization to the brink of the abyss and, with little provocation, push it over the edge. In the Phi Beta Kappa address that he delivered at the University of Minnesota on May 1, 1952, later published as "The Man of Letters in the Modern World," Tate voiced his apprehension:

21. See Tate, *Collected Essays*, 282–93, and *FD*, 1–17. See also *EFD*, 535–46.

I take it that we have sufficient evidence, generation after generation, that man will never be completely and permanently enslaved. He will rebel, as he is rebelling now, in a shocking variety of "existential" disorders, all over the world. If his *human* nature as such cannot participate in the action of society, he will not capitulate to it, if that action is inhuman: he will turn in upon himself. . . . Man may destroy himself but he will not at last tolerate anything less than his full human condition. (*FD*, 7)

It was the special responsibility of the man of letters in the twentieth century to recreate for the age an authentic and coherent image of man by sustaining the integrity, purity, and vitality of language. The man of letters had to reveal as much as he knew about the circumstances of modern life, however melancholy or dreadful they might be. He had to record the spiritual condition of man, which was inevitably his own, in order to enhance man's knowledge of himself in relation to other men, to nature, and to God. Indeed, Tate argued, the purpose of all literature was nothing less than the attainment of this kind of self-knowledge.

The disciplined use of language, Tate thought, formed the basis of any moral and social order worthy of the name. The man of letters had to be not only a poet but also a critic. For criticism was not merely a way of arguing that one piece of writing was superior to another. Criticism was meaningful, Tate reasoned, only insofar as it instructed the ignorant portion of mankind, among whom Tate always included himself, in the exercise of taste, the pursuit of standards, the application of judgment and discrimination, and the acquisition of self-knowledge. If literature failed to advance self-knowledge, which Tate defined as insight into man's relation to a social and spiritual order—and, indeed, the ability to make that order intelligible at all—then taste, judgment, and discrimination were meaningless words.

Literary men, perhaps since the fifteenth and unmistakably since the seventeenth century, had steadily diminished and finally abdicated their moral obligations by isolating themselves from the world. Their disdainful withdrawal from society hardly created a sensation any longer (in fact, few persons noticed), for it was the manner in which writers were expected to behave. Modern men of letters might comprehend the horror of life, but they could not do anything about it, for they were convinced that society was beyond redemption. In the minds of modern writers and their followers, literature had replaced religion. The mind and imagination of the man of letters became the repository of ultimate reality. The work of literature, far from describing, probing, and explaining the human condition, became an end in itself. The secular word replaced the sacred word, aesthetics replaced faith, the man of letters replaced God, thus establishing the superiority of human construct to divine creation.

Tate lamented that the Agrarians themselves had participated in this tendency by divinizing the South. The literary imagination became for them not only the medium through which the "truth" of southern history was to be revealed but also the means through which the spiritual destiny of the South was to be fulfilled. Like other modern poets, the Agrarians displayed the same arrogance as the scientists and social scientists, believing that they occupied a special place in history and that they possessed sufficient knowledge and power to change the very constitution of Being.

The modern poet exhorted the crowd. He desired to influence and stimulate his readers or listeners, who would, in the next moment, be influenced and stimulated by a news commentator, a political orator, or a stand-up comic. The poet may have "transmitted" something to his audience. He may have communicated with them. As Tate made clear, however, poet and audience shared nothing. The exchange may have been intense and exciting, but from it emerged no enlightened understanding of the human condition.

Tate believed that the self-indulgence of the modern men of letters would catch up with society and that chaos would result. Unless men of letters concentrated on illuminating man's relation to the unchanging source of Being, there was no possibility of reversing the cultural and spiritual fragmentation of Western civilization, which would eventually collapse. Without the disciplined use of language, men would forever remain slaves, manipulated and controlled by the debased language of mass communication. Author and reader had to experience a sense of spiritual communion in which the communicants were necessary to one another. Otherwise, they had no transcendent standard by which to judge human experience.

According to Tate, literature could not properly communicate any truth to men. Literature could not serve as a guide to better living, a primer of good manners, or a source of wisdom when faced with a moral predicament. Nor could it function as a substitute for religion, filling the spiritual void that ensued with the loss of faith. In Tate's view, literature was participation in the communion of common experience. All true works of literature, as opposed to pieces of propaganda written to support or refute some point of view, represented the recurrent discovery of the common human experience in history and the human communion with the transcendent. Tate wrote: "Our unexamined theory of literature as communication could not have appeared in an age in which communion was still possible for any appreciable majority of persons. The word communication presupposes the victory of the secularized society of means without ends. The poet, on the one hand, shouts to the public, on the other (some distance away), not the rediscovery of the common experience, but a certain pitch of sound to which the well-conditioned adrenals of humanity obligingly respond" (*FD,* 12).

Men of letters had to renew their dedication to creating a unified civilization in the West. Their true province was not the dissemination of novel distractions but the preservation of culture itself, of the manners, customs, values, and traditions by which a people lived. More important, men of letters performed the critical service of showing how civilization, which embodied men's temporal lives, was related to their "supratemporal" destiny, how history was, in fact, the means through which men came to understand their "supratemporal" destiny.

Men were inescapably creatures of history and community, Tate assumed, able to become fully human only in association with other human beings. Not only did they need to communicate with each other, though; they also had to experience communion through love. Communication that was not also communion was incomplete. It was therefore the duty of the men of letters to supervise the culture of language, to which the rest of culture was subordinate, in order to ensure that language was forwarding the ends proper to social and historical man: "Communion in time through love, which is beyond time" (*FD,* 17). The writer had to remind men that brotherhood developed not merely from the common experience of the human condition but also from the common experience of God's grace through Christ's love and sacrifice.

Throughout his long and distinguished career as a man of letters, Tate stressed the need to reunify Christendom. A society that had once been religious, he asserted, could not become secular without risking spiritual death, preceded by the usual agonies. Men could survive in a fragmented society, but they could not live as human beings. Without respect for the past or a knowledge of the traditions, rituals, and beliefs that once composed man's unified sensibility, life became an abstract series of random impressions: confused, perplexing, and incoherent.

Few twentieth-century men of letters have been more determined than Allen Tate to recover the original unity of Western civilization, to restore its culture, and to revitalize its faith. The significance of Agrarianism, as he always interpreted it, was an attempt not simply to revive the antebellum South but to create a historical situation in which men could reinvigorate their faith and attempt to bring about the spiritual unity of all Christians. Although he grew less hopeful in old age, Tate never relinquished the idea that an important phase of this cultural and spiritual transformation might take place in the South.[22] But, he wrote, "to try to 'revive' the Old South, and to build a wall around it, would be a kind of idolatry; it would prefer the accident to the substance."[23]

The changes that Tate hoped would occur in the spiritual life of modern man could not be exclusively southern; they would have to be greater than the South and have a meaning beyond southern history. In Tate's mind, southern history had not only to be assimilated to European history but to be subordinated to Christian revelation. Yet he never relinquished his commitment to the South. He believed that southern civilization perpetuated many of the virtues that had distinguished the unified order of Christendom.

Following his conversion to Roman Catholicism, Tate suggested that the South still represented the social order best fitted to sustain "humane life." He now saw in the South not a redemptive community poised to redeem men from history but an earthly community that offered an imperfect analogue to the City of God. The historic South at last provided for Tate the image of a Christian community in which men could experience the fullness of the human condition—a community in which the present could be joined to the past, the living to the dead, the fleeting to the everlasting.

22. See William Boozer, Interview with Allen Tate, New York *Times,* April 8, 1979, p. 11.

23. "A Symposium: The Agrarians Today," *Shenandoah,* III (Summer, 1952), 29.

5

DAVIDSON AND THE SOUTHERN TRADITION: THAT RAGE OF BELIEF

> "Ah, Truman Lane, you heard it well as I!—
> That rage of belief, the tears, the misery
> Quickened the flags of men right willing to die,
> Only such men could tell what once could be,
> Hear what we hear, see what we see."
> —Donald Davidson, "Late Answer: A Civil War Seminar"

AMONG THE CONFEDERATE DEAD

Early on Sunday morning, April 9, 1933, Donald Davidson stepped off a bus in Rome, Georgia. He was on his way back to Marshallville, Georgia, where he was spending a year-long sabbatical from Vanderbilt University in lodgings provided by his friend John Donald Wade. Hours earlier he had been a guest at Cornsilk, the Lytle family farm near Guntersville, Alabama, where the Agrarians had gathered to discuss making the *American Review* the official organ of their movement.[1]

The Agrarians had invited Seward Collins, then editor of the *Bookman,* to Cornsilk to exchange ideas, argue policy, and formulate strategy. A few weeks before the meeting, Collins had written to Davidson to solicit his help in founding a new journal in which conservative thinkers could publish their work.[2] He proposed to draw together in the pages of

---

1. See *SWMW,* 61–62. See also Paul K. Conkin, *The Southern Agrarians* (Knoxville, 1988), 106–10.
2. See Seward Collins to Donald Davidson, March 8, 1933, Donald Davidson to Seward Collins, March 18, 1933, Donald Davidson to John Gould Fletcher, April 7, 1933, all in Donald Davidson Papers, Special Collections, Jean and Alexander Heard Library, Vanderbilt University.

the *American Review* the writings of the New Humanists, the French Neo-Thomists, and the English Distributists, as well as those of the Southern Agrarians.

The meeting at Cornsilk was tense but festive, the lively talk continuing far into the night. Despite their enthusiasm for his offer, the Agrarians pressed their own demands and agenda on Collins, whom they mistrusted. Indeed, their association with Collins was turbulent and brief.[3] Yet when the time came for Davidson to board the bus for the long ride back to Marshallville, he was already devising new schemes to replace those that had hitherto ended in frustration and failure.

As he rode across the Alabama countryside, Davidson had no idea that this meeting would prove to be the last time the Agrarians assembled in one place. All the principal members of the group who could be present had been there: Allen Tate, John Crowe Ransom, Robert Penn Warren, Lyle Lanier, John Wade, Frank Owsley, and, of course, Andrew Lytle. In a few years these men would go their separate ways. The diaspora, in fact, had already begun. The Agrarians did not, for example, invite Herman Clarence Nixon to the meeting, though they still regarded him as a valuable member of their group. For his part, Nixon wrote an enthusiastic letter in support of the affiliation with Collins. John Gould Fletcher, who had been invited, was in a hospital in Little Rock, Arkansas, recovering from one of his periodic bouts of depression. The Agrarians excluded Henry Blue Kline and Stark Young from the proceedings. Neither man ever again participated in an Agrarian venture. Nevertheless, to Davidson in April, 1933, the future never looked more promising.[4]

Davidson delighted in the prospect of establishing a reliable outlet in which to continue the Agrarians' critique of modern society and defense of the southern tradition. He was even more enthusiastic about undertaking a new project in the company of friends. To Davidson, it seemed that the Agrarians once more possessed the means and the will to resume

---

3. For a more complete discussion of the Agrarians' intentions, misgivings, and disappointments regarding their association with Collins, see Mark G. Malvasi, "Risen from the Bloody Sod: Recovering the Southern Tradition" (Ph. D. dissertation, University of Rochester, 1991), 15–17 and the sources cited there in nn. 3–6.

4. See Conkin, *The Southern Agrarians*, 107.

the argument begun three years earlier with the publication of *I'll Take My Stand*.

But now he stood alone, waiting for the bus that would carry him on the last leg of his journey from Rome to Marshallville. It would be hours before the bus arrived. Tired of waiting, he decided to walk about the deserted city. He went first to the statue of the daring Confederate hero Nathan Bedford Forrest. Then he paused on the lawn of the municipal building before the bronze figures of a she-wolf suckling the infants Romulus and Remus. At last, Davidson climbed a high hill overlooking the city, from where he could see the junction of the Coosa and the Oostenaula Rivers.

He found himself in a lovely, old cemetery, wandering among the graves of Confederate heroes. His pace slowed. In the growing light of morning as he moved among the dead and read the headstones, Davidson imagined other fields on other mornings. He saw the young men in gray or butternut, poised for extinction, awaiting the command that would send them into battle. He heard their fierce yells and watched them surge forward. The thunder grew in his ears. He saw their bodies writhe and fall. He saw the bloodied faces, the startled, staring eyes, the gaping mouths, the twisted arms and legs. He witnessed the silent agony that fixed the moment forever in time.

Davidson felt irrevocably bound to the men who died fighting for this land. At that moment, he experienced none of the uncertainty or desolation that had overwhelmed another young man who stood at the gates of a Confederate cemetery, Tate's modern protagonist in "Ode to the Confederate Dead." Davidson did not hesitate before "the sagging gate"; he was not "stopped by the wall." Unlike the melancholy young man in Tate's poem who despaired of recovering, comprehending, or even remembering "the immoderate past," Davidson reaffirmed it without reservation. Every southerner who had kept alive "the fierce faith undying / And the love quenchless" recollected that past in his heart, knew it in his blood, possessed it in his bones.

Southerners, Davidson thought, carried their tradition in themselves. They knew from their own experiences, and from those of their ancestors, who they were and from where they came. They did not—indeed, could not—analyze their tradition. They did not need to, for they experienced it in their everyday lives, enjoying a timeless existence that bound the living to the dead and the unborn. What was once would be always, until the end of time.[5]

This common experience and the way of life that it engendered was the southern tradition. On that warm Sunday morning, as he walked among the dead, Davidson came upon a monument honoring his faithful ancestors with an inscription that epitomized his convictions about the South. These words expressed everything that he needed to know, to feel, and to believe:

> This monument is the testimony of the present to the future that these were they who kept the faith as it was given them by their fathers. Be it known by this token that these men were true to the traditions of their lineage. Bold, generous, and free, firm in conviction of the right, ready at their country's call, steadfast in their duty, faithful even in despair, and illustrated in the unflinching heroism of their deaths, the freeborn courage of their lives. How well they served their faith, their people know; a thousand battlefields attest; dungeon and hospital bear witness. To their sons they left but honor and country. Let this stone forever warn those who keep these valleys that only their sires are dead; the principles for which they fought can never die. (*SWMW,* 62)

Unless contemporary southerners deliberately severed the ties to their ancestors and betrayed their heritage, Davidson maintained, they could not but draw on the collective memories, judgments, and values of that community, past and present, that was the South. Twenty years later, in 1953, Davidson echoed these sentiments in a letter to his friend and former student Jesse Stuart: "Whenever a Southerner speaks in the manner native to him . . . he is always speaking not only with his own voice but with the voices of his foreparents. That is one of the big differences between being a Southerner and not being one."[6] For Davidson, the unity and continuity of the southern tradition all but negated the transformations of history, dramatic as those had been. To explore and illuminate the meaning of the southern tradition, he emphasized the permanent over the ephemeral, the eternal over the transient, the traditional over the historic.

5. See *SWMW,* 61–62; Allen Tate, *The Collected Poems of Allen Tate, 1919–1976* (Baton Rouge, 1989), 20–23; Donald Davidson, *Poems, 1922–1961* (Minneapolis, 1966), 43–46; and Thomas Daniel Young and M. Thomas Inge, *Donald Davidson* (New York, 1971), 92–100, 126–49.

6. Donald Davidson to Jesse Stuart, August 10, 1953, in Davidson Papers.

Davidson nevertheless placed the past at the center of southern experience. Like Tate, he sought to discover ways in which the past might function as a rebuke to the present. But Davidson went further: he also looked to the past to establish some essential, irrefutable, and unchanging vision of identity, order, meaning, and being.

Tate stressed the "historical consciousness," whereby modern men could locate an image of themselves in the past and place themselves in time. Davidson, too, declared that the modern crisis resulted from an incomplete knowledge or an outright repudiation of the past. His solution, however, lay not in devising some image or analog of the past in the present but in recreating the past in some tangible form. This quest rendered history irrelevant. Davidson's vision of the South was more pastoral than historical.

The southern past, Davidson suggested, was at least partially exempt from the historical circumstances that had created it and the human hands that had made it. Southern history was not subject to the contingencies of ordinary human history. Instead, in reconstructing the southern past, Davidson replaced the idea of history as a process of change with an image of the past as a lasting source of identity, order, meaning, and being.[7]

Davidson was less deeply engaged by modernity than was Tate. His sympathies lay almost wholly with the past, and despite his emphasis on the unity and continuity of the southern experience, he accepted the historical dislocation of the past from the present, a misfortune that he hoped Agrarianism could remedy. To Davidson, modern civilization had gone badly awry. The modern world could not be reformed or saved. It therefore had to be abandoned in favor of an older way of life in which men could once again sense their spiritual connections with one another, their ancestors, and their descendants. In such a world, they could know the joys and responsibilities of life in a community bounded by custom, ritual, and tradition.

Contrary to Davidson, Tate always carefully identified the plight of modern man as his own. Poems such as "Ode to the Confederate Dead" attest to Tate's involvement in the present.[8] Like his young protagonist,

7. Cf. Richard Gray's interpretation of Tate's use of history in *The Literature of Memory: Modern Writers of the American South* (Baltimore, 1977), 40–105.

8. See Louis D. Rubin, Jr., *The Wary Fugitives: Four Poets and the South* (Baton Rouge, 1978), 98–116; Radcliffe Squires, *Allen Tate: A Literary Biography* (New York, 1971);

Tate recognized the difficulty, perhaps the impossibility, of modern men reestablishing a direct link with the past. Modern southerners, in particular, could barely comprehend, let alone participate in, the world of their fathers. It was lost to them forever. "Our past," Tate once told Davidson, "is all but irrecoverable."[9] Southerners living in the modern world could hope only to posit a coherent image of the past that would enable them to preserve as many of the old ways and values as possible. Thus could they perpetuate something of the "humane life" for which their ancestors had fought and died.

Tate understood history in the context of Christian revelation. History, no matter how much he admired it or longed to believe in it, could never be an end in itself. To attribute any consequence to history, men had to possess some transcendent vision of reality against which to measure earthly life.

Davidson objected to Tate's conclusions, thinking his friend had compromised fundamental Agrarian principles. He deplored Tate's lack of resolve and aspired instead to establish a more incontrovertible basis of identity, order, meaning, and being. Although he shared Tate's horror at the barbarism of the modern world, Davidson did not agree that the reunification of Western Christendom under the aegis of the Roman Catholic Church would be the best way to effect a solution. It would be better, he thought, to revive the "gods of our fathers."

To that end, Davidson set forth the most elaborate, comprehensive, and intractable defense of the southern tradition to be offered by any thinker of his generation. He believed that the South was the last incarnation of that ancient, homogeneous, independent, and moral community of Anglo-Saxon farmers in which Thomas Jefferson had so eloquently placed his hopes for the future of mankind.

The meaning of the southern tradition, Davidson declared, could be apprehended without reference to European history or Christian revelation. America, and in particular the South, was not Europe but an alternative to Europe. Southerners were not the "last Europeans," as Tate

---

David A. Hallman, "Donald Davidson, Allen Tate, and All Those Falling Leaves," *Georgia Review* (1983), 550–59; and Allen Tate, *Collected Essays* (Denver, 1959), 248–62.

9. Donald Davidson, *The Spyglass: Views and Reviews, 1924–1930,* ed. John Tyree Fain (Nashville, 1963), 201.

had asserted. Davidson's objective was not, like Tate's, to revitalize classical-Christian civilization in the West. Instead, Davidson wished to restore the unity and continuity that he assumed had characterized human life long before men sought its meaning in the doctrines and dogma of Christianity. The traditional, agrarian South was not the culmination of the unified Christian society that had flourished in Europe during the Middle Ages. It was a historical manifestation of "the great vital continuum of human experience" that stretched further back in time than history could recall (*SRSY,* xvii).[10]

EUROPE AND AMERICA

Americans had turned their backs on Europe. They repudiated European corruption and decadence. Europeans had journeyed to America to escape the avarice, luxury, materialism, tyranny, and despotism of Europe. Davidson wrote to the novelist, poet, and editor Hervey Allen that he felt "the sense of separateness, of almost final separateness, from European concerns that must have dominated our pioneer ancestors."[11] In the vast, vacant spaces of the New World, unencumbered by the fears and superstitions of a moldering civilization, men could attain the liberty for which they hungered. There, weary Europeans would miraculously transform themselves into new men and unite in the pursuit of a unique and common purpose. They would become Americans, Davidson proclaimed, whose historical destiny it was to give humanity a second chance.

Americans would not live piled upon one another in large cities. Manufactures would not become their principal occupation. Never would they submit to an economic system calculated to subvert their autonomy and self-sufficiency, to keep them poor, weak, and frightened. Americans would remain on the land. Content to enjoy the blessings of the simple, rural life, Americans thus guaranteed their happiness and, at the same time, maintained their virtue. They also retained their independence, steadfastly refusing to become a servile people. Americans, so

10. See also Lewis P. Simpson, "Donald Davidson and the Southern Defense of Poetry," reprinted in *SRSY,* v–xviii, and *The Brazen Face of History: Studies in the Literary Consciousness in America* (Baton Rouge, 1980), 167–80, and Richard Gray, *The Literature of Memory,* 94–103, and *Writing the South: Ideas of an American Region* (New York, 1986), 271–72.

11. Donald Davidson to Hervey Allen, November 6, 1943, in Davidson Papers.

it seemed to Davidson, had fulfilled the ancient dream of creating "a more perfect union."

America, Davidson argued, was not so much a nation as a community, a collection of families living on the land, sharing the same values, commitments, and pieties. This traditional, agrarian community not only had escaped the worst evils of European civilization but had discovered the elusive secret of reconciling the demands of nature with the desire for human progress and thus of living in harmony with God, nature, and each other.[12]

From its inception, Davidson asserted, America had been a "traditional society of the New World type, considered in contrast to the anti-traditional society imposed by the industrial order."[13] If Americans had anything valuable to offer to the rest of the world's peoples, surely it was the creation and preservation of this traditional, agrarian society. For that accomplishment alone, Americans were justly celebrated. They had renewed hope in the future of mankind that had long ago withered in Europe.

America soon faced a crisis of its own, however. Before the Civil War, Americans, North and South, had remained faithful to the ideals and intentions of the first settlers and, later, of the Founding Fathers. The United States were a traditional society whose citizens were devoted to agriculture not only as a way of making a living but as a way of life. Gradually, almost imperceptibly, northerners seceded from the original America and set up a very different kind of society. Such action in itself might have been tolerable, though regrettable, had northerners not attempted to force southerners to go along with northern ambitions. Northerners imagined that their principles, attitudes, and aspirations would apply just as benevolently in Charleston and Savannah as they did in Boston and New York. Southerners, according to Davidson, had a different view, yet they would never have considered launching a south-

12. On the image of America as a New World paradise, see Hugh Honour, *The New Golden Land: European Images of America from the Discoveries to the Present Time* (New York, 1975). On the pastoral in literature, see Raymond Williams, *The Country and the City* (New York, 1973), and Lewis P. Simpson, *The Dispossessed Garden: Pastoral and History in Southern Literature* (Baton Rouge, 1983). For a convenient summary of Davidson's vision of America, see "A Symposium: The Agrarians Today," *Shenandoah,* III (Summer, 1952), 16–22.

13. "A Symposium: The Agrarians Today," 19.

ern crusade against the impending "Northern Holy War" that threatened to annihilate the South and the American Republic itself.[14]

Strife between South and North had existed since Jamestown and Plymouth were established on the shores of Virginia and Massachusetts, and it had continued even as the colonists affirmed their independence from Great Britain. Whether as colonial Englishmen or American citizens, though, the men inhabiting the New World had always found some way to compromise, some reason to make common cause and to reconcile their differences. Statesmen thus preserved the political equilibrium and sectional balance that characterized early national life in the United States.

The careers of John Adams and Thomas Jefferson symbolized for Davidson the vigilance with which Americans safeguarded their political freedom and their sectional stability.[15] Although bitter political rivals, both Adams and Jefferson made practical concessions for the good of the nation without sacrificing cherished principles. That Adams, Jefferson, and their contemporaries had been so successful at preserving equilibrium was no mean achievement. The pages of American history recorded the numerous tensions, difficulties, and setbacks that they experienced. Yet they persevered, and the Union endured.

These men acknowledged differing, sometimes opposed, sectional interests, but they fashioned a gentlemen's agreement to honor the differences and worked to foster unity within diversity. This arrangement, to which all parties gave free and mutual consent, represented the genius of American politics and demonstrated the efficiency and health of the American experiment. Of these facts, Davidson harbored no doubt.[16]

Northerners then betrayed the trust and mounted a powerful and imperious campaign against American ideals, positing their own sectional interests as the fictive national interest. When the citizens of the North attempted to translate their sectional preferences into national imperatives, the possibilities for compromise and reconciliation between the sections were all but lost.

14. See Donald Davidson, "*I'll Take My Stand*: A History," *American Review*, V (1935), 306–307, and *SRSY*, 174.

15. See *SRSY*, 207–209.

16. See Donald Davidson, *AL*, 266–69, "The Agrarian South: An Interpretation" (MS, 1936), 15–21, and "No Ammer" (MS, *ca.* 1939), 10–13, both in Davidson Papers.

The "Northern" or "New England heresy," as Davidson variously described it, portended the destruction of American liberty by perversely transforming republican ideals into the pragmatic, utilitarian philosophy of the market that had ruined Europe. He noted that Jefferson feared precisely the advent and dissemination of the ideology of the market in the United States. Jefferson had witnessed the dreadful collapse of French civilization first hand: the propertyless, starving masses; the angry, unruly mobs roaming city streets and the countryside; the tyrannical policies of a government undertaken in a vain attempt to keep order but concealing no illusions about the preservation of liberty. He knew of the appalling misery, the terrible suffering, the awful violence to which Frenchmen and other Europeans had been subjected by chance and circumstance. Having seen it with his own eyes, he had resolved to prevent similar conditions from prevailing in the United States.

Davidson argued that Jefferson understood clearly the differences between Europe and America and thoroughly grasped the requirements for ensuring the freedom of—and freedom within—the United States. Jefferson had not supported the revolution against Great Britain simply in the interest of establishing an independent, national government. He had, Davidson affirmed, loftier purposes: to nurture the development of a peaceful, agrarian republic in the United States. Southerners alone had faithfully adhered to Jefferson's original vision. Northerners, who had willfully abandoned Jefferson's piety for the land and rejected his counsel about the danger of manufactures, perverted his dream into an obscene nightmare.[17]

At the same time, Davidson held, Jefferson was not a doctrinaire agrarian. He never desired to exclude manufactures from the United States, and as a dedicated philosophe, he even welcomed technological innovations that promised to improve the condition of the human race. But he recognized how easily men could lose their liberty to the machine, how rapidly they could become enslaved to money and commerce, and how utterly they could forfeit their property and, hence, their virtue and citizenship. Davidson believed that Jefferson had foreseen the results of the industrial revolution and wished to avoid the crisis that had already befallen Europe and now imperiled the modern world.

17. See Davidson, "The Agrarian South," 15–21; Davidson, "No Ammer," 12–13; and Davidson, *The Spyglass,* ed. Fain, 230–32, 237–38.

Davidson's analysis of Jefferson begged numerous questions, especially questions of political economy. Davidson did not address the tension between Jefferson's vision of a virtuous, independent, agrarian republic and the economic and political policies that he and his successors adopted to ensure the Republic's survival. Jefferson's commitment to a simple, peaceful, predominantly agrarian social order ironically required an aggressive and expansive foreign policy that promised to draw the United States into a series of potentially damaging confrontations with other nations. His determination to acquire Louisiana and Florida, for example, arose from his concern for the immediate and long-term security of the United States. Not only did American commercial interests need protection, but there always lurked the danger that the Spanish might cede the territories to more formidable rivals such as France or Great Britain, which they did in the case of Louisiana, leaving a powerful foreign enemy entrenched on native soil.

Although Jefferson frequently exalted America's self-sufficiency, independence, and isolation from Europe—sentiments that Davidson apparently took at face value—the United States depended almost wholly on European markets. It required both a free international commercial order and the absence of any foreign competition on the North American continent. Americans could endure no restriction on access to those markets any more than they could tolerate foreign interference with the development of domestic markets. If the United States was forced permanently to become a world unto itself, either its agricultural surplus would greatly diminish for want of markets or a vast domestic market would have to be created to absorb the huge agricultural surplus. Jefferson found neither prospect inviting for political, social, economic, and moral reasons. The first option raised the problem of sustaining an active, industrious, and virtuous republican citizenry in an economically poor, backward, and isolated country. The second implied the need for large cities and large-scale manufacturing to provide home markets for surplus agricultural produce and employment for the propertyless and idle members of a populous and otherwise affluent society.

The tensions and contradictions in Jefferson's vision came into sharper focus during and after the War of 1812, when James Madison reoriented republican political economy toward the development of domestic manufacturing and the creation of an extensive home market. Implicitly acknowledging the logic of Alexander Hamilton's recommendations and policies of the 1790s, Madison admitted the necessity of integrating large-scale manufacturing and vast commercial enterprise into the original Jeffersonian conception of the healthy republican society.

The security and longevity of the American Republic thus depended less on an undying love of the land, a singular devotion to agriculture, and the establishment of stable, agrarian communities than on territorial and commercial expansion and the growth of domestic manufacturing, in other words, on imperialism, industrialism, and capitalism. Davidson remained largely undisturbed by such urgent questions and sought only the triumphant, uncomplicated revival of the agrarian past.[18]

John Taylor of Caroline, whom Davidson proclaimed "the philosopher and statesman of agrarianism," extended, refined, and applied Jefferson's original insights. Taylor formulated a political economy contrasting boldly with the one prevalent in Europe, which had surfaced in America under the aegis of Alexander Hamilton's radical efforts to promote industry and commerce. In awe of Taylor's contributions to agrarian thought, Davidson wrote: "The pages of Taylor's *Arator* and his *Inquiry into the Principles and Policy of the United States* are so prophetic and so applicable even to detail of present conditions that they might have been written for the campaigns of 1932 and 1936 rather than for the battle against the Federalists. And these pages, rather than the pages of Karl Marx's *Capitalism* [*sic*], would seem to be the proper guide for Americans who wish to interpret their history in the light of American conditions and preferences."[19]

18. I based the preceding discussion of Jeffersonian and Madisonian ideals and policies on the following sources: Drew R. McCoy, *The Elusive Republic: Political Economy in Jeffersonian America* (New York, 1982) and *The Last of the Fathers: James Madison and the Republican Legacy* (New York, 1989); Allen Kaufman, *Capitalism, Slavery, and Republican Values: American Political Economists, 1819–1848* (Austin, Tex., 1982), 3–36; Dumas Malone, *Jefferson the President: First Term, 1801–1805* (Boston, 1970) and *Jefferson the President: Second Term, 1805–1809* (Boston, 1974); Richard Buel, Jr., *Securing the Revolution: Ideology in American Politics, 1789–1815* (Ithaca, N.Y., 1972); Roger H. Brown, *The Republic in Peril: 1812* (New York, 1964); J. C. A. Stagg, *Mr. Madison's War: Politics, Diplomacy, and Warfare in the Early American Republic, 1783–1830* (Princeton, 1983); Marshall Smelser, *The Democratic Republic, 1801–1815* (New York, 1968); and Robert E. Shalhope, "Thomas Jefferson's Republicanism and Antebellum Southern Thought," *Journal of Southern History*, XLII (1976), 529–56, and *The Roots of Democracy: American Thought and Culture, 1760–1800* (Boston, 1990).

19. Davidson, "The Agrarian South," 20.

As with Jefferson, the distinction between American and European conditions formed the core of Taylor's ideas about society, politics, and agriculture. Taylor dismissed John Adams' conclusions that the danger to American liberty arose from the resurgence of a feudal aristocracy. He believed, in Davidson's analysis, that the real danger followed from the concentration of power in the hands of those who controlled money and credit, encouraged incorporation and monopoly, and promoted commerce and industry at the expense of agriculture.

In *Arator,* Taylor cited England as the prime example of a nation that had exploited agriculture and bestowed special privileges on industry and commerce. He warned that the same had happened in the United States when the federal government adopted Hamilton's economic proposals. Taylor predicted the future that would emerge from the imperial domination of industrial and commercial enterprise: the decline of a free, agrarian nation into a despotic state enslaved to money, credit, trade, manufacturing, and government. In the modern world, Taylor's worst fears had come to pass, though Davidson thought that even Taylor could not have foreseen the magnitude of the catastrophe.[20]

Davidson formulated a political economy that recapitulated the major premises of Taylor's argument: national welfare depended on sustaining agricultural prosperity and preserving republican liberty. Heeding Taylor's counsel and espousing the precepts advanced in *Arator* and *Inquiry,* Davidson insisted that the land represented the permanent source of wealth and virtue in any properly constituted society.[21]

At first glance, Davidson's political economy, like Taylor's, paralleled that of the French physiocrats. Despite their mutual emphasis on agriculture, however, Taylor and Davidson differed markedly from them. The physiocrats were statists; the main intent of their policies was to secure abundant and certain revenues for the state. Taylor and Davidson, both vehemently antistatist, feared that the government would extract revenue

20. See *ibid.,* 15–25. See also *AL,* 266–69; *RI,* 157–76; Robert E. Shalhope, *John Taylor of Caroline: Pastoral Republican* (Columbia, S.C., 1980); Duncan MacLeod, "The Political Economy of John Taylor of Caroline," *American Studies* XIV (1980), 387–406; and Paul K. Conkin, *Prophets of Prosperity: America's First Political Economists* (Bloomington, Ind., 1980), 43–76.

21. See John Taylor, *Arator, Being a Series of Agricultural Essays, Practical and Political: In Sixty-Four Numbers,* ed. M. E. Bradford (Indianapolis, 1977), 65–114; 308–24, and Davidson, "The Agrarian South," 19–21.

from the true producers of wealth, those who owned and cultivated the land, and would use it to promote industry and commerce.[22]

Davidson followed Taylor in rejecting, albeit for quite different reasons, the axiom of classical political economy that as fertile land was exhausted and marginal land forced into cultivation, the productivity of agriculture would inevitably decline. But Davidson missed a crucial point in Taylor's argument: the significance of labor in determining the value of land. Taylor thought that labor alone made land valuable. It was through labor that the value of land was maintained and even enhanced. Thus, men, by laboring in the earth, could improve upon the generosity of nature. Land, therefore, was not in theory subject to the law of diminishing returns. In fact, however, Taylor was quite concerned to arrest the declining fertility of the soil and to promote techniques that would increase the capital value of farms and plantations, thereby refuting those who argued for the inevitability of decline. Davidson, more or less, assumed the value of land to be a constant and overlooked the effects of labor so crucial to Taylor's analysis.[23]

For Davidson, the land was a gift that nature freely and generously proffered to mankind; it did not yield diminishing returns. A farmer who faithfully and conscientiously cultivated his freehold could expect indefinitely to reap the material and moral fruits of his labor. Subsistence farming and production for small, local markets would not deplete the soil. Only when farmers, beguiled by the lure of profit, planted cash crops did they imperil the fertility of the land.[24]

22. See George Fort Milton to Donald Davidson, September 9, 1930, in Davidson Papers. See also Elizabeth Fox-Genovese, *The Origins of Physiocracy: Economic Revolution and Social Order in Eighteenth-Century France* (Ithaca, N.Y., 1976); McCoy, *The Elusive Republic*, 41–46; and MacLeod, "The Political Economy of John Taylor of Caroline," 387–406.

23. See MacLeod, "The Political Economy of John Taylor of Caroline," 394–99, and Taylor, *Arator*, 130–312. On the efforts to reform southern agriculture during the antebellum period, see Eugene D. Genovese, *The Political Economy of Slavery: Studies in the Economy and Society of the Slave South* (New York, 1965), 85–153. For helpful summaries of the political economy of the eighteenth and early nineteenth centuries, see Mark Blaug, *Economic Theory in Retrospect* (3rd ed.; New York, 1978), and D. P. O'Brien, *The Classical Political Economists* (New York, 1975). For additional primary sources, see Malvasi, "Risen from the Bloody Sod," 38–39 n. 28.

24. Donald Davidson, "Dying Cities, Living Fields" (MS), in Davidson Papers, and "A Case in Farming," *American Review*, III (1934), 526–30.

THE SOUTHERN STRAND

Nowhere did Davidson explain how reliance on tobacco and cotton, crops grown almost exclusively for sale and export rather than for personal use and local consumption, influenced the development of southern agriculture or shaped the course of southern history. He avoided the issue by de-emphasizing the importance of the plantation, the planter class, and slavery and by concentrating instead on the family farm, the frontier, and the rugged, independent yeomanry. Davidson argued that the frontiersmen and the yeoman farmers did as much as, if not more than, the planters and the slaves to establish the southern way of life.

Davidson wrote that though he and his fellow Agrarians acknowledged the influence of the plantation, they remained "rather critical of the plantation, both because [they] felt its role had been over-emphasized and sentimentalized and because [they] were interested in correcting, for the modern South, the abuses of the plantation system." He explained: "We thought the role of the small farmer, or yeoman farmer, had been very underestimated. . . . Therefore we tended to push the plantation into the background of consideration and to argue the case of the yeoman farmer."[25] In Davidson's view, the distinctive character of southern life from at least the 1670s until the 1860s derived from many and varied sources, chiefly the availability of land, the remoteness of government, and the mobility of population. These ingredients coalesced to create a traditional, agrarian society on the southern frontier. In the South every citizen could reasonably aspire to land ownership. Easy access to fertile but inexpensive land, owned in fee simple, fostered the establishment of homesteads and naturally imparted the advantages of family life.

The distance and relative weakness of the federal government encouraged both independence and community: the determination to rely upon oneself and one's neighbors to build houses, plant crops, and fight Indians. Paradoxically, despite the predominance of family and community, people constantly moved into and out of frontier society, immeasurably complicating the organization of a disciplined labor force. To ease this difficulty, southern farmers turned to slavery.

The adoption of slavery to remedy the chronic shortage of labor satisfied Davidson that slavery was a necessary attribute of frontier life and

---

25. Davidson, "*I'll Take My Stand:* A History," 312.

not only of the "plantation system." Slavery added nothing significant or distinctive to southern life, the constitution of southern society, or the character of the southern people. Its introduction represented merely southerners' pragmatic attempt to solve specific and urgent economic problems.[26]

The plantation itself, Davidson argued, was a frontier institution, no less than the hunter's shack, the Indian fighter's camp, the trader's outpost, or the farmer's cabin. "The plantation . . . was itself held in check," he wrote, "and made to conform by farm and frontier" (SRSY, 208). Historians erred in thinking that the rise of the plantation system represented the mature stage of southern civilization that advanced as the frontier receded. It was a mistake, Davidson cautioned, "to imagine a chronological sequence in which hunter and Indian fighter come first, tree-girdling farmer second, and then, after these rough fore runners [sic], the elegant planter." He warned historians further: "Do not be misled by the elegance of dress or manners or architecture attributed to the plantation, generally held to be in contrast with the crudity of the frontier. That elegance, wherever it flourished, was just as much a part of the frontier as the supposed crudity."[27]

Hunter, trader, Indian fighter, farmer, and planter entered the frontier simultaneously and lived in close proximity to one another. Each did his part to extend the frontier, conquer the wilderness, and fashion southern culture. The planter may have been wealthier than the others and, of course, may have owned anywhere from 20 to 150 slaves, but those were superficial distinctions that did not fundamentally separate him from his more modest, rustic counterparts. However urbane, gracious, and charming he may have been, the planter exercised no more influence upon the configuration of southern society or upon the formulation of the southern world view than did the others. Southern society, composed of plantation, farm, and frontier, was blessed with the considerable benefits that such an admixture entailed.[28]

26. See Donald Davidson, "William Gilmore Simms and the Southern Frontier" (MS), in Davidson Papers, 24–27; Davidson, "No Ammer," 6–11; ITMS, 53; SRSY, 199–211, 223–27; and Donald Davidson to Frank Owsley, August 4, 1951, in Frank L. Owsley Papers, Special Collections, Jean and Alexander Heard Library, Vanderbilt University.

27. Davidson, "William Gilmore Simms and the Southern Frontier," 26–27.

28. See SRSY, 207–209.

By diminishing the historical importance of the planters and accentuating the historical importance of the yeomanry, Davidson hoped to demonstrate that the South was neither a purely aristocratic nor a purely democratic society, neither entirely the society of Thomas Jefferson nor that of Andrew Jackson. There was in the South, he wrote, "a fair balance between aristocratic and democratic elements" that sustained the original American ideals of balance, harmony, and unity within diversity (*ITMS*, 53). The aristocratic strain, proud and august, promised leisure, the cultivation of manners, and the pursuit of knowledge. The democratic strain, spirited and dynamic, insisted upon individuality, autonomy, and independence. Both kindled an ardent devotion to family and inspired a fierce loyalty to community. Together, the aristocratic and democratic elements shaped the southern tradition.[29]

Antebellum southerners, Davidson concluded, enjoyed a corporate life within a unified, agrarian social order that protected individual rights and liberties. In place of class consciousness and class distinctions, southerners substituted family and clan. The Marxian categories of "class," "class consciousness," and "class struggle" simply did not apply to the South.

Davidson did acknowledge that the Populist movement may have been an exception to this rule and represented an attempt to introduce "the class approach" into southern life. Insofar as that was the case, he argued, southerners instinctively rejected Populism. Then, too, Davidson thought, the Populists encountered trouble when they violated the racial orthodoxy of the South and solicited blacks to join their ranks. These two inexcusable errors, from Davidson's point of view, vitiated whatever good the Populists might have accomplished, explained the failure of the movement, and made easier the triumph of the "New South Bourbons," those southern leaders who, while publicly lamenting the downfall of the Confederacy, proceeded to mortgage the South to northern manufacturing and commercial interests.[30]

29. See also Donald Davidson, "The South and Intellectual Progress" (MS), 2–3; and "Poetry and Progress" (MS), 12, both in Davidson Papers.

30. See Davidson, "No Ammer," 10–11, 14–15. Davidson's use of the phrase "New South Bourbons" was somewhat idiosyncratic. Ordinarily the name denotes "a mossback reactionary devoted to things past, to ideas that no longer fitted changed conditions, to the Old South, and to the Confederacy" (George Brown Tindall, *The Persistent Tradition in New South Politics* [Baton Rouge, 1975], 5). For Davidson, the term signified instead the advocates of an industrial New South. On southern Populism, see Lawrence Good-

Nevertheless, Davidson had little use for Marxism. He questioned whether Marxian categories were applicable to the industrialized nations of Europe or to the industrialized states of the Northeast and Midwest. They certainly had no relevance either to the South of the 1850s and 1860s or to the South of the 1920s and 1930s. The prevailing sense of social equality among the people of the antebellum South and the dominant tradition of individual liberty suggested to Davidson that Marxian categories were at best metaphorical or rhetorical. At worst, the application of Marxian principles distorted southern reality.[31]

Davidson's response to Marxist critics was impassioned and succinct. Before the Civil War, he declared, southerners had already achieved what Marxists proclaimed to be the ultimate goal of their crusade: a classless society. Whatever their incidental differences, petty antagonisms, and minor disputes, southerners were bound together as members of a single family, conscious of their mutual interests, shared beliefs, and common values. Southern life, Davidson maintained, was grounded in experience and practice, rather than in a "series of pragmatic adjustments, capable of easy rationalization and also capable of quick change, so characteristic of modern life." (*SRSY,* 193). This "complex of attitudes" united southerners, eradicated the need for class consciousness, and prevented the formation of class distinctions. As a consequence, both aristocracy and democracy flourished in the antebellum South, complementing and reinforcing one another.

Historians who argued that the aristocratic planter somehow dominated the democratic yeoman and persuaded him to accept the ideal of chivalry and the code of honor confused cause with effect. The planter's prestige and leadership issued from, but did not engender, the universal standards of judgment, morality, and conduct that every southerner, from the humblest Georgia cracker to the most refined South Carolina planter, accepted as the basis of civilized life.

Slavery, for Davidson, was emphatically not the unifying agent of southern society, and in no sense did slavery conceal the planters' ex-

---

wyn, *Democratic Promise: The Populist Moment in America* (New York, 1976); Bruce Palmer, *"Man over Money": The Southern Populist Critique of American Capitalism* (Chapel Hill, 1980); Steven Hahn, *The Roots of Southern Populism: Yeoman Farmers and the Transformation of the Georgia Upcountry, 1850–1890* (New York, 1983); and Robert C. McMath, Jr., *American Populism: A Social History, 1877–1898* (New York, 1992).

31. See Davidson, "No Ammer," 11–13.

ploitation of nonslaveholding white men. Yeoman farmers entertained no ambitions to emulate the planter elite. Rather, they gloried in their individuality and independence and were content with their lot, however meager it might appear to modern liberals and socialists. The undying affection they felt for their leaders and the uncompromising trust they placed in them, Davidson asserted, reflected the sense of pride and confidence that the yeoman farmers had in themselves. The yeomanry readily deferred to the planters' natural superiority, for they had tried these men under exacting circumstances and found them splendidly courageous, wise, and generous, neither self-aggrandizing nor indifferent to the common good.

This "natural aristocracy of virtue and talent"—in Davidson's view it was in this sense alone that the planters constituted an aristocracy—had no desire to subvert democratic principles. The very structure of southern society precluded the abuse or subjugation of the common people. The yeoman farmers restricted the power of the planters by reserving to themselves the right to withdraw consent should legitimate authority deteriorate into tyranny. The convergence of aristocracy and democracy in the antebellum South explained the remarkable success that southerners had in attaining social unity and order without sacrificing individuality and liberty. The antebellum South, Davidson exulted, "was as complete a realization as we have any right to expect, of the kind of society that Jefferson visualized—the society in which democracy could flourish and maintain itself without artificial stimulation" (*SRSY,* 207).

The easy interplay between planter and yeoman and the intimate connection between plantation and frontier typified the organic social relations that characterized the antebellum South. These unique social and political arrangements, which preserved unity within diversity and ensured the balance of individual liberty and social order, also had important moral implications. Conscious of the complexity of experience, southerners distrusted abstract theories and grand proclamations. Apprehensive about utopian visions of perfect worlds, southerners, Davidson wrote, never forgot that "there were snakes in Eden" (*SRSY,* 240). They accepted life as they found it, in all its mystery, ambiguity, contingency, and contradiction.

Bound by a kinship of the blood, southerners displayed a fervent pride of ancestry and a fierce sense of personal honor. At the same time, they were remarkably indulgent toward the frailties and the inconsistencies of human nature. Awed by the unpredictable and uncontrollable power of nature, they cherished the land with a love both possessive and fearful. They knew that God would be merciful toward them, forgive them their trespasses, and provide for their needs. In the event of the Lord's displeasure, they could still rely on the old folks at home. Southerners could live life as it came, without giving much thought to the morrow. They would be ready for whatever the morrow might bring as long as they heeded the wise old ways of their fathers and of their fathers' fathers before them. So it had been, and so, they believed, would it always be "unto all generations of the faithful heart."[32]

THE YANKEE CHALLENGE

Left to their own devices, antebellum southerners would have remained forever content to celebrate the virtues with which their ancestors had endowed them. Fate, however, proved unkind. Courteous, serene, and affable in social matters, conservative, independent, and pious in civic matters, southerners had no wish to interfere in the private affairs of their neighbors, to say nothing of the internal affairs of the North. They were satisfied to live and let live. Northerners were not so complacent.

Northerners, especially those from New England, could not imagine a land so perverse and corrupt that the presence of evil neither disturbed the people's composure nor impeded their happiness. Pragmatic, self-righteous, and fanatical, northerners saw clearly their obligation to eradicate evil and to bring the Word, or the wrath, of God to their fallen brethren. To begin reforming southern society, northerners assailed the most conspicuous and peculiar of southern vices: slavery.[33]

Thus did Davidson trace the origins of antislavery sentiment, abolitionist agitation, and civil war. At his most charitable, he depicted northerners as well-intentioned but woefully ignorant zealots embarked on one of their periodic campaigns to improve God's handiwork, an annoying, but relatively harmless, distraction. Less charitably, Davidson saw northerners as neither benevolent nor obtuse but as calculating and subversive. Their actions were motivated by economic and political consid-

---

32. See *SRSY,* 213–27. See also *ITMS,* 28–60, and Davidson, "The Agrarian South," *passim.*
33. See *SRSY,* 131–53, 169–91, 261–84. See also Davidson, "*I'll Take My Stand:* A History," "The Agrarian South," and "The South and Intellectual Progress."

erations, not by any selfless desire to rescue slaves from the lash or to save southerners from their own sinful natures.

Northerners pursued an economic program and a political agenda that they believed southerners somehow jeopardized. They were unconcerned with questions of moral rectitude and social justice. Let the South be damned, if its damnation served northern purposes. Their main intentions, Davidson maintained, were to augment their wealth by promoting industry and commerce and to defend their growing political power by any means necessary.

In their attack on slavery, not only did northern ministers, editors, and politicians seek to win public support for such diabolic measures as the tariff, internal improvements, commercial expansion, and industrial development. They also sought to discredit their southern antagonists as enemies of progress, civilization, and humanity. When vague antislavery sentiments hardened into militant abolitionism, northern leaders took advantage of the situation and fabricated tales of southern wickedness and depravity calculated to shock and appall even the most callous and unregenerate. Hysterical reformers and conniving politicians such as Ralph Waldo Emerson, Harriet Beecher Stowe, Theodore Dwight Weld, Horace Greeley, and that triumvirate of archvillains William Lloyd Garrison, Charles Sumner, and John Brown conspired to spread horrible rumors about slavery and to tell sinister lies about the imperial ambitions of the so-called slavocracy.[34]

This deliberate and heinous plot effectively induced Abraham Lincoln, a moderate opponent of slavery but hardly a foe of the South, to misinterpret southern attitudes and intentions. Lincoln came to believe, despite overwhelming evidence to the contrary, that southerners proposed to transform not only the United States but the entire Western Hemisphere into a vast slave empire. He was convinced that southerners, unable to subdue the North, meant to sever their ties with the Union and to create an independent nation.

Lincoln could not abide a challenge to the sanctity of the Union any more than he could permit southern interests to triumph over national (which Davidson charged were actually northern) interests. But, he concluded, Lincoln was sadly mistaken about southern aims. Southerners

---

34. See Donald Davidson, "The New South and the Conservative Tradition," *National Review*, September 10, 1960, pp. 141–46, and "The Agrarian South," 4.

had no wish to subvert the Union, no imperial ambitions, and no yearning to intervene in northern affairs. They longed only to be left alone to live their lives in peace. If provoked, however, they vowed to fight unto the last man.[35]

The tragedy of the Civil War, in Davidson's opinion, was not as much the outcome, dreadful enough for the South, as the event itself. He conjectured that the war did not have to take place, and probably would not have, had the North not forced the issue. Northerners, not southerners, had rebelled against American ideals and the American way of life. For almost a century, American statesmen had nurtured a delicate balance between the sections based on mutual consent and rational compromise.

By 1860, aroused by lusty dreams of the great fortunes to be amassed through industry and commerce, northerners abandoned that beneficent arrangement and repudiated the constitutional heritage of the United States. To conceal their apostasy, northerners denounced southerners as traitorous peddlers in human flesh who were little better than savages themselves. They lamented that southern obstinacy on the slavery question left them no choice but to force compliance with the laws of nature and nature's God. Lincoln, foreseeing disaster, declared that the nation could not endure half-slave and half-free: it had to become all one thing or all the other. Spoken in good faith and in the naïve hope that northern appetites could be sated and southern honor appeased, these words, in effect, rent the Union in two. Only after Lincoln had uttered them did the conflict between the North and the South become "irrepressible."

Northerners, Davidson felt sure, cared little about freeing the slaves. The Emancipation Proclamation of 1863, which liberated slaves in states still in "rebellion" against the Federal government, was a desperate political maneuver contrived to rekindle waning northern enthusiasm for the war. The North prosecuted a vicious and bloody war not on behalf of the slaves but to gratify despotic politicians who wished to subjugate the South politically and to enrich acquisitive manufacturers, merchants, and financiers who wished to exploit it economically. Since 1865, the victors had obscured their real motives, portraying their cause as the progressive fight not only to liberate the slaves but to wrest control of the nation from reactionary southerners who preferred to destroy the

35. See Davidson, "The New South and the Conservative Tradition," 142.

Union rather than to relinquish their prerogatives and their power. Davidson resolved to tell the other side of the story and at last to reveal the ugly truth of northern aggression concealed beneath the abolitionists' humanitarian rhetoric.[36]

Sophistical, ignorant, and prejudiced, northern partisans—and southern liberals such as Stringfellow Barr, Gerald Johnson, Virginius Dabney, and George Fort Milton, who sympathized with the northern position— depicted the antebellum South as a backward, stagnant region peopled by dull and witless yokels who mindlessly resisted progress.[37] In times of political crisis and social tumult, Davidson argued, his ancestors instinctively appealed to the guiding principles of Jefferson's philosophy. They were more perceptive and discerning than abusive northern partisans or puzzled southern liberals imagined.

Southerners' strict adherence to Jeffersonian ideals convinced them that the "common man" had an integrity that no government had the right to disdain or violate. Ordinary citizens could be better trusted to make considered and wise decisions about their lives than remote governmental officials, who would likely intrude into local or private matters that did not require intervention. Government, southerners presumed, could easily become an instrument of oppression. "There has never been a government anywhere in the world," Davidson wrote to Harvey Broome, "that did not in the end abuse its power."[38] Southerners resoundingly condemned the tendency, so clearly visible in the North, toward the consolidation of power and staunchly resisted all forms of

---

36. See *AL,* 266–70.

37. See Allen Tate, Donald Davidson, and John Crowe Ransom to Stringfellow Barr, September 9, 1930, Donald Davidson to J. J. Finney, November 6, 1930, Donald Davidson to Ferris Greenslet, October 18, 1933, Stringfellow Barr to Donald Davidson, February 15, March 11, 1930, Allen Tate and John Crowe Ransom to Stringfellow Barr, September 20, 1930, Stringfellow Barr to Allen Tate, Donald Davidson, and John Crowe Ransom, September 25, 1930, George Fort Milton to Donald Davidson, June 7, September 9, 1930, February 26, 1931, George Fort Milton to the Editor of the *New Republic,* February 18, 1931, and Herman C. Nixon to Donald Davidson, May 5, 1931, all in Davidson Papers. See also Davidson, "No Ammer," and George Fort Milton, *The Age of Hate: Andrew Jackson and the Radicals* (New York, 1930), *The Eve of Conflict: Stephen Douglas and the Needless War* (Boston, 1934), and *Abraham Lincoln and the Fifth Column* (New York, 1942).

38. Donald Davidson to Harvey Broome, April 25, 1948, in Davidson Papers.

despotism that would enslave them, whether military, political, or economic.

Although Jeffersonian doctrine had long enjoyed special currency among southerners, events required that they alter their outlook to combat the very innovations that Jefferson had feared. The democratic principles that southerners revered had no meaning apart from an agrarian social order. Southerners had little confidence that democracy could prosper or survive in an industrial regime. How could southerners defend agrarianism against the menace of northern industrialism? How could they proclaim themselves the true heirs of the Jeffersonian tradition while northerners castigated them as slaveholders, using the same egalitarian arguments that Jefferson himself had once so effectively leveled against King George III?

Jefferson had clarified the grievances against Great Britain and paved the way for American independence. Davidson, though, like many of his antebellum forebears, came to see egalitarianism itself as the problem. Most antebellum southern social theorists repudiated the Jeffersonian ideal of equality among men and made careful distinctions between liberty and equality. Equality of condition or of opportunity, they alleged, could never be a precondition or a goal of political and civil liberty. To link equality and liberty would, in the end, destroy both. The northern attempt to conflate liberty and equality would result in the "tyranny of the majority," which, in practical terms, meant the oppression of the South, the destruction of southern interests, and the elimination of southern institutions.

To counter the threat of northern domination, southern thinkers, led by John C. Calhoun, urged that the southern states, already bound geographically, establish social, political, and economic ties. Initially, Davidson thought, Calhoun and others had considered the assertion of states' rights sufficient to guarantee the interests of the states against the encroachments of the federal government. State conventions composed of democratically elected delegates could prevent the operation of injurious federal laws within state borders. With the failure of nullification in 1832, however, Calhoun and the South gradually committed, Davidson argued, to the doctrine of state sovereignty.

Prior to the adoption of the Constitution, Davidson insisted (following Calhoun), the several states had been independent and sovereign. By mutual agreement, the states had created the Union and had established the political and legal mechanisms whereby it functioned. Should membership in the Union become onerous or detrimental, an individual state or a group of states had the right to reassert their original independence. When, in the 1850s, shrewd and ruthless northern politicians seized control of the federal government and used its power to restrict southern freedom, thwart southern interests, and endanger southern welfare, Calhoun's successors prepared to exercise the principle of state sovereignty: secession.

Davidson contended that the question of state sovereignty should have remained at the center of the political controversy of the 1850s and 1860s. Unfortunately for the South, northerners effectively concealed their coup d'etat behind a relentless barrage of antislavery rhetoric. Under the strain, southerners allowed slavery, which should have remained at most a minor issue, to become the focus of their defense of agrarian republicanism.[39]

This tactical blunder seriously impaired the southern cause, for it enabled northern provocateurs to set the terms of the debate. Casting themselves as the virtuous champions of liberty, progress, and civilization, they compelled southerners to subordinate all other considerations to the slavery question. Slavery, Davidson reiterated, had no great significance for southern society, remaining a mere vestige of colonial days. In time, he surmised, southerners themselves would have found some orderly and peaceful means of dispensing with slavery had self-righteous northerners not interfered. But northerners demanded that the South do away with slavery immediately, however much emancipation disturbed social and political order.

Southerners, of course, refused. They recognized that Yankees benefited from slave labor while denouncing slavery as an outrageous social, political, and moral evil. Northerners could savor the luxury of a clear conscience; southerners had to be realistic. They knew that blacks could never be absorbed into white society. The presence of a large, unruly, alien population would threaten the traditional social order that they had taken such care to erect. Davidson summarized his view: "As for the

39. See *AL*, 3–38, 115–17, and Davidson, "The Agrarian South," 12–13. On the nullification controversy, see William W. Freehling, *Prelude to Civil War: The Nullification Controversy in South Carolina, 1816–1836* (New York, 1965), and Richard E. Ellis, *The Union at Risk: Jacksonian Democracy and the Nullification Crisis* (New York, 1987).

Negroes, their case seemed insoluble except on a realistic basis. No matter what fine theories there might be about the inalienable rights of man, the Negroes were in the South, their rights had already been alienated, and no Southerner could conceive that black slaves could be changed overnight into high-minded Jeffersonian democrats" (*AL,* 269).[40] Having devoted such attention to slavery, though, southern apologists lent credence to northern allegations. They allowed the abolitionists to transform the formidable southern defense of agrarianism and republicanism into an ill-fated defense of slavery.

The defects of the southern argument notwithstanding, southern thinkers and statesmen abandoned Jefferson's precept of radical egalitarianism. To the misfortune of all, however, their northern counterparts insisted on a rigid application of Jeffersonian egalitarianism within the glorified image of the federal Union. Northerners denied that their defense of the Union and their commitment to equality endangered the interests or the liberties of southerners. The awful war that ensued, Davidson concluded, was not an engagement between the forces of progress and those of reaction but a struggle between two discrete and antithetical varieties of liberalism: the "romantic liberalism" of the North and the "realistic liberalism" of the South.

Davidson's characterization of the South as in any sense liberal may seem curious and surprising, but there was a certain logic to his argument. It flowed from his determination to repel the charge that the South constituted a reactionary slave regime. By contrasting the realistic liberalism of the South with the romantic liberalism of the North, he could reveal the flaws in northern declarations of moral superiority. For all their inspired talk about the rights of man, northerners had made not a moral but a sentimental choice. They could vilify the slaveholders and decry the enslavement of blacks without having to accept the consequences of their demands. As the spirit moved them, they could clamor for the South to free its slaves, for they did not have to live with the consequences of their momentary heart's desire.

Southerners knew better. Realistic rather than sentimental, southerners made a moral choice to care for their slaves as their ability and circumstances permitted. They constructed a social order that included the slaves, providing them with an acknowledged, secure, and comfortable,

40. See also *SRSY,* 209–11.

if inferior, status. It was, therefore, the very essence of liberalism that northerners accept southern differences and permit southerners to develop their own way of life. It was the height of illiberalism, or of romantic liberalism, for northerners, who misunderstood the complexity and particularity of slavery, to flaunt abstract notions of "liberty," "justice," and "equality." To dictate to southerners how they ought to live, how they had to organize their society, and how they should treat their black dependents only added insult to injury. That, Davidson insisted, was precisely what northerners had done.

Northern victory assured the abolition of slavery, reduced the South to an economic colony within the United States, and isolated the South from the community of nations. The triumph of romantic liberalism unleashed exactly those destructive forces against which Calhoun, and before him Jefferson and Taylor, had warned. The war years and the immediate postwar period witnessed the dawning of the machine age, the consolidation of the industrial regime that promised to enslave conquerors and conquered alike. With the advent of industrialism and the decline of agrarian republicanism came the Leviathan state, the huge, centralized government that mercilessly exacted servile obedience from its subjects. Together the machine age and the Leviathan state marked the end of the old republic that northern armies had presumably fought to save.

THE DEGRADATION OF THE SOUTH

Despite the collapse of the southern nation, the bonds among the southern states grew stronger. After the war, the former Confederates were united not only by mutual interests but by the shared feelings of resentment, humiliation, and loss. Southerners had laid down their arms but had not renounced their principles. "In the end," Davidson wrote, "the South remained more determined than ever before in its economic and cultural sectionalism" (*AL*, 269).

Surrender did not take place at Appomattox. General Lee conceded military defeat, nothing more. Even the "tragic era" of Reconstruction did not, in Davidson's mind, signal the finality of southern capitulation to the industrialized North, but Reconstruction did begin the slow erosion of the traditional South.

Davidson minced no words in relating the malevolent intentions of the Radical Republicans. Reconstruction was a conspiracy of mad partisans willing to undertake such Draconian measures as the enfranchisement of former slaves to confirm and secure their political power. Under the leadership of Representative Thaddeus Stevens of Pennsylvania and Senator Charles Sumner of Massachusetts, the Radicals, who included in their company "Beast [Benjamin] Butler," "treacherous [Edwin] Stanton," "disreputable [James M.] Ashley," and "grotesque Ben Wade," maliciously and utterly subverted the Constitution of the United States. Davidson concluded that Reconstruction was a conspiratorial revolution "to which the slightest gilding of mistaken idealism cannot possibly be applied."[41]

However clandestine their transactions, the Radicals' objectives were far from mysterious: seize control of the federal government and use it to their and their political cronies' advantage. The best one could say for them, Davidson thought, was that they were intelligent, persistent, and audacious. While others celebrated or mourned the outcome of the war, the Radicals prepared to win the peace. They refused all gestures of reconciliation (even the few that were forthcoming). The Radicals knew that they had to silence and impoverish white southerners and reduce the South to a political and economic colony of the North. To accomplish this task they instigated a viciously repressive campaign, confiscating southerners' property, abridging their rights, and extolling the vision of "black heels on white necks" as the sine qua non of justice.[42]

Toughened by the rigors of war and the adversity of Reconstruction, white southerners resisted northern efforts to humble and dominate them. They defied and toppled the puppet governments, removing the carpetbaggers from power. They expelled the scalawags, who had betrayed country and clan. For the security and welfare of both races, whites reasserted their authority over the hapless and puzzled blacks, who were unfit to assume the responsibilities that freedom entailed. This struggle, heroic in Davidson's eyes, eventually prompted northern politicians to effect a compromise with their disaffected southern neighbors.

With the Compromise of 1877, northerners showed signs of recovering their common sense. They left old wounds to heal and abandoned the enmity and resentment that they felt toward southerners. During this "gentle, almost heavenly time of peace," Davidson wrote, southerners

41. *The Spyglass*, ed. Fain, 218.
42. *Ibid.*, 222.

"were allowed without much restraint to follow our poverty-stricken, unprogressive, and on the whole happy Southern path" (*SWMW,* 31). The settlement proved too good to last. The expectancy and optimism that augured universal prosperity and progress disguised the stench of new malignancies, masked the triumph of expediency over principle, and concealed the reappearance of the Radical Republicans' selfish creed. Southern leaders, tired of war and poverty, thought that at last they, too, could participate in the "Great Barbecue." They lost touch with the old community of plain folk that they had pledged to serve and made a separate peace with the Yankees. It was not the peace of Robert E. Lee, Thomas J. "Stonewall" Jackson, or Nathan Bedford Forrest but the "Peace of Henry Grady." Davidson characterized this lapse as a "lamentable error." For all its grandeur, Grady's vision of a new and radiant civilization in the South was, it seemed to Davidson, too closely akin to the powers of darkness.[43]

When the "New South Bourbons" transferred their allegiance from agriculture to industry and commerce, they disrupted the continuity of southern history. Their capitulation to northern business and commercial interests was more conclusive and damaging than Lee's surrender at Appomattox. Even as the Bourbons wistfully recalled the lost glory of the Old South, they wondered whether Yankee ways might not, after all, be preferable. Lee, Davidson thought, could not have imagined, and never would have condoned, such speculation. Unlike the leaders of the New South, Lee could distinguish between good and evil. He understood, too, that evil at times prevailed.

Davidson remained unforgiving. He acknowledged that the Bourbons could explain their defection by appealing to the principle of self-preservation. With their land ravaged by war and occupation and with no prospect of quick recovery, they convinced themselves that industrialism furnished the way out. Davidson, in fact, argued that the Bourbons perhaps expected to avenge the Confederacy by wreaking some unspecified financial havoc in the North. Consequently, they welcomed business and industry to the South, hoping to trade political favors for money, power, and prosperity. It was a devil's bargain.[44]

43. See *ibid.,* 223–24; *SWMW,* 33; *AL,* 270–71; and Donald Davidson, "Robert E. Lee: The Soldier" (MS), in Davidson Papers.
44. See *AL,* 272–80, and *SRSY,* 240–42. For a survey of post-Reconstruction southern political and social history, see C. Vann Woodward, *The Origins of the New South,*

More distressing than the imprudence of the politicians was the inexcusable duplicity of the southern liberals, who became enchanted with northern culture and society. Liberals of the immediate postwar generation were primarily educators, like Edwin A. Alderman, or journalists, like Henry Grady and Walter Hines Page. To these men, Davidson opined, the South suddenly appeared cheap, dilapidated, and inferior. Davidson believed that Alderman, Grady, and Page, like Barr, Milton, Dabney, and Johnson in the 1920s and 1930s, conditioned southerners to accept northern definitions of liberty, democracy, justice, and progress.[45]

Confident that industrial prosperity would create the material foundation for a vigorous, democratic civilization in the South, southern liberals since the 1880s had repudiated much of their heritage and embraced science and industry as the salvation of mankind. To Davidson's disappointment, they convinced the young men of the postbellum era to turn their backs on the past and to build the future according to the lax precepts of fashion and expedience. Young southerners who had been reared under the new system of public education remained virtually uninstructed in the southern past. What knowledge they did possess came from northern textbooks or from books that took the northern point of view. Their liberal mentors had taught them that wealth equaled success and that success resulted from the expansion of industry and commerce. They believed in progress and thought it depended wholly upon objective scientific investigation. Politics, therefore, was unimportant.

Southerners' political struggles to maintain their traditions, so the liberal argument went, actually prevented them from enjoying the advantages of modernity. As long as southerners persisted in their aberrant

---

1877–1913 (Rev. ed.; Baton Rouge, 1971); Edward L. Ayers, *The Promise of the New South: Life After Reconstruction* (New York, 1992); William J. Cooper, Jr., *The Conservative Regime: South Carolina, 1877–1890* (Baltimore, 1968); Paul M. Gaston, *The New South Creed: A Study in Southern Mythmaking* (New York, 1970); Tindall, *The Persistent Tradition in New South Politics;* Jonathan M. Wiener, *The Social Origins of the New South: Alabama, 1860–1885* (Baton Rouge, 1978); Dwight B. Billings, Jr., *Planters and the Making of a "New South": Class, Politics, and Development in North Carolina, 1865–1900* (Chapel Hill, 1978); and James Tice Moore, "Redeemers Reconsidered: Change and Continuity in the Democratic South, 1870–1900," *Journal of Southern History,* XLIV (1978), 357–79.

45. See Donald Davidson, "The Trend in Literature," in *Culture in the South,* ed. William Terry Couch (Chapel Hill, 1935), 183–215.

behavior, the South would remain stagnant, idle, and languid. The liberals and their protégés applauded the growth of southern cities, the emergence of a native industrialism, and the gradual accommodation to the machine. They emphasized sophistication over wisdom, experimentation over tradition, and liberation over morality. Stressing the poverty of the old-fashioned southern farmer, they confirmed their contempt for agrarianism.[46]

Southern liberals consciously discredited the old agrarian tradition. They complained that southern life consisted of little more than lynchings, chain gangs, the Ku Klux Klan, hookworm, pellagra, poor whites, and a few aging patricians who did everything in their power to make the blacks miserable. There were too many one-horse farms worked by illiterate tenants, too many Baptist preachers, and too many old colonels. There were too few schools, colleges, paved roads, symphony orchestras, public libraries, skyscrapers, cotton mills, steel factories, and labor unions. If southerners would forget the ways of their fathers and grandfathers and put their faith in science, industry, and public education, liberals vowed to make of the South a New Jerusalem. But, Davidson wondered, at what cost to southerners' autonomy, self-respect, and humanity?[47]

Captivated by ideas of reform, improvement, and progress, the liberals loved the South in a manner philanthropic rather than filial. Careless and foolhardy, they surrendered their identity as southerners and thereby sanctioned the North's spiritual conquest of the South. They substituted for agrarianism a way of life at once vulgar and sterile.[48] The charming, graceful neighborhoods of Charleston and Savannah, Davidson feared, would soon come to resemble the ghastly slums of Cleveland, Detroit, and Chicago. The spacious, picturesque farms that seemed to grow out of the land around Marshallville, Georgia, or Guntersville, Alabama, might soon be surrounded or replaced by the ugly factories of Pittsburgh, Pennsylvania, or Youngstown, Ohio.

As the stewards of the modern scientific-industrial order, liberals counseled that the factory was the emblem of the future, the farm a relic of the past. Young men should flee the country and the farm for the city and the factory, where they could earn more money than they had ever

46. See *AL,* 72–75, 280.
47. See *SRSY,* 254–57.
48. See *AL,* 274–79.

seen. Liberals seemed unconcerned that, along the way, these young men would trade their independence for the conformity of the labor union and the strictures of the shop floor. Progress, too, had its price, but, the liberals reassured everyone, things would turn out all right in the end.

For Davidson, industrialism caused more problems than it solved and perpetuated more suffering than it alleviated. In the South especially, industrialism rendered endemic social diseases that might otherwise have been quite temporary.[49] The industrial revolution was the sinister instrument of northern imperialism. The diffusion of industrialism reduced the South to colonial dependency and imposed an unvarying uniformity in place of the traditional diversity of southern life. Liberals, northern and southern, hailed science and industry as the sovereign principles of organization in the modern world. Southerners, Davidson interpreted liberals to argue, ought thus to forfeit their preferred way of life to secure the blessings of technological efficiency and economic prosperity.[50]

Liberals told southerners to build dams to generate the electricity that would illuminate their farmhouses. Never mind that acres of farmland would be flooded and countless farms, even entire towns, would now be under water. Everything would turn out for the best. Liberals instructed southerners to prompt their state legislatures and chambers of commerce to plow under green fields, level rolling hills, and pave dirt roads to engineer efficient superhighways that would ease the travel of gawking Yankee tourists. They would make money in the long run. Never mind that they sacrificed their culture and traditions and became the mortgaged serfs of northern capitalists. Liberals urged southerners to alert physicians and social scientists to the unsanitary conditions of southern life and to assist them in getting rid of outdoor privies and installing indoor plumbing. They would be better people for it.

The farmer and his family might have all the modern conveniences that industrialism could provide: a toilet, a bathtub, electric lights, and paved roads. The farmer's pockets might bulge with money. Did these transformations enhance the standard of living? Perhaps. Had they enriched the quality of southern life? Davidson unambiguously answered no.

49. See "A Symposium: The Agrarians Today," 16–22.
50. See *SRSY,* 240–42, and Donald Davidson, "Where Are the Laymen? A Study in Policy Making," *American Review,* IX (1937), 456–81, "The South and Intellectual Progress," 7–8, and "The Agrarian South," 1–10.

Neither the farmer, his wife, nor his sons and daughters any longer heard grandpa's stories, strummed guitars, picked banjos, or sang the old folk ballads. Instead, they listened as the crackling voice on the radio told them what to think, what to believe, and what to do. To the liberals' delight, they learned what soap to use, what magazines to read, what clothes to wear, what cigarettes to smoke. They learned new standards of right and wrong and new definitions of good and evil calculated to bring them up to date. In the process, however, they endangered, and perhaps squandered, their inheritance.

Davidson did not think that expenditure, acquisitiveness, and display were in themselves the agents of the modern crisis. Consumerism was merely a symptom of a more serious malady. He did not worry that indoor plumbing would corrupt the hardy southern yeoman stock, but he never tired of telling liberal reformers that flush toilets would not improve a man's character. Davidson did not begrudge southern farmers the necessities of life, or even a few of the amenities. He knew how hard they had worked for them. He worried, though, that the propagandists for industrialism would induce men to make a necessity of every luxury.

Spokesmen for industrialism posited an image of life made up of an endless series of material satisfactions and private indulgences. They believed that there was nothing that could not be bought or sold, exhorting men always to spend more than they had and to want more than they needed. Davidson tried to dissuade southerners from exchanging their values, their traditions, and their souls for the artificial comforts that ingenious industrialists and advertisers had devised.[51]

He did not believe that southern farmers had willfully exhausted their land by planting only staple crops. They did not intentionally cut down forests to make a profit from selling the lumber. They preferred instead to nurture the land that had so long provided for them and their families. In the capitalist world, however, the preferences of southern farmers no longer mattered. They were constrained to exploit the land that they loved because they needed to survive, and to survive they needed money. The farmer had to put shoes on his children's feet and clothes on their backs. Perhaps his wife, too, needed a new hat or a warm coat. The roof on the barn needed repairing. The old wagon could use a fresh coat of paint. Some new tools would certainly be useful. Nor could the farmer

51. See Davidson, *The Spyglass,* ed. Fain, 238, and *AL,* 10–11.

forget that he owed the bank a mortgage payment and owed the government a share of his meager earnings. The ravaged lands of the South, Davidson proclaimed, were not a symbol of southern avarice or malignity but mute testimony against the tyranny of the money economy and the Leviathan state. The farmer, ensnared by forces beyond his control, had to get money for many reasons:

> [To] placate the sucking tentacle-tip of the money octopus flung far to seize him . . . money for more taxes for still more public improvements—new roads, new courthouses (with *steel* filing cabinets), and new bureaus upon bureaus; money for interest on the national debt, covered by bonds gilt-edged, good as gold, offering Hamiltonian conveniences to banks and security-venders; money for the new Northeastern idea of insurance, to hedge him against the liabilities and calamities forced upon him by the system and to bury him when, lifeless, moneyless, and propertyless, he delivers his soul to his Maker and his body to a mortician who is one of the highly valued members of the Chamber of Commerce. (*AL,* 114–15)[52]

Industrialism and the money economy were more devastating to the South than was Sherman's march to the sea. Add science to the already volatile mix of money and machine, Davidson predicted, and the compound would produce catastrophe. Since the early seventeenth century, men came more and more to accept science as the arbiter of truth, but the skepticism that science engendered offered a wretched foundation upon which to establish a stable social and political order. Science bred doubt rather than conviction, suspicion rather than faith. It presented no guide to moral conduct and no definition of the good life. Science, in Davidson's view, denied the very possibility of the good life. According to the scientists, there was only biological life; value judgments were meaningless.[53]

The scientific method, operating on man's fundamental conceptions of life, produced a world without mystery. Man, nature, and God were no longer worthy of reverence or even simple respect. Man was a mere collection of coordinated biological and chemical functions, with perhaps a few of Dr. Sigmund Freud's repressed sexual impulses and neurotic

52. See also Davidson, "The Agrarian South," 8–14.
53. See *SRSY,* 240–42; *AL,* 340–42, 353–54, and Davidson, "Poetry and Progress," 3–5.

complexes thrown in. Nature existed for man's pleasure, to be conquered and exploited at will. God was a concept to console the faint-hearted or to pacify the hard-headed, narrow-minded fundamentalist.[54]

The order that emerged from the purview of modern science was, in essence, a permanent disorder that rendered all previous social and political arrangements obsolete. Science thrust society into such furious uncertainty and instability that it became imperative to institute the rule of force to maintain even the semblance of order. Under the dispensation of the scientific-industrial regime, Davidson asserted, men were incapable of exercising the freedom to which rational consideration entitled them. The modern world was a barbarous place, at once pitiless and humorless, devoid of love and laughter. In such a world, violence became the only expression of power and authority.[55]

How, Davidson wondered, could modern men retain "spiritual values against the fiery gnawing of industrialism"?[56] Fanatical devotion to the machine threatened to destroy the continuity of human history and to extinguish human life itself. The present dominance of industry did not confirm its goodness, demonstrate its permanence, or ratify its superiority. Even as industrialism became more entrenched and as Americans became more dependent on technology, Davidson remained adamant that nothing about industrialism justified the belief that it would last forever.

Industrialism had not fulfilled, nor could it fulfill, the extravagant promises made in its name. Industrialism could not guarantee individualism or equality. It was not the source of happiness or the agent of enlightenment. The industrial regime did not bring uninterrupted prosperity. On the contrary, Davidson asserted, industrialism was the focus of evil in the modern world. In "The Agrarians Today," a symposium published in *Shenandoah* in 1952, he reassessed his original interpretation of industrialism and found that even after twenty-five years it required no amendment:

> Industrialism . . . has provided more and better automobiles, airplanes, refrigerators, and weapons of war—including the atomic bomb. And

54. See Davidson, "Poetry and Progress," 3–5, and *SRSY,* 259–62.
55. See Davidson, "Where Are the Laymen?" 456–59, 480, and *SRSY,* 3, 124–26, 226–27.
56. Donald Davidson to R. N. Linscott, April 9, 1922, in Davidson Papers. See also *SRSY,* 67, and Davidson, *The Spyglass,* ed. Fain, 237–38.

it has also become a party to the infliction of war, death, and destruction on an unprecedented scale. It has wasted our resources to the point of danger. It has degraded society, perverted education, and undermined religion. It has invaded, abridged, and all but destroyed our constitutional liberties, and now threatens to convert our government into a totalitarian regime. It has spread confusion and suspicion; it has begotten corruption and treason; it has reduced millions to a state of groveling servility and fear.[57]

By the 1920s, Davidson conceded, industrialism already dominated the North. To those northern politicians and southern liberals and to businessmen of both sections who advocated massive industrialization, it seemed a foregone conclusion that the South would also succumb to its sway in time. Davidson resisted but recognized that industrialization and commercialization spread like a cancer throughout the South. Respected members of chambers of commerce slithered on their bellies to entice some petty manufacturer of pants or socks or shoes to take up his tax-exempt residence in their midst. Assuredly, there were serpents in Eden.

Worse, those southerners who wanted to bring industrialism to the South proceeded without considering the ways in which it would disrupt the traditional, rural communities that had escaped the harshest aspects of modernity and had sustained the southern way of life. What was to become of these agrarians, these heroic descendants of the yeoman farmers who had settled the South more than two centuries before? They were inarticulate, at least in the modern idiom of liberals, social scientists, and capitalists, but they were neither irresponsible nor stupid.

Apprehensive, discontented, and perplexed, these traditional southerners, Davidson was certain, would welcome a candid assertion of southern principles and a forthright defense of southern values. He believed that the salvation of the South had to come from within. The plain folk of the South needed to find a way to calm their fears, to assail their enemies, and to remind themselves of who they were and from where they came. Davidson resolved to give it to them.

57. "A Symposium: The Agrarians Today," 17.

6

DAVIDSON'S DEFENSE OF THE SOUTH:
A LAND STILL FOUGHT FOR

> . . . Earth
> Is good, but better is land, and best
> A land still fought-for, even in retreat
> For how else can Aeneas find his rest
> And the child harken and dream at his grandsire's feet?
> —Donald Davidson, "Lines Written for Allen Tate
> on His Sixtieth Anniversary"

THE NEW FEDERALISM

By the 1930s, the United States had endured seventy years of uncontested
northern rule. The resulting spectacle of chaos and debauchery was unprecedented in history. "A sense of crisis weighed strong upon me," Davidson recalled years later (SWMW, 42). He had to do something before
it was too late. This was no time for mere aesthetic contemplation; the
time had come to act. Davidson wrote to R. N. Linscott in 1927: "The
South, I believe, has arrived at a crisis. It has always possessed great individuality which under modern influences it runs great risk of losing.
To return to its spiritual unity the South . . . must become conscious of
and not repudiate whatever is worth saving in its tradition." [1]

What was the southern cause of the 1930s? Davidson was convinced
that it was still the good cause, but he wondered how he could convince
modern men not likely to be well disposed toward it. What words, what
images could he use? He returned to first principles. Dedication to ag-

---

1. Donald Davidson to R. N. Linscott, April 9, 1927, in Donald Davidson Papers,
Special Collections, Jean and Alexander Heard Library, Vanderbilt University. See also
Donald Davidson, "Poetry and Progress," MS in Davidson Papers.

riculture was the characteristic attribute of southern life. Any defense of the South had to originate with a defense of agriculture not merely as a system of production but as a way of life. The modern crisis had deeper roots than the antipathy between North and South. In *I'll Take My Stand,* the Agrarians asserted that it began in the irreconcilable conflict between agrarianism and industrialism. In "The Trend in Literature," published in 1935, Davidson elaborated: "The war of cultures in our time . . . is a war between urban civilization—which is industrial, progressive, scientific, anti-traditional—and rural or provincial civilization—which is on the whole agrarian, conservative, anti-scientific, and traditional." [2]

In that modern "war of cultures," Davidson mounted a defense of the South in an attempt to restore some "true and commanding" image of the southern past. He knew, though, that such an effort would not be enough. The southern cause of the 1930s, as Davidson defined it, was actually the recovery of the past. The "Lost Cause" was not completely lost. The southern agrarian tradition did not perish with Confederate defeat. It lay submerged, buried and forgotten beneath the rubble of history. Davidson proposed to resurrect southern agrarianism as the one sure alternative to the confusion, sterility, and decadence of the modern world.

Not only could southerners restore the past; they had to do so or remain forever lost amid a thousand barren novelties and bizarre fantasies that promised happiness but delivered only misery. In their steadfast conservatism and proud backwardness, southerners actually preserved the secret that could empower them to reconstruct southern, and possibly American, society. The cause of the South, Davidson declared, was nothing less than the cause of civilization. He read *I'll Take My Stand* as the first volley in the southern counterattack against Leviathan, the battle of civilized society against the barbarism of science and industry under the direction of the "modern power state."

In extolling the South, Davidson abandoned the defensive posture of the southern liberals, whom he detested. He rejected the "defeatism" of Walter Hines Page and Henry Grady; he condemned the servile collaboration of George Fort Milton and Stringfellow Barr, who saluted the new carpetbaggers and begged them to make the South a part of modern

2. Donald Davidson, "The Trend in Literature," in *Culture in the South,* ed. William Terry Couch (Chapel Hill, 1935), 198.

industrial society. The Agrarian movement of the 1930s, Davidson announced, marked the first time since 1863 that southerners had gone on the offensive. He prepared to lead the fight.[3]

The Agrarian program offered the only means of relieving the modern crisis. Agrarianism entailed a return to the land. The rehabilitation of the landowning farmer was of first importance to the South, to the nation, and to civilization itself. More than promoting an agricultural restoration, Agrarianism proposed to dismantle the industrial system. The invasion of industrialism, Davidson warned his friend John Gould Fletcher, had to be dealt with pragmatically. To that end, he demanded that the federal government withdraw economic subsidies from industry and legal protection from corporations in order to eliminate monopoly and the "privilege of irresponsibility."[4]

National policy supported the industrial regime. Economists, social and political scientists, and politicians who promoted industrialism apparently assumed that industrial prosperity would "trickle down" to the exploited farmers. In effect, Davidson argued, they supposed that the debtor could pay off his debts if his creditor did not succumb to bankruptcy. To help the creditor (who was none other than the undisciplined and profligate capitalist) to avoid bankruptcy, the federal government granted him an endless series of tax exemptions and economic subsidies. To Davidson, such measures looked too much like socialist maneuvers designed to create a state-financed and state-controlled economy.[5]

Agrarianism, in Davidson's conception, provided a practical alternative to corporatism, centralization, and monopoly in any of their various guises, whether capitalist, socialist, or fascist. An agrarian society ensured the wide diffusion of property rather than the concentration of property in a few hands. The distribution of real property, in turn, gave all citizens a stake in society. With the acquisition of property, all citizens became vital members of the community resolutely committed to maintaining

---

3. See the following by Donald Davidson: "*I'll Take My Stand*: A History," *American Review*, V (1935), 301–21; "The 'Mystery' of the Agrarians: Facts and Illusions About Some Southern Writers," *Saturday Evening Post,* January 23, 1943, pp. 6–7; *AL,* 261–84; "The South and Intellectual Progress," MS in Davidson Papers; "The Trend in Literature," 202; and *SWMW,* 31–62.

4. Donald Davidson to John Gould Fletcher, December 12, 1937, in Davidson Papers.

5. See Donald Davidson, "No Ammer" (MS, *ca.* 1939), 13–14, in Davidson Papers.

the social order. They had no desire or need to exploit nature or to cheat their neighbors, as did men ravaged by industrialism. They were independent. Whatever they or their families required they made with their own hands, grew with their own toil, or bartered from neighbors who did.

Agriculture and the kind of craftsmanship that went with it were labor-intensive, and labor, Davidson believed, was not an evil to be avoided but a joy to be savored. He proposed that labor-saving, or, as he called it, "labor-evicting," machinery be strictly regulated or altogether prohibited. He opposed production for a mass market and instead favored production for use or for local markets. Only an agrarian economy, which Davidson conceived of as a virtual autarky, guaranteed a modicum of security and comfort without engendering the human casualties attendant upon industrial capitalism. Agriculture may have sold fewer goods and generated less revenue than industrialism, but such considerations did not discourage Davidson. He expected farming not to produce wealth but to ensure human welfare.[6]

Although the South was inescapably part of the modern capitalist social and economic order, Davidson insisted that it must have the freedom to define its role within that society and economy. Southerners must not abridge their liberty or allow others to usurp it. It was not a question of whether southerners would accept or reject progress but a question of what sort of progress they would have. Whose idea of progress should southerners adopt? Should they listen to H. L. Mencken? Henry Grady? Norman Thomas? Oswald Garrison Villard? John Dewey? Franklin D. Roosevelt? Or should they listen long and hard to their neighbors and their kin, to their pas and their grandpas, to their consciences and their hearts?

Davidson answered plainly. The lover of humanity had no choice but to reject the enforced mechanical conformity of industrialism and embrace the humane dignity of traditional, agrarian society. Any idea of progress that would hold southerners' attention, Davidson wrote to A. C. Aswell of *Forum,* could not be "insensitive . . . to the demands of an old tradition and way of life, deeply ingrained, surely worth salvaging

6. See Donald Davidson, "The Restoration of the Farmer," *American Review,* III (1934), 96–101, "The First Agrarian Economist," *American Review,* V (1935), 106–12, and "*I'll Take My Stand:* A History," 301–21.

in some parts." He continued: "I should like to see the South retain its character, not melt into the general mass. And I think the 'intellectuals'. . . are going to get an 'intellectual movement' under way only by working out ideas of progress that really have some relation to the Southern tradition."[7] Davidson feared that unless southerners reserved the power to determine the fate of the South, they could preserve few of its distinctive qualities. In the modern world, science and technology mandated that southerners could not maintain their self-respect and yet adhere to their traditional way of life. They would have to sacrifice one or the other, and almost certainly they would lose the greatest moral necessity of a living culture: their genius as a people. If the South were to survive, southerners had to return to the culture of the land, which had been the original foundation of the American Republic and which remained the foundation of the South long after it had disappeared elsewhere.

The traditional, agrarian South, whatever its imperfections, was the best alternative to the industrialized society of the North, which was revolutionary in its every manifestation. The time had come for every southerner to rediscover his heritage, reclaim his identity, and exclaim: "I am what I am. I cain't be no ammer!"[8]

In subtle and imperious ways, southerners were continually urged to forget their origins or to remember them with shame and to merge into the frenzied, anonymous world of modernity. Southerners, Davidson feared, felt increasingly constrained to conform to fashion and to get in step with the national procession. "Cosmopolitanism," the designation that Davidson applied to this phenomenon, was the virtue trumpeted by the modern, industrial age. Cosmopolitanism, however, did not operate virtuously. It homogenized diversity and eradicated individuality. Those transformations would prove catastrophic to southerners, rendering them, and every other people, unexceptional. If cosmopolitanism prevailed, one people would become like every other people. Everywhere they would dress alike, talk alike, read the same books and magazines, buy the same products, listen to the same radio programs, and watch the same movies. Cosmopolitanism would reduce human beings to inter-

7. Donald Davidson to A. C. Aswell, October 2, 1927, in Davidson Papers. See also Donald Davidson to John Donald Wade, March 3, 1934, in Davidson Papers.

8. Davidson, "No Ammer," 16.

changeable parts, a fitting tribute to the pervasive influence of Henry Ford.[9]

Davidson, for his part, refused to pay tribute to Ford or to any of his kind. Ford was perhaps the most dangerous man in history. With the lure of money and the machine, he tempted the world as Lucifer had tempted Christ. In a day of apparent prosperity and progress, Davidson was not prepared to forsake the southern tradition in pursuit of faddish and startling innovations. Most southerners, he felt certain, were with him. Although at times they despaired of preserving the historic character of southern life, southerners instinctively sensed that the South was unlike other regions of the United States. So adamantly and frequently had they insisted on that point throughout their history that they appeared ignorant, quixotic, backward, and stupid.

As an alternative to the "cosmopolitanism of the world-city," Davidson proposed the "philosophy of provincialism." Provincialism, according to him, had a special appeal in the South. It rested not on abstract reason but on concrete experience, not on new but on old, established foundations. Provincials rebelled against the standardization that accompanied science and industry. They believed in unity, not uniformity.

Yet provincials did not thoughtlessly reject "the new" out of hand. In times of "mass-thinking," Davidson wrote, they kept an independent mind. They did not exalt themselves beyond the station proper to mankind or pretend to be something that they were not. They remained self-possessed and maintained the integrity of their souls. At the same time, they graciously tolerated difference, for the aesthetic of provincialism certified that beauty and harmony in the social order, as elsewhere, emerged not from narrow correspondence and equivalence but from widest possible diversity and discrimination.[10] To survive, southerners had to become good provincials. They had to avoid at all cost the taint of cosmopolitanism, which would dilute or subvert their native inheritance.

"Sectionalism" was the political expression of "the provincial habit of mind." Americans of the machine age deluded themselves that there was a sovereign national culture. In the United States there was no national

9. See Donald Davidson, *The Spyglass: Views and Reviews, 1924–1930*, ed. John Tyree Fain (Nashville, 1963), 237–38, and Donald Davidson, "Where Regionalism and Sectionalism Meet," *Social Forces*, XIII (1934), 23–31.

10. See Davidson, *The Spyglass*, ed. Fain, 3–7.

culture, Davidson countered, but a congeries of sectional cultures that flourished in New England, the Midwest, the South, and the West. Apart from these sectional cultures, the fictional national culture did not exist.

Davidson professed no abstract loyalty to the nation. He was devoted to the loose, historic confederations that were the United States. "The kind of nation that requires me to heave a sacrificial sigh and immolate my cherished sectional peculiarities, hopes, pleasures, and means of life on the altar of some theoretic national good," he wrote his friend John Donald Wade, "is not the nation that I hope the United States will become."[11]

Although often unacknowledged, sectionalism was a "living form" in all periods of American history and the effective reality of American life. The structure of each section was determined by its "permanent physiographic situation," in a word, by its geography, and reinforced by the tendency of peoples of similar ethnic background to settle in the same place and foster the cultural traditions to which they were accustomed. Environment thus shaped the economics and, to a certain extent, the culture of each section. Davidson's analysis of sectionalism, however, involved more than a rigid environmental determinism. He was also concerned with "political sectionalism," for it was in the realm of politics that a people articulated and addressed the forces that united them and the tensions that divided them.[12]

Davidson defined "political sectionalism" as the inclination of a group of states, bound in geographical contiguity and united by social, cultural, and economic ties to think and, on occasion, to act in common. Throughout the history of the United States, Americans had decided few issues according to the precepts of some uniform political economy or political philosophy. Although national in scope, debates over the tariff, internal improvements, the Bank of the United States, slavery in the territories, the income tax, the popular election of senators, the minimum wage, and women's suffrage were all sectional issues. Even foreign wars, which might engender nationalist sentiment, invariably provoked a disproportionate sectional endorsement or opposition.

No other nation in the Western world, Davidson asserted, displayed sectional alignments on major questions of policy and politics with such

---

11. Davidson to Wade, March 3, 1934, in Davidson Papers.
12. See *AL,* 45–47.

regularity and conviction. Yet the Constitution granted no legal status or political recognition to the sections. The Founding Fathers, intent on creating a nation out of assemblies that claimed independent sovereignty, took only the states into legal regard and made them the focus of political activity.

Both the states and the federal government were abstract devices abstractly conceived. They were no more than convenient mechanisms of organization. The sections, on the contrary, were organic. The states and the federal government were artificial constructs; the sections were natural. Neither archaic vestiges of the past nor sentimental fictions of the present, the sections were continuous and permanent entities that still exercised a powerful influence on national life. Sectional diversity was essential to national unity; differentiation was a prerequisite of unification. The United States, unique among the nations of the world, was a sovereign nation composed of identifiable and self-reliant sections. No definition of the "United States of America" could be complete if the sectional component was excluded.[13]

American history, according to Davidson, was not the story of the gradual and steady evolution of a unified, national culture majestically proceeding from a recognized center. The history of the United States was shaped by a series of sectional conflicts, often approaching violence and once erupting in war but more often mediated through conciliation and compromise. "The phenomenon of which these clashes and compromises are manifestations," Davidson concluded, "is sectionalism, no matter how assiduously historians and politicians may veil its appearance under one or another sort of euphemism" (*AL,* 24).

The euphemism for sectionalism that most troubled Davidson was the "regionalism" of sociologists Rupert B. Vance and Howard W. Odum.[14]

---

13. See *ibid.,* 3–19.

14. See the following works by Howard W. Odum: "Regionalism vs. Sectionalism in the South's Place in the National Economy," *Social Forces,* XII (1933), 338–54; "The Case for Regional-National Social Planning," *Social Forces,* XIII (1934), 6–23; and *Southern Regions of the United States* (Chapel Hill, 1936). See also the following works by Rupert B. Vance: "The Concept of a Region," *Social Forces,* VIII (1929), 208–18; "The Geography of Distinction: The Nation and Its Regions, 1790–1927," *Social Forces,* XVIII (1939), 168–79; *Human Geography of the South: A Study in Regional Resources and Human Adequacy* (Chapel Hill, 1932); and *Regionalism and the South: Selected Papers of Rupert B. Vance,* ed. John Shelton Reed and Daniel Joseph Singal (Chapel Hill, 1982).

Regionalism subordinated the region to the nation, whereas sectionalism extolled the section as the only practical foundation for nationalism. Odum and Vance eschewed politics, whereas Davidson favored a politics of "sectional reciprocity." Blindly optimistic, Odum and Vance never imagined that a sectional interest could disguise itself as the national interest, seize control of the federal government, and pursue sectional aims unscrupulously concealed as national purpose. Davidson denounced those forms of sectionalism that pretended to nationalism.

For seventy years, northerners assumed that their opinions and beliefs, no matter how thoroughly northern, were the only truly national sentiments. All opinions and beliefs identifiable as southern were sectional and thereby subject to derision. As a consequence, northerners had long assumed it their right to interfere in the domestic affairs of the South and to violate the integrity of that section. The northerners' self-righteousness and arrogance, Davidson told Wade, was "simply unendurable."[15]

It was imperative to formulate a new theory of federalism that formally endorsed sectionalism and assured the vitality of the sections within the national polity. The reconciliation of nationalism and sectionalism was the foremost political obstacle for those who wished to perpetuate democratic institutions and republican government in the United States. History should have taught Americans that it was unwise to disregard the existence of sections in such a large and diverse nation. Should the equilibrium between the sections again break down, as it had during the 1860s, not only the nation but civilization itself would be in peril.

In Europe, where no federal principle existed, only violence and conquest could end the constant scramble for power. Such circumstances gave rise to the Leviathan state, to fascism and communism, to a politics of terror. The United States, Davidson feared, was not immune to such influences and could easily recapitulate the sorrowful history of Europe if Americans did not vigilantly guard their sectional prerogatives. Unless the present generation courageously faced the problem of the relations of the sections to the nation, some future historian would no doubt pause in his lecture and declare: "*At this point regional differences passed beyond the possibility of adjustment under the Federal system, and here, therefore, began the*

15. Davidson to Wade, March 3, 1934, in Davidson Papers. See also Davidson, "Where Regionalism and Sectionalism Meet," 23–31, and *AL*, 51–52.

dismemberment of the United States, long since foreshadowed in the struggle of the eighteen-sixties." Davidson considered other options, too: "But he [the historian] might state a different result, now before us as a possibility: *At this point the ordinary processes of Federal government failed to serve the national purposes. A dictatorship ensued*" (*AL,* 109–10).

The greatest hazard to prolonged sectional equilibrium was the very device that Odum and Vance would employ to establish it: regional planning on a national scale. Planning, Davidson reasoned, inclined toward tyranny. Would federal intervention into traditional sectional arrangements actually incorporate sectional considerations into the democratic process? Under the deliberate scrutiny and thoughtful supervision of Odum and Vance, Davidson conceded, perhaps it would. But what if the process fell under the sway of such extremists and radicals as V. F. Calverton, Granville Hicks, Edmund Wilson, or Michael Gold? These men and their comrades agreed that the Leviathan state was the only way to maintain order while securing for mankind the benefits of technological change and industrial prosperity. In their hands, planning would become an instrument of totalitarianism. They were interested only in effecting a scientific, regimented society and an efficient, corporate economy and would gladly trade political freedom for economic security.

In their conception of the ideal society, the precision of scientific calculation replaced the unwieldy operation of tradition. Coercion became the exclusive sanction of their "scientific politics," which gave no quarter to liberty and diversity. The "Functionalists," as Davidson called them, would bring democratic sectionalism viciously "to heel with the lash of a dictatorial whip." [16]

This revolutionary proposition was native not to the United States but to the Soviet Union. Sectionalism was not compatible with social planning. Indeed, from Davidson's point of view, sectionalism provided an automatic and natural restraint upon the vast centralization and consolidation of wealth and power. The assurance of sectional reciprocity and autonomy diminished the possibility of civil war or revolution and guaranteed the continuation of constitutional government. What would happen, Davidson wondered, if by some extraordinary turn of fortune, the United States came to approximate the condition of the Soviet Un-

16. Davidson, "Where Regionalism and Sectionalism Meet," 29–30; *AL,* 102–28.

ion? "What are we going to do then?" he asked Wade. Davidson shuddered at the consequences he imagined for the South:

> Will you be content, John Wade, to see your plantation divided up between the relations and friends of Richard, the yard boy, and Tom, the field hand? And will you be charmed to teach the milder English classics (those not too-too colored with "bourgeois" sentiment) and the greater Russian classics to a class where kinky heads and blond tresses mix in critical appraisal, and do not ever nod politely—and all this for a pittance, or for nothing, while you live with your aged mother (for whom you cannot get medicine) in an apartment designated by the central committee.[17]

To avert this unpleasantness, Davidson recommended the creation of "regional commonwealths" to supplant the states as the seats of local government. These regional commonwealths would constitute the basis for a "New Federalism," which would protect the sections from the economic exploitation and political imperialism to which they had formerly been subjected. If such arrangements did not form a more perfect union, they might still form the type of union that suited American traditions, preferences, and realities.

These regional commonwealths would have to have the power to tax and regulate "foreign" enterprises that would despoil them. Regional councils would exercise some authority over capital investment, the money supply, and credit within sectional boundaries and would have every right to limit the industrial monopoly that endowed one region with a virtual right of conquest over another. Perhaps, Davidson conjectured, the regional commonwealths should also possess a veto power, similar to Calhoun's doctrine of the concurrent majority, to enable citizens to overturn abominations that others tried to force on them.

Ideally, regional commonwealths should nurture agriculture and promote small business in order to encourage men to stay at home and collect modest but adequate returns from their investments and their labor. Industrialism, by definition, was imperial; agrarianism, by nature, was not. Davidson insisted on complete sectional reciprocity: the rights and powers granted to one section had to be granted to all. He obviously believed that agrarianism would ensure sectional autonomy and, thus, the liberty of the South better than would industry and science.

17. Davidson to Wade, March 3, 1934, in Davidson Papers.

This New Federalism, though applied to all sections, would be especially advantageous to the South in at least three important respects. The system of regional commonwealths would give southerners the power to curtail or eliminate the absentee ownership of farmland by Wall Street speculators or southern expatriates who had retired to the splendor and luxury of New York or Los Angeles. More important, the New Federalism would shield southern schools from the influx of propaganda aimed at the very heart of southern culture and would entrust southerners themselves to preserve the biracial social structure without resorting to furtive evasion or to raw violence.[18]

Davidson disavowed any inclination to use the New Federalism to retaliate against northerners for the old injuries that their ancestors had done to the South. He made it clear, however, that southerners would not again permit the South to be hemmed in, humiliated, denied recourse, and offended by the assumption of superior piety. The South belonged to the men and women who dwelt there, and they would be governed only by their own consent. Southerners had simply to look into their hearts to know what they had to do if provoked. Davidson admitted his true beliefs to Wade: "I don't know whether I am a sectionalist or a regionalist; but I know I am a Southerner. . . . After all, what we are reviving is the South, under any name or ism you please."[19]

RACE AND THE SOUTHERN TRADITION

The legal, political, intellectual, and moral assault on segregation, which began as early as the late 1930s, gave Davidson an opportunity to put the New Federalism into practice. He welcomed the challenge and rushed to the defense of southern values and institutions.

Davidson's interpretation of the "Negro question" had much of the simplicity and allure of the modernist nostrums that he detested. White supremacy, like slavery, he declared, was a negligible issue in southern life and history. There was no "Negro problem" in the South. It existed only in the fevered imaginations of northern liberals, radicals, and idealists. Blacks preferred the few rights and the inferior status traditionally accorded them in the South, for they knew that the alternative would

18. See *AL,* 121–28.
19. Davidson to Wade, March 3, 1934, in Davidson Papers.

be to possess no rights at all. Northerners, who had a woefully inadequate appreciation of southern race relations, could never understand or accept that resolution.

Northern sociologists, politicians, and reformers, the spiritual heirs of John Brown, William Lloyd Garrison, Wendell Phillips, Charles Sumner, and Thaddeus Stevens, had unfortunately learned nothing from their predecessors' mistakes. In their arrogance, they again mistook appearance for reality. They self-righteously presumed to know what was best for the South and proceeded thoughtlessly to interfere with southern institutions and arrangements of long standing. The abolitionists sought political and social justice for the slaves. Not only did they fail to achieve their objectives; they also perpetuated injustice and ruin upon white southerners. And southerners had long memories.

The abolitionists made slavery a topic of political controversy, just as the "social missionaries" of the 1930s, 1940s, and 1950s transformed segregation into a question of social justice and moral rectitude. There was, Davidson contended, nothing inherently proper or improper, moral or immoral about southern race relations. White southerners had simply devised the best method to maintain a congenial social order under their particular circumstances.

The biracial system, he declared, had always represented whites' concessions to blacks, not whites' oppression of blacks. Davidson recoiled at the suggestion that white southerners had set out to inconvenience, humiliate, subordinate, exploit, or punish blacks. The preservation of "separate-but-equal" status demonstrated no ill will toward blacks but rather positive concern for whites.

Southerners had accepted the outcome of the Civil War and had assented to the passage of the Thirteenth Amendment. They had objected, however, to the enactment of the Fourteenth Amendment, which proscribed the abridgment of Negroes' rights of citizenship, and the Fifteenth Amendment, which secured the vote for the former slaves. The Fourteenth and Fifteenth Amendments, Davidson protested, were ratified through "fraud and force." The Reconstruction governments that voted for ratification were the precise moral equivalents of "the Quislings and Vichyites." All loyal Americans, whether northern or southern, should regard them with similar contempt.

Davidson believed that the South was under no legal obligation or moral compulsion to observe the provisions of the Fourteenth and Fifteenth Amendments. At most, southerners owed the laws only grudging and technical obedience. Neither amendment had ever enjoyed much popularity in the South, whereas the various state laws that fortified racial segregation won approval from an overwhelming majority of southerners. Davidson assumed that approval to be self-evident. Agitation over racial discrimination and attempts to upset the biracial system could thus only come from precocious northern blacks, uninformed social scientists, liberal reformers, or rabid communists.

Davidson acknowledged that the southern racial code forbade blacks from participating as equals in white society. At the same time, that code did not prevent blacks from flourishing within the context of the biracial social order. Segregation, for him, was not an expedient way of excluding or expelling blacks from southern society but a way of defining the mutual obligations that bound members of the one race to those of the other. It marked the conditions of tolerance and coexistence between whites and blacks. The southern system of race relations thereby maintained the peace and tranquility that naturally characterized southern life whenever circumstances allowed for the realization of its native genius. Violence ensued only when blacks, or those who presumed to speak for them, defied the racial orthodoxy. The biracial system itself did not engender conflict, as its critics supposed. On the contrary, it was designed to preclude conflict by diminishing both the reasons for dissension and the rewards of confrontation.[20]

About the ultimate purpose of the biracial system, however, Davidson remained implacable. White southerners did not intend for blacks to suffer needless disgrace or to come to harm, but they instinctively understood that any elevation in the status of blacks could only result in their own degradation. Southerners would never willingly sacrifice their privileges to pursue the doubtful advancement of blacks. Southern race relations thus had less to do with upholding white supremacy than with maintaining racial purity and ensuring white survival. For Davidson,

20. See the following by Donald Davidson: "A Sociologist in Eden," *American Review*, VIII (1936), 177–204; "Gulliver with Hay Fever," *American Review*, IX (1937), 152–72; "The Class Approach to Southern Problems," *Southern Review*, V (1939), 261–72; "Agrarianism and Politics," *Review of Politics*, I (1939), 114–25; "Preface to Decision," *Sewanee Review*, LIII (1945), 394–412; "The New South and the Conservative Tradition," *National Review*, September 10, 1960, pp. 141–46; and "No Ammer."

southern race relations were not a matter of power and status but a matter of life and death.

The overwhelming and obvious fact about race in the South, for Davidson, was that whites remained unmistakably white and blacks remained irredeemably black. The status of blacks in the South, he conceded, may have represented an injustice, but if injustice was necessary to temper racial animosity, then so be it. Whatever material advantages white southerners gained from black labor were more than offset by the burdens they endured on blacks' behalf. Blacks were economic, social, and political liabilities, whose presence painfully taxed southerners' already meager resources. The alleged discrimination against blacks was also a source of tension between North and South. Northerners did not have to meet blacks face to face day after day. They could castigate southern whites for their ill treatment of blacks whenever they sensed an opportunity to abuse or exploit the South.

Given these circumstances, Davidson contended that white southerners displayed remarkable generosity and indulgence toward blacks. Even whites' generosity and indulgence, though, had their limits. White southerners had never agreed to accept blacks as equal members of society. They denied blacks equal social participation not only because they considered them unworthy of equality but, more important, because they were determined to prevent racial amalgamation. On this point, Davidson left no room for equivocation or doubt:

> This South rather likes the Negro than dislikes him; at any rate it is used to him, values him for reasons not always selfish, and wishes him no harm. It would be glad to see him have better housing and more money, if such things can be had without impoverishment of the already insecure white South. But . . . it will not support a program of improvement that implies a change of status; in particular any equality that implies race amalgamation. . . . The white South does not wish to make this sacrifice. It is a simple matter of self-preservation, about which there can be no argument. The white South prefers to remain white, and that is all there is to it.[21]

Davidson's candor is admirable, but he never pretended to objectivity. "Do remember," he reminded his friend William Yandell Elliott, "that I am an ardent partisan who doesn't like to surrender, once I am convinced

21. Davidson, "Gulliver with Hay Fever," 169–70.

and committed."[22] Davidson was indeed a partisan, fully committed to justifying the prevailing southern race relations and fully convinced of the efficacy and probity of segregation. Although clearly a matter of personal preference and political expedience, Davidson's acceptance of racial segregation was also necessary to his understanding of southern culture and history. His conception of the South as the enduring source of identity, order, meaning, and being in the modern world depended on the subordination of blacks and the maintenance of racial purity among whites.

Miscegenation was, therefore, an unspeakable atrocity, the annihilation of racial purity, an unmitigated disaster. White blood that passed into the black race ceased to be white, but black blood that passed into the white race remained black. The purpose of the southern racial code was to prevent black blood from passing into the white race and thereby polluting it. The customarily brutal penalty imposed on a black man who sexually violated a white woman was thus to be expected.

Few white men, Davidson supposed, consorted with black women. For that perverse minority who could not control their impulses, legislatures throughout the southern states had uniformly forbidden miscegenation. The legal prohibition against it, not those white men who strayed or faltered, represented the social norm of the southern white community.

The presence of mulattoes among the black population offered no conclusive proof that southern whites had violated their own principles and strictures. Indians, Spanish explorers, French colonists, and later Union soldiers had all availed themselves of black women and contributed to the interracial combinations. There was also a tendency among black men themselves, Davidson proposed, to select as sexual partners or mates lighter-skinned black women. Since he found it virtually impossible to trace the lineage of blacks over long periods of time, Davidson decided that observation was a better guide than speculation to demonstrate racial composition. The marked physical differences between blacks and whites in the South was evidence enough to convince him that white southerners neither condoned nor indulged in "irregular alliances."

22. Donald Davidson to William Yandell Elliott, February 21, 1960, in Davidson Papers. Elliott was a member of the Fugitive Group but did not participate in the Agrarian movement.

Blacks were also culturally inferior to whites. Slavery, which Davidson argued had no constitutive effect on white culture, had left blacks without culture. The twentieth-century descendants of the slaves continued to suffer from this legacy of cultural dispossession. The enactment of anti-lynching legislation, the elimination of the poll tax, the establishment of the fair employment practices commission, or even the passage of a federal law to encourage the mixing of the races could not compensate for that deprivation. The many previous attempts to legislate blacks into political and social equality had failed miserably. History, custom, and tradition regulated the pattern of race relations in the South. The rule of law could displace history, custom, and tradition only if the law was supported by military force.

Southerners had long confronted the consequences of their decisions and actions. They were not given to romantic illusions or utopian dreams. They understood that southern race relations were a cultural and historical matter into which the law entered at its peril. Irresponsible legislation, in all likelihood, would only make a bad situation worse. Every direct assault upon southern race relations thus far, Davidson wrote, had "shifted it into a new complex of difficulties, so that the problem, instead of being solved, has taken a new form and introduced new perplexities." His evaluation noted the negative effect of such legislation on democracy itself: "Meanwhile, what incidental gains the Negro may seem to have made have been offset by the harm done to the nation as a whole through unforeseen applications of the legislative acts. Instead of being . . . an organic part of the process of democratic evolution, the various attempts to legislate the Negro into equal status may be viewed as a notable disruption of that process."[23] There was, Davidson concluded, no easy solution to the problem, save perhaps for that tried and true southern remedy: patience and forbearance.

Davidson's argument subtly contradicted his assertion that blacks had no culture and were fit only for slavery, from which they derived innumerable benefits. If slavery stripped blacks of their native culture, as he suggested, then he had also to admit that they had once had a culture and that slavery had harmed them by destroying it. Davidson left these implications unexamined, considering neither proposition conjointly but affirming both independently.

23. Davidson, "Preface to Decision," 403.

He did not retreat. He never repudiated his stand on segregation, never modified his views on race relations, never abandoned his racism. As the years passed, he grew even more exacting in his analysis of racial issues. Following the decision of the Supreme Court in the case of *Brown v. Board of Education of Topeka,* Davidson embarked on a mission to save the old order. In 1954, he helped to found, and later directed, the Tennessee Federation for Constitutional Government, an organization that he hoped would concentrate local resistance to court-ordered school desegregation.

As head of the federation from 1955 until 1959, Davidson wanted to do more than write pamphlets and deliver stump speeches. Through the federation, he wanted to influence events, at least in Tennessee, if not the nation. He sought to organize opposition to the integration of public schools in the towns and counties across the state in an attempt to subvert the practical operation of the Brown decision while mounting a legal challenge to the constitutionality of the law. In 1955, Davidson wrote to Wade to describe the activities and objectives of the Tennessee Federation for Constitutional Government:

> Our Tennessee organization is at last a going concern. Apparently our first announcements may have had some definite effect on the Tennessee situation. Up to the time when we broke the news, it seemed as if the State educational authorities would very likely follow the line of "voluntary compliance" with the Supreme Court decision. We have seemingly stopped, or slowed down, that process, by simply announcing that the Tennessee Constitution, which prohibits educational "integration," is still in force and any school boards who might try to desegregate would be subject to legal action; and that, when and if a Federal court in Tennessee might declare the segregation clause of the state constitution null and void, we would then go into court (state court) and seek an injunction to restrain educational officials from the use of state funds, on the ground that the entire educational clause (and not merely the sentence referring to segregation) will be void, and there will be no authority for the use of funds for desegregated schools. The school boards and other officials were really hoping that some organized group would take this position, and we know from various sources that they do welcome our move.[24]

24. Donald Davidson to John Donald Wade, August 4, 1955, in Davidson Papers. For Davidson's views on southern race relations, see also Donald Davidson to John Pomfret, December 12, 1937, Donald Davidson to William Terry Couch, October 12,

From Davidson's point of view, blacks' struggle for civil rights was "nauseating and terrifying."[25] The implications were unimaginable. The civil rights movement threatened the ideal of racial purity, which Davidson took to be the foundation of civilized order in the South.

Throughout his life, Davidson at times had difficulty distinguishing between honest disagreement with his ideas and personal attack on his character. After 1954, it had become nearly impossible for him to differentiate one from the other when the discussion of racial segregation arose. He could not attribute good will to anyone who wished to debate that issue. Debate was useless, for, in Davidson's mind, there was only one side to the question.

The men and women, white and black, who welcomed the integration of public schools in the South, Davidson concluded, had been duped and manipulated. The leaders of the movement for integration were either cynical or mad. They would resort to any measures to get what they wanted. Freedom and advancement for blacks concerned them but little. If anything, Davidson thought, they were more interested in demeaning and punishing southern whites. That motive explained the blacks' quick turn to violence, despite the numerous protestations against violence that the Reverend Martin Luther King, Jr., and others had uttered.

Davidson singled out Dr. King for special reproof. As the emerging leader of the early civil rights movement, King came to symbolize for Davidson both the cynicism and the madness that he believed characterized blacks' fight for equality and liberation. King was a fraud. In 1963, Davidson wrote Allen Tate that it was only a matter of time before the white South would be locked in a mortal struggle of unprecedented violence. Blacks, not whites, Davidson asserted, would initiate the violence, but because King preached the gospel of nonviolent resistance and because southern whites had once again adamantly refused to accom-

---

1948, Donald Davidson to Louis D. Rubin, Jr., October 16, 1953, September 2, 1955, Donald Davidson to Frank Chodorov, May 28, 1954, Donald Davidson to Jesse Stuart, May 29, 1954, Donald Davidson to Russell Kirk, June 10, 1955, Donald Davidson to William E. Dodd, November 23, 1955; Donald Davidson to Floyd G. Watkins, June 11, 1956, Donald Davidson to Thomas J. B. Walsh, April 24, September 2, 1956, Donald Davidson to Allen Tate, May 30, 1963, Donald Davidson to M. E. Bradford, August 7, 1966, and Donald Davidson to Laura Virginia Hale, n.d., all in Davidson Papers.

25. Davidson to Kirk, June 10, 1955, in Davidson Papers.

modate to someone else's idea of justice, progress, and civilization, the media would miscast King as the hero and southern whites as the villains. Davidson thought trouble was coming and knew whom he might blame for it: "A period of great violence *may* now be in prospect. We have not really had it, up to now, not from the Southern side, despite what you may have seen on T-V, heard on radio, on [*sic*] read in the press. . . . The saintly Dr. King, though a professed Ghandi-ite, by no means wears a loin-cloth or the equivalent or subsists on a bowl of rice with a pinch of salt."[26]

Tate demurred. He, too, had long believed in racial segregation and black inferiority. Tate remarked to Lincoln Kirstein in 1933: "I belong to the white race, and I am convinced by the experience of my race with the negro that when two such radically different races live together, one must rule. I think the negro race is an inferior race." The situation would not have been substantially altered, Tate continued, even had "we had a superior race like the Chinese in our midst."[27] He would still have favored white rule as the means of maintaining social order. For Tate, the issue was never as simple as affirming the racial superiority of whites. Rather, he advocated white rule in defense of the South's community and culture, which he believed would not survive without the stern imposition of racial homogeneity. The world, however, had changed since the 1930s. Although Tate may still have thought blacks innately inferior, by the late 1950s and early 1960s he saw no way humanely to enforce the segregation of blacks in the South.

Tate did not welcome integration with enthusiasm. He told Davidson that he would feel "uncomfortable" in an integrated South: "It would not be my world. I would not know how to conduct myself."[28] But Tate understood that more was at stake than his own preferences. Resistance to desegregation, he warned Davidson, would turn the rest of the nation against the South, invite federal intervention, and once more transform the South itself into a bloody battleground. For what? The South could

26. Davidson to Tate, May 30, 1963, in Davidson Papers. See also Davidson to Bradford, August 7, 1966, in Davidson Papers.

27. Allen Tate to Lincoln Kirstein, May 10, 1933, in Allen Tate File, *Hound and Horn* Papers, Beinecke Rare Book and Manuscript Library, Yale University. Kirstein, who later founded the American Ballet Theater, was at this time the editor of *Hound and Horn.*

28. Allen Tate to Donald Davidson, October 19, 1962, in Davidson Papers.

not possibly win. White southerners had no means, except sporadic violence, with which to oppose the federal mandate and defeat integration.

The doctrine of nullification, in Tate's opinion, was no longer applicable and had, in fact, been discredited. The states were no longer sovereign but reserved to themselves only paltry local rights that did not threaten the sanctity and power of the centralized federal government. Individual states had no authority to "nullify" federal legislation. Secession had once been a respectable idea, but no nation could admit the practical validity of the right of secession even if the constitution legally provided for it. The only justification for secession, Tate declared, was its success. The right of secession presupposed the ability to wage war to achieve separation. Could Tennessee alone, or the southern states combined, now make secession viable? The question required no response.[29]

Tate anticipated the future of race relations in the United States and awaited the coming of integration as stoically as he could. He saw only one course available to white southerners. They should not simply assent to federal regulations but should assume control of the movement toward integration and accomplish it in a traditionally southern way, with order, moderation, and dignity. Tate had already proposed a similar approach to Frank Owsley as early as 1943. In a letter to Owsley, he wrote:

> Perhaps we can stir up something in the South. I am in favor of a manifesto signed by Southern leaders, to the following effect: that the race problem is a Southern problem, and will be handled openly and responsibly by the South; that within the framework of "equitable segregation" the negro can ultimately be given economic opportunity along with equal rights before the law, as the prosperity of the South permits; and that all attempts of the East and North to use the Federal power to interfere with the Southern way of dealing with these problems will be resisted. If Southern leaders do not frame some such policy I predict that the North will completely undermine the South; if they do frame it, I am convinced that much of the agitation from this quarter will be disarmed, and that the negroes themselves will cooperate with the Southern white leaders.[30]

29. See Tate to Davidson, October 19, November 23, 1962, both in Davidson Papers.

30. Allen Tate to Frank L. Owsley, November 18, 1943, in Frank L. Owsley Papers, Special Collections, Jean and Alexander Heard Library, Vanderbilt University.

By making concessions to blacks, Tate hoped, southern whites might actually maintain and strengthen the traditional social order.

Either with the help of white southerners or at the insistence of the federal government, however, blacks would integrate the public schools. The integration of public facilities would soon follow, and eventually blacks would have the vote. Yet, Tate reassured Davidson, enfranchisement would not automatically incline blacks to live among whites. Once they could vote, blacks might take control of those towns and counties in which they had an electoral majority. Most whites would surely move elsewhere, and de facto segregation would result, not through coercion but by choice. Segregation, Tate speculated, would be reestablished in the South on a voluntary, rather than a compulsory, basis.

Davidson could not have disagreed more fully with Tate's attitude and assessment. It was impossible for him to be as sanguine as Tate about the future of southern race relations. In his analysis of southern history and culture, Davidson could permit blacks no poetic or historical voice. He could allow them neither to tell their own story nor to interpret its meaning. Under no circumstances could he consider their having a political voice: the ability and the authority to alter their condition. Blacks had to remain forever inarticulate, forever docile. Consigned to the background of southern history and life, blacks were the hewers of wood and the drawers of water. To assign them a greater role would be reckless. Blacks were constrained to accept the definition and the status that whites imposed on them. They had no choice.

Davidson's vision of the South was, in the end, predicated less on white supremacy and black inferiority than on racial homogeneity. White supremacy represented not his ideal but his accommodation to the black presence in the South. To safeguard racial purity, Davidson preferred blacks and whites to live apart, but racial heterogeneity in the South made white supremacy necessary. If blacks were to live among whites at all, they had to submit to white rule. On no other basis could whites tolerate their proximity.

In advancing his vision of white racial purity and preeminence, Davidson virtually ignored blacks. Tate noted that Davidson did not deal adequately with blacks, and especially with slavery, in his numerous discussions of matters southern. In a retrospective essay on *The Fugitive* published in 1962, Tate complained that "Mr. Davidson's Old South has always seemed to me to leave about half of the Old South out of account:

the half, or third, or whatever the figures were, that included the Negro" (*MO*, 37–38). By overlooking blacks and denying the centrality of slavery to the antebellum southern social order, Davidson evaded the critical question of class antagonism between slaveholding and nonslaveholding whites. The presence of a wealthy and dominant slaveholding class, whose status, wealth, and power rested on the right of property in man, challenged Davidson's vision of southern whites unified as a homogeneous race. The existence of rival social classes maneuvering for power belied his declaration of organic unity among southern whites. Unless this characterization of racial unity stood, Davidson's interpretation of southern history was in jeopardy. To be sure, Tate's analysis of slavery as destroying the organic unity of the South implicitly suggested that Davidson's fear had come to pass.

His objections notwithstanding, slavery did provide the basis of status, wealth, and power in the antebellum South. It created and sustained a plantation community that was the foundation of southern civilization. The slaveholding class dominated blacks and exercised hegemony over nonslaveholding whites. A minority of the white population, the slaveholders commanded such esteem and wielded such influence that they, not the yeomen, formulated the southern world view and shaped the southern way of life. The planters set the tone of southern politics, society, culture, thought, and religion. The traditional southern emphasis on family, community, honor, elegance, leisure, learning, and faith was the pride and the province of this class of aristocratic slave owners. Slavery unified southern civilization, created a social ideal that nonslaveholding yeomen aspired to emulate, and consolidated the economic and political power of the slaveholding gentry.

Davidson would not have appreciated this interpretation. He rejected, if he ever considered, the notion that the antebellum South was a slave society. Diverting attention from slavery, he sought to demonstrate that the South was an agrarian society locked in a battle against the deadly encroachments of industrialism.

THE HEROIC SOUTH

Had the South won its war for independence, Davidson believed, the world would have been a better place. The responsibility to articulate and detail the enduring virtues of the southern way of life, even in defeat, fell chiefly upon southern men of letters. To recommend that southern writers self-consciously advocate the southern tradition carried grave risks for southern literature. Davidson admitted the danger that literature might degenerate into propaganda but argued that such concerns were overshadowed by an even more serious threat. Southern writers needed to mount a deliberate counteroffensive, for their enemies had launched a deliberate attack. There would be no southern writers and no southern literature, except in the purely formal and technical sense, unless the southern tradition again became a vital component of American life. Writers could not isolate their defense of poetry from their defense of the South.[31]

Southern men of letters had a unique opportunity to contribute to the general rebellion against modern American life and the growing dissatisfaction with metropolitan culture. Their struggle for literary and cultural self-determination might come to represent an exciting and important moment in the general renewal and reformation of American life and letters within the citadels of agrarianism, provincialism, sectionalism, and conservatism.

The revival of the southern tradition, Davidson quickly added, had to accompany the revival of southern society. No longer could southern writers feel ashamed of their heritage. No longer could they accept northern descriptions of the South as a disgraceful example of bigotry and fanaticism. No longer could they acquiesce in the progressive formula of industrialism, liberalism, and public education. They had to disavow the progressive ideal as the betrayal of everything they cherished. There was no reason to contort themselves into awkward conformity with a world view that they found repugnant.

The historic conservatism, repose, affability, generosity, humor, and piety that distinguished southern society had an abiding relevance and worth. Southern writers had to reassert their attachment to the southern tradition and their reverence for the southern way of life. "We come back to our life, finally," Davidson wrote, "because it matters most of all, and literary issues are minor by comparison." The way to establish a southern tradition in literature was to reestablish it in life. Realizing that ambition was, for Davidson, at the core of the Agrarian movement:

31. See Davidson's remarks in *Fugitives' Reunion: Conversations at Vanderbilt, May 3–5, 1956*, ed. Rob Roy Purdy (Nashville, 1959), 181.

Our total purpose was to seek the image of the South which we could cherish with high conviction and to give it, wherever we could, the finality of art in those forms, fictional, poetical, or dramatic, that have the character of myth and, therefore, resting on belief, secure belief in others, and, unlike arguments, are unanswerable, are in themselves fulfilled and complete. Such was the total purpose, of which the so-called "Agrarian" movement was but a declaratory preface. . . . [It was] the South against Leviathan, or in more positive terms, the South for the Southern tradition and our heritage of Western civilization. In the modern world there is no other way for the Southern writer to enjoy and use his rightful heritage and still be in any true sense a Southern writer. (*SWMW,* 60–61)[32]

To begin the quest for a heroic image of the South in which men could put their faith, the southern man of letters had to repudiate the supremacy of industrialism and depose science as the god of modernity. This was no doubt a desperate act, but the times demanded it.[33] Southern writers could not expect ordinary southerners to appreciate the beauty and importance of southern literature or the relevance of the southern tradition as long as they were dazzled by the discoveries of science or the products of industry. Any novel, any poem, any drama, any essay was meaningless unless it addressed the essential problem facing mankind in the modern world, which, as Davidson stated it, was "the remaking of life itself" (*ITMS,* 51).[34]

If Americans were to recover their virtuous way of life, they had to abandon industrialism and return to the land. The traditional, agrarian society kept the family intact, secured hearth and home, and provided stability, leisure, and peace for its inhabitants. The South offered a continuous illustration, through more than three hundred years of history, of such an agrarian community. Rooted in "family, blood-kinship, clanship, folk-ways, custom, community," southern society was "stable, religious, more rural than urban, and politically conservative" (*SRSY,* 172).

32. See also Davidson, "The Trend in Literature," 199–210, and *AL,* 93–96.

33. See Donald Davidson, "Agrarianism for Commuters," *American Review,* I (1933), 238–42, and *The Spyglass,* ed. Fain, 230–32.

34. See also *SRSY,* 3–22, 156–79, 254–66, and Donald Davidson, "The Talking Oaks of the South," *Shenandoah,* V (1953), 3–8, "The Trend in Literature," 183–210, *AL,* 65–101, 240–57, 339–46, and "Poetry and Progress."

The agrarian tradition existed as an organic and spiritual bond among southerners.

The experience of being southern was immanent. It was also ineffable, virtually unmediated by concepts or words. It was not, however, incomprehensible. The southern poet could discover and describe the genius of his people. He alone could reveal what they truly were, for poetry—the word spoken or, preferably, the word sung—conveyed the irreducible continuity of human existence, the "myth that is truest memory."[35]

Discovery and description remained separate from experience. No poet could tell all that he knew about being southern. He could relate certain values, sentiments, and beliefs that southerners held in common. He could depict their customs and rituals. He could capture their idiom and the cadence of their speech. To define what it meant to be southern, though, was beyond his talents and capacities. The southern tradition, Davidson believed, was an organic whole composed of indivisible parts and was not subject to analysis. His vision of the southern past was normative rather than analytical, rhetorical rather than dialectical. To be a good southerner one had to feel, to believe, and to act like a good southerner.

Davidson's assertion, though tautological, was not meaningless. He labored to find a language that would enable him to speak about permanence. He sought to limit or eliminate transience, inconstancy, and change from the southern tradition. In place of history, process, and change, he offered a vision that confirmed an unchanging southern identity. He eschewed history. The essential, elemental South was not in process, was not changing, was not becoming but was the immutable source of identity, order, meaning, and being.

Investing the South with a powerful destiny, he relied on the southern past not only to validate the southern tradition, to revitalize southern culture, and to vilify modernity but also to explain the meaning and purpose of life on earth. To violate the organic unity and continuity that characterized the southern tradition, therefore, meant violating the very essence of nature. Indeed, Davidson dissolved the distinctions between the order of southern society and the order of nature: nature and society were joined in the organic social order of the South. Such for Davidson was the real significance of Southern Agrarianism.

35. Donald Davidson, *Poems, 1922–1961* (Minneapolis, 1966), 24.

Davidson saw the present and the future almost wholly in terms of this heroic southern past, but his vision of the southern past was no mere invention or fabrication. It contained more than an element of truth. He was, however, concerned with far more than what had actually happened. The truth that captivated him was not a factual but a moral truth. He wanted less to know than to believe, to experience a pervasive act of faith. He aspired not only to understand the southern past but to sanctify it.[36]

Tate emphasized the futility of Davidson's quest. Davidson, Tate charged, had forgotten that all men, southerners included, were bound and circumscribed by their historical circumstances. When Davidson sang the glories of the heroic southern past remembered in the blood, he presupposed the existence of a unified sensibility that was inconceivable in any age but especially so in the modern. Tate detected in Davidson's thought a willful and desperate attempt to manipulate and control history. Davidson exhibited what Tate called the "mythic consciousness," not the "historical consciousness." He had lost the sense, Tate wrote, that the South "was the home of a spirit that may also have lived elsewhere and that this mansion, in short, was incidentally made with hands" (*ITMS*, 155 n. 1).[37] The South was, Tate asserted, a living community of human beings subject to the ordinary conditions and limitations of history: progress, change, and decay.

Davidson posited an image of the South as an almost tribal culture, isolated from modernity. The southern social order was grounded in a militant southern fundamentalism, which defied all rational attempts to define or dismiss it. In such a world, men did not understand themselves by what they might become at some unspecified moment in the future. They understood themselves by what they were from long experience.

Davidson longed to reconcile the characteristically modern separation of the individual and the community, the self and society. He wished to negate the artificiality of manufactured experience and to restore the original animating spirit of the humane life. Men could partake of their

36. For a lucid distinction between "history" and "the past," see J. H. Plumb, *The Death of the Past* (Boston, 1970), 11–17.

37. See also Lewis P. Simpson, "Donald Davidson and the Southern Defense of Poetry" (rpr. *SRSY*, v–xvi), and *The Brazen Face of History: Studies in the Literary Consciousness in America* (Baton Rouge, 1980), 167–80.

full humanity, he believed, only by participating in society. In the modern scientific-industrial order, however, men existed in seclusion from one another and were divided against themselves. Participation in society, and therefore the full realization of humanity, was impossible under modern conditions. Davidson attempted to eradicate the problems of modernity by reestablishing the ancient unity and continuity of human life that bound men together in a community of the living, the dead, and the unborn.

The reconstitution of traditional, agrarian society and the revitalization of the heroic southern past would end the antagonism between self and society. For Davidson, the interpsychic conflict between individuals and the intrapsychic conflict of the self were not inherent, ineradicable parts of the human condition. Under the right circumstances, men could resolve the psychic and social tensions that haunted them.

Davidson was explicitly reactionary, not nostalgic or sentimental. He did not wistfully pine for the "good old days" but yearned to recreate or approximate the past in some concrete, palpable form that would enable men to reconstitute more humane social relations than modernity allowed. He affirmed that if men lived under the gentle auspices of the humane tradition and fostered a stable, organic, agrarian social order, they could alter the conditions of human existence. A regenerate agrarian society in the South would thus surely cultivate "free" and "whole" men as readily as it produced corn, cotton, and wheat.

Instinctively, Davidson comprehended that science, industrialism, and rationalism jeopardized his vision. Scientific-industrial society did not need the past as much as did the traditional, agrarian society that it replaced. The cultural, intellectual, and emotional orientation of modern scientific-industrial society was toward change, process, and the future. Science and industry, Davidson insisted, were by their very nature revolutionary and destructive of the organic continuity of human life. They continually accelerated the processes of change. Like wild fire burning out of control, science and industry disfigured or consumed all that they touched. Modern men were, therefore, in danger of forgetting the past or, worse, of making it a curiosity that no longer commanded fidelity and belief. Davidson feared the consequences of the dissolution of the past. He regarded the southern past as an enduring source of identity, order, meaning, and being, and he recognized the continuing need for such a source in the modern world.

There was no other humane basis upon which to reconstruct a social order short of returning to "some kind of simple pastoral life." But the agrarian life moved neither backward nor forward. Its pattern was not linear. Agrarianism wanted nothing to do with the illusion of progress or the illusion of decadence. Davidson's version of agrarianism encompassed the past, present, and future in an intricate narrative that uncovered the deeper continuities of human existence: "Life is a timeless cycle, not a line, and the agrarian life establishes man within that natural cycle, where he belongs. Those who have argued the contrary are now seeing what it costs to support an industrial order, when it becomes the order of life; when indeed it gives orders, as it must, not only in the factory and office, but everywhere."[38]

Davidson's view of the southern tradition in the end assumed not only a heroic but a mystical aspect.[39] He envisioned the spiritual secession of the South from modernity and the spiritual unification of southerners in that "great vital continuum of human experience to which we apply the inadequate term 'tradition'" (*SRSY*, xvii). Since Appomattox, Davidson proclaimed, the cause of the South was "the cause of civilized society as we have known it in the Western world, against the new barbarism of science and technology controlled and directed by the modern power state." He concluded, "In this sense, the cause of the South was and is the cause of Western civilization itself" (*SWMW*, 15).

Despite his defense of segregation, which has indelibly fixed his reputation, Davidson proved a serious and insightful critic of modernism, an aspect of his thought frequently obscured as we grow more unwilling to forgive previous generations for the sin of not being like us. Indeed, he identified the central dilemma of modern life. He saw that science, technology, and the power state, the very forces supposed to liberate men from toil, drudgery, and tyranny, were paradoxically the authors of human bondage, exploitation, and suffering.

As the power and influence of rationalism, science, and technology grew, Davidson asserted, violence, chaos, and absurdity would result. In such a world, beyond human comprehension, proportion, and control,

---

38. Davidson, "The 'Mystery' of the Agrarians," 7.

39. See Randall Stewart, "Donald Davidson," in *South: Modern Literature in its Cultural Setting*, ed. Louis D. Rubin, Jr., and Robert D. Jacobs (Westport, Conn., 1961), 248–59, esp. 253–54.

men could no longer live without sacrificing the essence of their humanity. For Davidson, who lived in a world that he had no part in making and did not want, the crisis was at hand. He dramatized it in "Fire on Belmont Street," the epilogue to his most ambitious and controversial collection of poems, *The Tall Men:*

> Citizens, awake! Fire is upon you, fire
> That will not rest, invisible fire that feeds
> On your quick brains, your beds, your homes, your steeples,
> Fire in your sons' veins and in your daughters',
> Fire like a dream of Hell in all your world.
> Rush out into the night, take nothing with you,
> Only your naked selves, your naked hearts.
> Fly from the wrath of fire to the hills
> Where water is and the slow peace of time."[40]

Davidson's language in "Fire on Belmont Street" linked the image of a house fire raging out of control to the biblical prophecy that fire would be the agent of earthly destruction and, finally, to the image of the eternal fires of Hell that burn but do not consume. The forces of modernity, Davidson concluded, had produced a nightmare world that sent men and women fleeing from their homes in search of a sanctuary to harbor them.

Davidson counseled spiritual and, wherever possible, literal secession from modernity. Only two options remained: submission or war. Davidson opted for the latter course and became something of a guerrilla fighter against modernity in an effort to preserve the ideals and traditions of the South that he cherished. In "Sanctuary," he again took the stand from which he had never retreated:

> I only know
> This is the secret refuge of our race
> Told only from a father to his son,
> A trust laid on your lips, as though a vow
> To generations past and yet to come.
> There, from the bluffs above, you may at last
> Look back to all you left, and trace
> *His* dust and flame, and plan your harrying
> If you would gnaw his ravaging flank, or smite
> *Him* in his glut among the smouldering ricks.

40. Davidson, *Poems,* 181.

The issue for Davidson was victory or death. There was no compromise. Defeat meant annihilation. Victory meant freedom:

> . . . You may lie
> On sweet grass by a mountain stream, to watch
> The last wild eagle soar or the last raven
> Cherish his brood within their rocky nest,
> Or see, when mountain shadows first grow long,
> The last enchanted white deer come to drink.[41]

The men who would preserve the world that their fathers made had to return to the place where the beech trees drooped their boughs and the dark cedars grew with stubborn roots caressed by warm, primeval rains. They had to flee the modern world and get back to the great, good earth, to "a land still fought-for."

Nonetheless, there is a lingering melancholy, even fatalism, in Davidson's poem. It is "the last wild eagle" that soars, the "last raven" perched in its "rocky nest," and "the last white deer come to drink." These doubtless are the last free men. Whether they will survive and whether there will be others like them, Davidson did not say. Such questions haunt us still.

41. *Ibid.,* 73.

7

THE SOUTHERN CONSERVATIVE TRADITION
IN RETROSPECT AND PROSPECT: GENERATIONS
OF THE FAITHFUL HEART

Young men, the God of your fathers is a just
And merciful God Who in this blood once shed
On your green altars measures out all days,
And measures out the grace
Whereby alone we live;
And in His might He waits,
Brooding within the certitude of time,
To bring this lost forsaken valor
And the fierce faith undying
And the love quenchless
To flower among the hills to which we cleave,
To fruit upon the mountains whither we flee,
Never forsaking, never denying
His children and His children's children forever
Unto all generations of the faithful heart.
— Donald Davidson, "Lee in the Mountains"

John Crowe Ransom, Allen Tate, and Donald Davidson participated in and advanced a tradition that had long before their time constituted the most searching critique of American national development and of the more disturbing aspects of the modern world. This southern conservative tradition, which originated in reaction to the excesses of the Enlightenment, the French Revolution, and the industrial revolution, was from the beginning deeply critical of modernity.

Among its intellectual and spiritual heirs, Ransom, Tate, and Davidson agreed wholeheartedly about the evils of the modern world. Industrial-

ism and its handmaiden, science, had distorted and enslaved human intelligence and will, rendering life hurried, brutal, and mercenary. Men
worked no longer to enjoy the satisfactions of labor but to attain the
material rewards attached to it in a capitalist economy. They worked hard
because they had to, knowing that if they did not, any one of a thousand
other men was prepared to take their place. This exchange of freedom
and dignity for a mere livelihood and a craven security was far from
gratifying. The servants of the scientific-industrial regime, devoted to
productive efficiency, strove to eliminate anything that inhibited its realization. Religion, manners, hospitality, conversation, leisure, sympathy,
romance, and art served no purpose in conducting the business of life.

Apologists for industrialism maintained that education would rectify
the spiritual deficiencies that modernity bred. They proposed to employ
cultural experts to instruct men and women in the amenities, rescuing
culture from the deadening rigors of the assembly line, the blast furnace,
and the bookkeeper's ledger. Ransom, Tate, and Davidson disagreed.
They argued instead that men could not hope to revitalize "culture" by
"pouring in soft materials from the top" (*ITMS,* xliii–xliv). Culture
rested upon a material base and constituted the substance of the way men
thought, felt, and lived. A traditional culture could not be sustained in a
society committed to unbridled industrial capitalism. To attempt such a
reconciliation was naïve at best, arrogant at worst, and would only make
men and women more wretched and disconsolate by forcing them to
conform to a system that enslaved them.

For Ransom, Tate, and Davidson culture was an "imaginatively balanced life lived out in a definite social tradition . . . deeply founded in
the way of life itself—in its tables, chairs, portraits, festivals, laws, marriage customs" (*ITMS,* xliv). The most felicitous social arrangements,
they discovered, emerged from the history of the antebellum South, for
southern history offered a legacy from which to undertake the defense
of family, community, and tradition. Living together agreeably on the
land, holding in common a set of values, beliefs, customs, and practices,
southerners confounded the dehumanizing hegemony of science and
industry. The alienated, atomized individuals who peopled the modern
world could only appeal to some totalitarian government, some tyrannical Leviathan, to order their woeful lives and to end their confused
suffering. No such entreaty came from southerners, who were the sworn

enemies of the bureaucratic state that imposed such a perilous conformity upon its citizens.

Ransom, Tate, and Davidson sought to establish a social order that nurtured a sense both of personal independence and of public responsibility. No state, they believed, could ensure a proper balance between freedom and authority. Only a community in which no man was accountable only to and for himself could sustain this ideal of a unified social order that protected the individuality of all its members. The traditional, agrarian South represented such a community, formal and hierarchical yet flexible enough to accommodate individual aspirations and talents. Southerners prospered under this providential dispensation, savoring all the happiness and freedom to which their individual gifts entitled them.

Ransom, Tate, and Davidson concurred about the nature of the modern crisis and the evils of the modern world, but they often sharply disagreed about the character of southern society and the meaning of southern history. When they took their stand in 1930, they knew well what they opposed but could not consistently agree about what they advocated. Their champions and their adversaries alike have too long assumed a monolithic uniformity among them, yet the Agrarians themselves never fully or systematically articulated the divergences in their thought.[1] Almost from the first, however, they recognized that important and subtle differences existed.

In the earliest days of the Agrarian movement, Ransom, Tate, and Davidson, each in his own way, envisioned the South as a redemptive community on a divine mission within the vast drama of history. For them, being southern constituted a spiritual identity. They recognized Prometheus, Faust, and Satan as the summary figures of modernity and offered the image of the southern patriarch—pious, unselfconscious, conservative, even reactionary—as a moral alternative. The old southern gentleman yielded to his tradition and to his God.

Throughout his life, Davidson remained the most faithful to this ideal, yet even he altered it significantly. For Davidson, the experience of being southern became an existential condition sufficient in itself. Southern existence required no transcendent spirituality to give it meaning. Southerners who had not renounced their heritage knew in their blood and

---

1. For an exception, see Paul K. Conkin, *The Southern Agrarians* (Knoxville, 1988).

in their bones what it meant to be southern. Southern history and community, Davidson proclaimed, may have extended the hope of salvation to the modern world, but redemption from that history and that community themselves remained unnecessary.

Allen Tate identified the "mystical secularism" that commanded Davidson's imagination. John Crowe Ransom accused Davidson of indulging in romantic fancy. What Tate interpreted as gnostic heresy and Ransom perceived as marvelous nostalgia, Davidson accepted on faith. He could not entirely embrace Tate's belief in Christian revelation, and he condemned Ransom's growing devotion to the independent Republic of Letters. Neither religion nor art separated from the southern tradition held much meaning for Davidson.

Tate's affirmation of the irony and tragedy of southern history remains compelling. His contention that the Agrarians and their antebellum forebears attempted to create a religion from the secular, historical experience of the South stands as timely counsel against the arrogance and audacity of modern intellectual and political life. The full spectrum of history, including southern history, did not constitute for Tate an end in itself. The temporal was but an aspect of the eternal, and the mundane became intelligible and meaningful only with reference to the transcendent. All human activity had to be subordinate to divine will and revelation.

Ransom's participation in the Republic of Letters challenged the foundation of the southern tradition in a way that Tate's membership in the Roman Catholic Church did not. Liberated from the intricate bonds of prescriptive community, modern men of letters transferred the focus of history from society to self and located truth not in the mind of God but in the mind of the writer. Despite the allure of an aesthetic vision that posited the irreducible multiplicity of a nature not wholly subject to scientific inquiry or subservient to rational analysis, Ransom's solution to the dialectical conflict between tradition and modernity, the predominant theme in the cultural history of Western civilization since the Renaissance, estranged him from the original intentions of the Agrarian movement and from the original southern critique of modern alienation and rootlessness.

Davidson was quick to recognize and to condemn the implications of Ransom's thought. He admonished southern writers to surrender their vocation and undertake the more important and formidable task of reconstructing a social order that would again accommodate art. Davidson suggested that men of letters become citizens and statesmen, even if they had to sacrifice a measure of their identity and autonomy as writers to do so.

The burden fell on subsequent generations of southern conservative thinkers to address the disagreements that beset their predecessors. These new "defenders of the faith" not only had to rescue the southern tradition from opponents eager to discredit it but had to clarify and elaborate the Agrarians' original statement of principles. No disciples have worn the mantle of southern conservatism more elegantly or effectively than Richard M. Weaver and M. E. Bradford.

Weaver and Bradford shared a deep concern with the present difficulties and the future prospects of the southern conservative tradition. Following Davidson, they argued that southerners alone remained faithful to the ideals of the Founding Fathers and that southerners have been most American when they have been most southern. Secession was an act not of haughty defiance but of loving patriotism. For Weaver and Bradford, as for Davidson, the South was the most genuinely and pristinely American section of the country.

A student of Donald Davidson and John Crowe Ransom at Vanderbilt University and of Cleanth Brooks at Louisiana State University, Richard M. Weaver was the first thinker to attempt a systematic reevaluation of the southern intellectual tradition.[2] In his magisterial study *The Southern Tradition at Bay,* which he began during the early 1940s as a doctoral dissertation under Brooks's direction but which remained unpublished until 1968, Weaver asserted that northerners had looked to American history to certify their own nascent world view. But he could find little rationale to justify such an appropriation, save that Federal troops had won a bloody victory in a great war.

The dead could not speak. Defeat forced the living into silence. Even when southerners did venture to articulate their ideas, values, and beliefs, few Americans, northern or southern, felt compelled to pay attention.

2. On Weaver, see *RWWA,* 73–82; Donald Davidson, "The Vision of Richard Weaver: A Foreword," in *STB,* 13–24; Lisa Jane Tyree, "The Conservative Mind of the South: Richard Weaver" (M.A. thesis, University of Arkansas, 1988); and Brenan R. Nierman, "The Rhetoric of History and Definition: The Political Thought of Richard M. Weaver" (Ph.D. dissertation, Georgetown University, 1993).

Virtually by default, the North, the "majority section," appropriated and articulated the meaning of America.

In Weaver's view, the generation of southerners who came of age after the War for Southern Independence had little success in imposing their ideals on the nation and the world. Maligned and forgotten, they scorned their patrimony or managed only a stupid and inept defense of it. Southerners failed to cultivate their foremost virtues and neglected to invoke their "mandate of civilization." They may have lost their struggle for independence and in the process relinquished any opportunity to attain wealth, prestige, and power, but the tradition that their ancestors forged and passed on to them deserved preservation and allegiance. "If the world continues its present drift toward tension and violence," Weaver wrote in "Aspects of the Southern Philosophy," "it is probable that the characteristic Southern qualities will command an increasing premium."[3] For though the southern tradition did not present the image of accomplishment, prosperity, and triumph, it kept from extinction virtues integral to civilized life.

The southern tradition offered a core of resistance to the most powerfully corrupting forces of the modern age: rationalism, positivism, and science. While modern men exhausted themselves pursuing false gods, southerners stayed at home and worshiped the old-fashioned God of their fathers. Bitterly reviled, southerners nevertheless refused to countenance the domination and exploitation of nature, sensing that such ventures invited only confusion, immorality, and degradation.

Even in their mute and easily ridiculed veneration of the past, southerners knew better than to expect automatic, inexorable progress toward a level of civilization presently beyond human conception. The history of their region eradicated the utopian tendencies that they might once have entertained. The mechanical, thoughtless dogmas of science eased the modern conscience by promising peace and prosperity without the usual exertion and suffering. Men deluded themselves that "a great machine appeared to have been set in motion" to liberate them from their responsibilities to order their lives and to govern their world (*STB,* 31).

The southern tradition, alternately, enabled men to see that civilization lay not in the accumulation of wealth and power but in the moral

3. *The Southern Essays of Richard M. Weaver,* ed. George M. Curtis III and James J. Thompson, Jr. (Indianapolis, 1987), 208.

and aesthetic conceptions with which men's imaginations informed reality. Civilization required a sense of discipline, restraint, and piety toward God and nature. As fallible and finite creatures, men should endure joyously their submission to nature and their humility before God. "We must admit," Weaver wrote, "that man is to be judged by the quality of his actions rather than by the extent of his dominion" (*STB*, 32). Civilized men sought to invest life with meaning, not as individuals but as members of a solemn community inspired by a shared reverence for the past and a common vision of the future.

Modern men had abolished both the past and the transcendent as dimensions of meaning. They shed their inhibitions, wanting no constraints imposed upon their ambition. Impatience, egotism, and vanity attained epidemic proportions among them. Weaver feared that modern men, enclosed in the artificial environment of the city, not only had abandoned their piety toward nature but had lost their "sense of the difficulty of things," the knowledge that all human accomplishments required toil and sweat. Expecting science to gratify their hearts' desires, they fell to cursing and blaspheming when the world resisted their manipulation and control. Selfish, pampered, and naïve, the modern men who inhabited the urban wasteland enacted frightening reprisals against nature and humanity when they did not get their way.

Southerners had a more reserved demeanor and more modest expectations. Dispossessed of their homeland and their history, suffering all the indignities of a conquered people and an occupied nation, southerners clung fiercely to their traditions and neither pitied themselves nor lamented their fate. They accepted what they could not change. Even in defeat they approved the contingencies of nature and the vicissitudes of the human condition more gracefully than their sophisticated and prosperous northern counterparts. Trusting in God to bless and keep them and their loved ones, southerners acquired a penetrating wisdom and a tragic spirituality amid the wreckage of their world.

The intellectual effort expended in defense of slavery, Weaver conceded, vitiated southern assertions of moral superiority. If antebellum southerners did not achieve a complete reconciliation between their moral aspirations and their social reality, they nonetheless displayed greater sensitivity and conscience than the fanatics who proclaimed the equality of all men. Southerners realized that men possessed vastly diverse intellectual and moral endowments and that to judge all men alike would be an injustice to their individuality.

Men could attain their full stature as human beings only in relation to, not in isolation from, other men. If they wished to avoid a return to the state of nature, which Weaver regarded as a Hobbesian "war of all against all," then men fortunate enough to have been favored with exceptional aptitude had to bear responsibility for the welfare of those less auspiciously situated. As Christian gentlemen, southern slaveholders thus saw it as their obligation to care for the unfortunate creatures whom God had entrusted to them. Weaver, like virtually all of the antebellum proslavery theorists, maintained that aristocracy and patriarchy, which placed some men in the service and under the protection of others, constituted the best, if not the only, means of perpetuating a Christian social order in the modern world.

Southerners understood that the ability to formulate and enforce these kinds of social distinctions gave the true measure of civilization and constituted the one sure way to impose order on an indeterminate and perplexing world. They expressed little sympathy for the bewildered moderns who shrugged that the world was incomprehensible or who protested that it could not be other than they imagined it. The modern quandary arose, Weaver ascertained, from adherence to the pernicious doctrines of radical individualism and equality. He declared categorically that no man was ever born independent and free and that no two men were ever born equal. That egalitarianism had emerged as a generally desired social philosophy troubled him, for it threatened to obliterate the sources of discrimination and therefore the standards of judgment that demarcated civilization from savagery.

Without a vision of order preserved and disseminated by men of virtue, character, and intellect, civilization would collapse into a barbarism and chaos that would inevitably engender despotism and tyranny. Only style distinguished the uncivilized brute who seized power by force from the cultured demagogue who beguiled the unthinking masses. Americans of the 1950s and 1960s had embraced faulty definitions of words like "discrimination" and "segregation." These terms did not denote some unnatural pattern in human affairs that excluded some men from the benefits of society. Instead, they constituted an intuitive process of discretion, refinement, and taste whereby the "coarser natures, that is, those of duller mental and moral sensibility, [are] lodged at the bottom and those of more refined [are lodged] at the top" (*STB,* 36–37). Ideas of rank and inequality, Weaver asserted, were not inimical to liberty, for only an intelligible order made freedom possible.

Denial of such ostensibly self-evident propositions scandalized Weaver, as it had antebellum southern thinkers. Southern political theory, Weaver argued, provided a mechanism and a rationale to establish social order; northern political theory reduced to a series of unattainable yearnings or, worse, to the onset of lawless competition. The political romanticism of the North confined life to the narrow context of practical judgment and material interest. Northerners regarded as antiquated and absurd southerners' attachment to custom, tradition, and community, none of which immediately enhanced scientific utility, technological efficiency, commercial activity, or profits.

Weaver, who concerned himself with the spiritual character of society, applied the term *Yankee* as the ancient Greeks had used the term *barbarian.* *Yankees* represented the apotheosis of the insipid but savage bourgeois world that Weaver decried. In a letter to his friend and mentor, Donald Davidson, he clarified his thinking: "By the term 'bourgeois' I really meant the American philistine, the sort of person who thinks that the greatest thing in life is to own and display a Buick automobile. It seems to me that it is this soulless, desiccated middle class which has done most to destroy the concept of non-material value. The levelling process results in everyone's being pushed into it. Its characteristic mentality is a perfect ideological befuddlement. The Common Man of Henry Wallace's Common Century would be a member of this class."[4] The South, on the contrary, was "*the last non-materialist civilization in the Western World*" (*STB,* 391). Southern civilization extended refuge to the virtues of the spirit, to the sentimental affinities of the imagination that had no demonstrable connection with mere survival or profit but that ratified the dignity of human nature.

Weaver did not use "sentimental" in the usual sense of a nostalgic longing for some object, place, or person now gone. By "sentimental" he meant instead the attachment to those ideas and beliefs through which men defined themselves and through which they reaffirmed their identity and their convictions. In *Ideas Have Consequences,* he wrote of "the un-

---

4. Richard M. Weaver to Donald Davidson, February 28, 1948, in Donald Davidson Papers, Special Collections, Jean and Alexander Heard Library, Vanderbilt University.

sentimental sentiment" as the agent that restrained the minds and disciplined souls of men in their quest to fashion a "metaphysical dream of the world." The "unsentimental sentiment," that deep and abiding fidelity to old forms, customs, and traditions, refined, cultivated, and civilized men and women, moving them from "a welter of feeling to an illumined concept of what one ought to feel." Culture, for Weaver, was thus "sentiment refined and measured by intellect."[5]

The destruction of the sentimental and the spiritual dimensions of life, Weaver maintained, reduced human beings not to animals, who had their own kind of dignity, but to debased and ruined men. The dissolution of traditional bonds, the fragmentation of life, the confusion of values, the inability to distinguish good from evil anticipated the coming disorder. Weaver's already mounting sense that Western civilization had arrived at a crossroads only deepened as he witnessed the grave consequences that attended the rise and spread of communism and fascism in Europe and the astonishing violence of World War II. Under such circumstances, what did it profit men to study lost causes?

In his apologia for the South, Weaver did not merely chronicle the incidents and personalities, the ideas, policies, wars, and treaties that were the most conspicuous aspects of history. He also evaluated the revolutionary forces of modernism from the perspective of a traditional, religious, agrarian order. He removed events from the realm of temporal accident and sought to establish their meaning as universal moral lessons. Weaver spoke for the South but, like Davidson, attempted to find in southern history permanent values that explained more than the struggles of a particular people living in a particular place under particular circumstances.

Southerners, according to Weaver, displayed two characteristic but catastrophic shortcomings in their encounters with the modern world. First, no southern philosopher emerged to articulate the southern world view in a systematic way, to state categorically the fundamental assumptions and principles upon which that world rested, "to show why the South was right *finally*" (*STB*, 389). The South had no Thomas Aquinas, no *Summa theologiae*.

The second great southern failure, more difficult for Weaver to forgive, was the surrender of initiative. Since 1865, southerners, though full

---

5. See Richard M. Weaver, *Ideas Have Consequences* (Chicago, 1948), 18–23.

of dreams, had no faith in their own imprimatur. Too many of them accepted northern interpretations of history and northern definitions of culture and success. They read books written by northern authors, while those by southern writers gathered dust on the shelf. They imitated northern ways and northern manners, which suggested to Weaver that a deep sense of incompetence and inadequacy balanced the vaunted southern arrogance and conceit. A consciousness of failure enveloped the South, making it impossible for southerners to vindicate their way of life.

However inadequately southerners may have defended humanism, sentiment, tradition, and Christianity, the convictions for which they fought, though out of fashion, had not yet expired. The achievement and promise of the South, Weaver argued, posed a challenge to the modern world to abandon the demonic forces of science and technology and thereby to save the human spirit. Only restoration of a "non-materialist society" could rescue humanity from the nihilism that would result from spiritual timidity and moral defeat. Weaver uttered a message of salvation, not a call for reform. He urged southerners to recover the initiative that they had lost, without awaiting northern approbation.

The recreation of a religious world view, the finest attribute of the South, would halt the decline of civilization in the West. Christianity would impress upon the modern world a splendid image of mankind ennobled by communion with God through Christ. Living under this religious dispensation, modern men could discard the random truths of science and materialism, which brought a false equality in their wake and which were democratic and egalitarian only in the most treacherous sense. "We all stand today at Appomattox," Weaver lamented, "and we are surrendering to a world which this hypostatized science has made in our despite" (*STB,* 393–94). Under the iron fist of science, men enjoyed the debased equality of slavery.

Religion, morality, and art would again enable men to experience the drama of life and to feel the transformative power that accompanied the struggle between good and evil. Scientists and positivists had devised a sanitized universe in which men at best occupied the position of sophisticated automatons. Those who were yet intellectually and spiritually vital, however, wanted a challenge. They longed to live out the ancient wisdom that men must suffer unto truth. The failure to reinstate the religious world view, moral sentiments, and aesthetic sensibilities to their former primacy summoned harrowing possibilities for Western civilization: malaise, ennui, decadence, collapse.

The tone of dark foreboding that from time to time entered Weaver's writing suggested not only a deepening pessimism about the likelihood of reversing the dissolution of the West but also a growing resolve to forestall decline. In *Ideas Have Consequences,* he recognized that among those who predicted the end of the world were many who had a death wish. They hoped that the end would come soon, for they had lost the ability to cope with life. But nothing was more certain, Weaver wrote, "than that we are all in this together." He elaborated: "Practically, no one can stand aside from a sweep as deep and broad as the decline of a civilization. If the thinkers of our time cannot catch the imagination of the world to the point of effecting some profound transformation, they must succumb with it. There will be little joy in the hour when they can say, 'I told you so.'"[6] Weaver at times feared the worst. His generation watched ancient empires fall and ancient faiths crumble. They saw cities obliterated, populations displaced or destroyed, nations decimated. For four centuries men had grown increasingly confident that they had achieved a level of intellectual independence that rendered the ancient restraints superfluous. Having attained the very summit of human progress, though, modern men now beheld unprecedented eruptions of hatred and violence. Modern men, Weaver declared, echoing the words of Saint Matthew, lived amid "great tribulation, such as was not since the beginning of the world."[7] They had squandered their rich estate, and as the crisis deepened, they grew more and more apathetic about the consequences.

Modern men, Weaver concluded, had lost their moral orientation, had become "moral idiots," unable to respond to the perversion, brutality, or challenges of their world. Heartless and indifferent, they lived not immorally but amorally, without the capacity even to measure their descent and degradation. The unceasing belligerence against everything that stood outside the self was but a single manifestation of the modern crisis. The barbarian, who denigrated and destroyed all that was different and unfamiliar, and the neurotic, who mistrusted and manipulated others, were, for Weaver, the characteristic personalities of the modern age. Both

6. *Ibid.,* 187.
7. *Ibid.,* 2.

impiously put men before God, usurping the power to dispose of others' lives.

Indeed, modern men could not credit the reality of other selves. They lacked the imagination and the sympathy to appreciate and respect other lives or to recognize that the sanctity of their own lives depended on the existence of a beneficent human community. Mystified by their curious disaffection from nature and humanity, modern men could not discover in reason or science a remedy for their affliction. In their confusion they adopted a cure far worse than the disease that ravaged them.

Weaver returned to the South for an antidote. "The Old South may indeed be a hall hung with splendid tapestries in which no one would care to live," he wrote in *The Southern Tradition at Bay*, "but from them we can learn something of how to live" (*STB*, 396). The sense of obligation, humility, honor, and faith embodied in the southern tradition offered the most complete image of a Christian community in the modern world and thus held out the only humane promise of sparing Western civilization a cataclysmic end.

Like Richard Weaver, M. E. Bradford reacted against the solipsism and alienation that define the modern spirit. Private judgment alone, he insisted, was insufficient to determine proper conduct and appropriate belief. Too often history has recorded individual acts of piety ostensibly undertaken to promote the general welfare—acts that, in reality, represented the apotheosis of the self at the expense of humanity. Bradford, too, ordained the superiority of community, rich in history and tradition, as the authoritative instrument of public governance and private morality. "Extreme individualism *and* subjectivism *and* interiority," he wrote, "are the reverse side of collectivism and oriental subservience" (*RI*, i). As a self-declared Whig and republican, Bradford formulated an interpretation of American history that enabled him to recover, articulate, and emphasize the eighteenth-century tradition of civic humanism that presumed individual rights derived from social obligations.

As a southern conservative, Bradford wanted to do more than merely preserve or restore traditional social and political arrangements. In the preface to *The Reactionary Imperative*, he carefully distinguished between the "conservative impulse" to resist change and the "reactionary imperative" to operate according to a set of normative principles. Conservatism was not enough. Echoing Tate, Bradford declared that reaction was necessary, for in the spiritual, intellectual, and political milieu of the late twentieth century merely to conserve sometimes meant to perpetuate the outrageous and the horrible.

To justify inhumanity and brutality by anticipating perfection in the future was not, for Bradford, politically tenable or morally acceptable. It was the method of the decadent bureaucrats or blood-thirsty gangsters who masqueraded as committed public servants or respectable statesmen. It was better, Bradford maintained, to invoke the image of former happiness and to insist on a restoration that approximated older, time-tested arrangements.

From Bradford's point of view, the contemporary predicament required the southern reactionary to become self-conscious. Menaced by the Promethean will-to-power and the Faustian illusion of omnipotence, the reactionary must force himself to carry out perilous acts of private judgment to revive a tradition that will render such acts superfluous, if not impossible. Bradford's dilemma coincided with Tate's and, in another way, with Davidson's attempt to reverse the roles of mind and society as the models of consciousness and history. "The argument that the conservative mind is always in difficulty when it becomes aware of itself *as conservative* but is rarely articulate until thus provoked," Bradford asserted, "is an accurate description of a painful paradox" (*RI,* iii).

He acknowledged the validity of Tate's insight that modern southern conservatives must take hold of their tradition "by violence." Neither Bradford nor Tate intended revolutionary violence, as many of their critics pretended. Instead, Bradford, like Tate, understood as "violence" the wrenching effort to turn mind against itself, to use reason to achieve essentially nonrational, spiritual ends. As Bradford frequently noted, twentieth-century southern conservatives inherited a magnificent legacy from the wise men who established the American republic, for they had found a "better guide than reason."[8]

The men who incited and fought the American war for independence, according to Bradford, did not aspire to "invent" a new nation to satisfy a commitment to some imprecise ideology. They merely sought to preserve the liberties that they, as British subjects, had long enjoyed. King George III and Parliament willfully altered these bonds, unjustly

8. Bradford adopted this phrase as the title for his collection of essays about the American Revolution.

depriving the colonists of their former autonomy. The king substituted tyranny for legitimate authority and thus forfeited his right to rule. His American subjects no longer owed the Crown allegiance. They had not only the right but the duty to throw off the oppression and to conserve their old way of life, even if such an act of preservation required war.[9]

In Bradford's estimation, the American Revolution was not innovative but conservative. The colonists took up arms against the British to perpetuate a cherished heritage and way of life. The "rebels" believed that they faced a vast conspiracy among the king's ministers and certain members of Parliament to deprive them of their birthright. They thought that the government had fallen into the hands of men no longer concerned for the colonists' security, property, or posterity. They had no designs upon seizing the king's power but simply desired to resign from his domain and to carry with them the traditions and the laws that had formerly regulated their lives.

Although they did in the end create an independent nation, Americans began with a disposition to establish a new unity based on old and familiar precedents. The Crown itself forced independence upon them with repeated efforts at coercion and, at last, with its resort to violence. If they hoped to retain their identity as a free and independent people, maintain their sense of rectitude, and earn a place of honor in the memories of their descendants, the colonists had no choice save to respond as they did.

The principal document of the Revolution, the Declaration of Independence, embodied the colonists' aspirations. In it, Bradford argued, Thomas Jefferson did not speak *ex cathedra* about the natural rights of man; his purposes were more limited. The body of the Declaration consists of a bill of particulars detailing the "abuses and usurpations" of George III. Apart from its immediate historical context and its reliance

---

9. This interpretation of the American Revolution was generally held in the antebellum South. See especially William H. Trescot, *The Diplomacy of the Revolution: An Historical Study* (New York, 1852). On Trescot, see Eugene D. Genovese, *The Slaveholders' Dilemma: Freedom and Progress in Southern Conservative Thought, 1820–1860* (Columbia, S.C., 1992), 76–85, and David Moltke-Hansen, "William Henry Trescot," *Dictionary of Literary Biography*, XXX, 310–19, and "A Beaufort Planter's Rhetorical World: The Contexts and Content of William Henry Trescot's Orations," *Proceedings of the South Carolina Historical Association* (1981), 120–32.

on the tradition of English common law and constitutional precedent, the Declaration of Independence, for Bradford, remained unintelligible.

Jefferson alleged that the removal of British subjects across the sea did not entail the alienation of their rights as subjects of the Crown. But the new forms of taxation imposed on them and other related offenses against the "immunities and privileges granted and confirmed" in the royal charters and "secured by their several codes of provincial law" exposed them now to such unwarranted deprivation. The colonial charters, Bradford interpreted Jefferson to have said, had become worthless.

By law, custom, and blood the North American colonies were part of the English *res publica* until the Crown severed that historic connection. With the enactment of the Prohibitory Acts in August, 1775, the king classified the colonists as "rebels" almost a year before they claimed that designation for themselves. Jefferson's Declaration, Bradford contended, demonstrated that the colonists believed both king and subject were accountable to law and that they occupied their different stations and enjoyed their diverse rights and privileges only within and under the law.

In Bradford's interpretation of the American war for independence, George III was the outlaw who had violated his sacred trust as regent. The colonists appear as unusually conservative and prudent men determined to stay within the confines of the law. Only when the Crown systematically denied them direct representation, confiscated their property, quartered hostile troops among them, and ignored their entreaties did they at last take up arms against his majesty's government.

Jefferson's silence on certain matters in the Declaration of Independence was, for Bradford, as revealing as his utterances. The Declaration represented the colonists' official bill of divorcement from the king, a response to proceedings already initiated by a petition filed against them in his behalf. Tory sentiment and indifference notwithstanding, the colonists as a people were largely united in their desire to separate from England and voiced their collective will through elected representatives assembled in local conventions.

Hence, Bradford concluded, Jefferson spoke of liberty and equality as corporate, not as individual, rights. In the Declaration, Jefferson staked nothing on an assertion of the universal natural rights of individual men. The only rights that men possessed, and the only rights that the colonists were prepared to defend, were their rights as citizens within the corporate bonds of a society governed by law. The traditional American definitions of freedom and equality, Bradford wrote, have thus been "a 'social bond individualism'—a freedom which has as its precondition the survival of an anterior social identity." Thus, he argued, "whatever we have said of the Declaration of Independence, we begin to think socially by assuming that specific rights are determined by an individual's place in the social reality, are measured by that reality and are inseparable from it" (*RI,* 139).

All men were created equal in their right to expect from government the freedom from bondage, from genocide, and from the unlawful expropriation of property. It was inconceivable to Bradford, as it was to the Founding Fathers, that an individual be granted boundless freedom without purpose, merely to satisfy private whims and personal desires. The law that united men as citizens within the polity guaranteed them liberty and equality only as members of society. No such assurances attended upon life in the state of nature. If men were free and equal in that mischievous abstraction called the state of nature, as a few of the Founding Fathers themselves sometimes conceded, they were also unprotected from coercion, exploitation, and violence.[10] Men who really wished to enjoy full equality, Bradford suggested, could live alone in the forests, where natural rights were admitted, until the wolves arrived.

The "self-evident" truths upon which Jefferson discoursed, Bradford maintained, were thus assembled as historical evidence against the king's offenses and not asserted as categorical statements of principle to demonstrate the equality of individual men. It was obvious, that is, "self-evident," to every reasonable man that no people should have to endure the denial of the rights and securities that alone made civilized life possible. "If even the Turk and the infidel would not as a people submit to a government such as George III proposes to impose through Lord [William] Howe's army," Bradford explained, "how can Englishmen be expected to agree to that arrangement?" (*BGR,* 40).[11] Such were the "inalienable rights" to resist tyranny with which the Creator had endowed all men.

The Declaration of Independence and the Constitution of the United States, Bradford insisted, are in perfect accord on the question of equality. By conscious design, the Constitution was written as an extremely lim-

10. See *RWWA,* 31.
11. See also M. E. Bradford, *A Worthy Company: Brief Lives of the Framers of the United States Constitution* (Marlborough, N.H., 1982).

ited document establishing a legal framework and a governmental structure to complement Americans' common origins and purposes. The
Constitution rested on a prior bond existing between the several free and
independent states and did not annul that autonomy and independence
when adopted. The Declaration of Independence was a necessary prelude
to the Constitution, making possible the free act of ratification in the
constitutional conventions that assembled in the states.

The contents of the Declaration, however, are not implicit in the
Constitution, Bradford pointed out. Numerous specific rights not men-
tioned in the Declaration of Independence are affirmed in the Constitution. More important, he noted, the Constitution withholds particular
rights that liberal scholars and critics have long thought inherent in the
Declaration. The Constitution does not provide for equal suffrage in state
or federal elections, nor does it sanction equal rights for women, certain
religious dissenters, blacks, or Indians. The Constitution endorsed slavery
and even guaranteed continuation of the slave trade until 1808.

Nonetheless, the adoption of the Constitution completed the work
begun in the Revolution. It secured for these Englishmen-become-
Americans the right to a limited and representative government. Although they initially had to alter and eventually to abandon their English
identity to safeguard their birthright, the Americans did so for no "light
or transient causes," and they prepared to suffer the consequences of their
temerity. When English tyranny liberated the colonists from the traditional source of prescriptive law, they sought a new mechanism through
which to sustain a lawful political order. Until they could devise such a
means, as William Henry Drayton of South Carolina stated, no true
liberty could exist among them.

Representatives of the people, drawing on their unique history and
genius, thus composed and authorized a new constitution to replace the
defunct English constitution. A living covenant that grew out of their
collective experience, the Constitution remained sovereign only insofar
as it enhanced the natural associations that already existed between free
men: the ties of family, friendship, neighborhood, community, church.

The Constitution directed the operations of government and defined
the appropriate ways of conducting the political affairs of the Republic.
Committed to upholding specific procedures rather than to realizing ultimate objectives, the Founding Fathers had the judgment and foresight
to build into their regime prudential impediments designed to mitigate

against whatever ideologies their less thoughtful descendants tried to enact. A strict reading of the Constitution, Bradford thought, would clarify the qualifications that it imposed on the scope and agency of government. It neither prescribed nor defended the rights of man outside the context of society. It neither proposed nor elaborated a millennial vision of the future but reflected and codified the historical experience of a particular people.

In its origins, Bradford argued, the United States was a "nomocratic" rather than a "teleocratic" republic. Applying terms borrowed from the English political philosopher Michael Oakeshott, he reasoned that the Founding Fathers refused to divinize the state or to seek salvation in politics.[12] Christian faith and common sense suppressed that tendency. Experience instilled in their hearts a distrust of remote and arbitrary authority that imposed its own agenda on local affairs. It also made them wary of embracing "large purposes" and hostile to using government to achieve some rational, contrived, predetermined end ("teleocracy") rather than to preserve an already flourishing way of life ("nomocracy").

Southerners, throughout their history, resisted teleology. They came to the New World not to find a New Eden or to found a New Zion but to obtain more land, a larger freehold, than they could have acquired in the old country. The Englishmen who settled in Virginia and Carolina were not in intellectual and political rebellion against their English heritage, like those who arrived in Massachusetts during the seventeenth century. Southerners remained faithful to their distant king, but circumstances required important adjustments and modifications in their inheritance. They did not duplicate the village life that prevailed in the English countryside, nor did they recapitulate the dogmatic politics of the English court. The South was from the beginning coincidentally republican, without a theory to describe the practice. Southerners tolerated the few royal placemen and officials who lived among them, and they welcomed the few garrisons that defended them from pirates, Indians, and the French, Dutch, and Spanish. But they grew restive at the prospect of unfriendly authorities wielding arbitrary power in colonial affairs.

Cautious, discerning, and worldly, southerners had little patience with the a priori rights of man and refused to utter unwarranted pronounce-

12. See Michael Oakeshott, *Rationalism in Politics* (New York, 1962) and *On Human Conduct* (Oxford, 1975).

ments on human nature. They preferred instead to operate from history, precedent, and circumstance and had no commerce with abstract theories of justice, liberty, and equality. They had settled certain fundamental questions about the nature and meaning of existence before they undertook serious deliberation about a preferred response to a particular situation. The need to belabor first principles or to reinvent their world each time they determined a course of action did not occur to them.

For such people, Bradford argued, reality inclined to be formal and external rather than idiosyncratic and subjective. Southerners rejected as inappropriate to a constitutional regime the "Puritan habit of mind" that ceaselessly probed the metaphysical foundations of reality. The colonists who journeyed to New England honored no authority but reason, accepted no truth except the absolute, had no preference save for restless innovation. Southerners, on the contrary, relished the comforts of their inherited religious and political identity. Their deepest convictions remained unspoken.

Informed by a sense of history, a humble view of human nature, and a modest hope for the future, southerners assumed the goodness of God's creation and the decency of their civilization. Those who carried forward the southern tradition were men who did not get "too good for their raisin'," who could not imagine their identities or their rights outside of or anterior to a network of extended families linked by blood, marriage, religion, and cooperation in a common enterprise. They were not alienated men. "From the high road which leads to a 'faraway country' and from the topless heights of the 'imperial self,'" Bradford wrote, "they kept their distance, and thus avoided some of the Faustian temptations contained within the ambitious, proud example of most Renaissance, Enlightenment, and Romantic thought: the equation, in a series of historic steps, of personhood with will, intellect, and sensibility" (*RI*, 121). It was this patrimony that antebellum southerners fought a great war to vindicate and defend.

The War for Southern Independence, Bradford declared, was as reactionary as the American Revolution. The historic southern conservatism asserted itself in the sectional conflict to oppose the extension and consolidation of centralized government and to affirm the merit and worth of an established way of life. Until agitation over slavery quickened in the late 1810s and early 1820s, American statesmen resisted the temptation to use the power of the federal government to regulate or to reform domestic economic, social, and political relations.

The Missouri debates of 1819 and 1820 marked the first of many attempts to alter existing arrangements, dictating that states could gain admission to the Union only after satisfying certain federally mandated requirements that determined the status of blacks within their borders now and in the future. The original thirteen colonies had not been constrained by this unprecedented proscription. The opponents of slavery employed what Bradford described as "chiliastic language" and appealed to millennial imperatives to justify their violation of the sacred trust of the Constitution. Their radical disposition augured the coming of a war that, from Bradford's perspective, would discredit the original motivation for union and would disgrace the accomplishments of the Founding Fathers.

Lincoln's election in 1860 tolled the death knell for the Union that Lincoln himself so desperately wanted to save. According to Bradford, as the leader of a "Puritan people," Lincoln prosecuted a bloody war against the Confederacy, which he misidentified as an imperial slavocracy. Lincoln excused and even encouraged the barbarism of Union troops in direct correspondence to the evil that he discerned among his southern neighbors, whom he had made his enemies. Bradford's principal objection to Lincoln's politics derived from Lincoln's interpretation of the Declaration of Independence as embodying the "deferred promise" of equality. Lincoln's "second founding," in Bradford's view, introduced for the first time in American history the prospect of endless social upheaval and political revolution. For Lincoln had dedicated himself to realizing the proposition that equality of opportunity and equality of condition were the foundation and purpose of union.

Lincoln distorted the meaning of American history, Bradford insisted, and his "martyrdom" removed him beyond the reach of dispassionate historical inquiry and honest critical assessment. Lincoln's political gnosticism, he concluded, fundamentally altered the character of the nation, distancing future generations from the republicanism of the Founding Fathers and initiating much of the confusion that has tormented American political life in the twentieth century. According to the myth that surrounds this "melancholy man from Illinois," the corporate life of the United States depended for its continuation on the shedding of sacred blood. Lincoln became, Bradford announced, the American version of the "dying god."[13] Christ may have "died to make men holy," but Lincoln "died to make them free." Even in death, he altered the course of American history.

Bradford's chief indictment concerned Lincoln's duplicity about the status and future of blacks in the United States. To unify disparate elements within the northern electorate, Lincoln assumed a moral position on slavery that he incorporated into his political and military policies. But what began as a strategy designed to win votes and sustain an increasingly unpopular war, Bradford maintained, had more durable and unfortunate consequences.

Lincoln's insistence that the Declaration of Independence implicitly condemned slavery and obligated whites to honor that pledge threatened a radical transformation of American society. This moral posturing cost him but little. His claims to moral superiority rested not on a specific appeal for Negro rights but on an abstract appeal for the universal rights of man. A commitment to the doctrine of natural rights, Bradford insisted, "which will not challenge the Black Codes of Illinois, which promises something like them for the freedmen in the South, or else offers him as alternative the proverbial 'one-way-ticket to nowhere' is a commitment of empty words." He noted it was "only an accident that the final Reconstruction settlement provided a bit more for the former slave—principally, the chance to vote Republican; and even that 'right' didn't last, once a better deal was made available to his erstwhile protectors" (RWWA, 145). Lincoln's grand rhetoric concealed the enactment of legislation to prevent blacks' migration to the North, the elaboration of a northern system of racial segregation and discrimination, and the exploitation of black labor throughout the country.

The hypocrisy and cynicism that Bradford saw as distinguishing Lincoln's public career bequeathed to subsequent generations of northerners a piously self-congratulatory political inheritance. During the more than 130 years since Lincoln's assassination, his spiritual progeny have developed the habit of concealing their larger political agenda behind the facade of racial tolerance and generosity. Bradford contended that northern radicals, from the abolitionists to the Radical Republicans to the New Left, used blacks to further their own political ends while making only minimal improvements in the conditions that prevailed among the

13. See RI, 219–27. See also RWWA, 143–56.

objects of their apparent beneficence. The radicals who ostensibly spoke for blacks, whether in the 1860s or in the 1960s, consistently promised more than they could deliver or, indeed, than they were willing to give.

During the "Second Reconstruction," this northern, specifically New England, predilection became national orthodoxy. The "civil rights revolution" that occurred during the last thirty-five years represented, in Bradford's opinion, the first and only time in American history the nation capitulated utterly to the millennial tendencies that compose part of its collective identity. Bradford discouraged these millennial dreams of perfection and submitted that procedures undertaken artificially to elevate blacks and other "minorities" constituted the most perilous of reforms. The effort to improve the lot of blacks invited the abolition of both liberty and the only equality that Americans should universally approve: simple equality within the circumscribed scope of the law.

Employment quotas, forced busing, welfare entitlements, economic subsidies, and the other products of affirmative action legislation, Bradford thought, intended to ensure not only equality of opportunity but an ultimately impossible equality of condition. These astonishing measures negated every statutory and historical right of American citizenship in the interest of achieving some teleological abstraction known as an integrated, egalitarian society.

The logic of Lincoln's doctrine of Union, that the United States must "be all one thing or all another," shattered the delicately balanced multiplicity that historically characterized the American experience. Have the changes encouraged by the civil rights movement, enacted in Congress, and defended through the courts, Bradford asked, been worth all the damage inflicted on the Constitution of the United States? The turmoil of the civil rights crusade risked the conversion of a nomocratic, customary, procedural government into a teleocratic instrument that politicians and bureaucrats could harness to accomplish whatever changes they desired. Bradford wondered whether "the tradition of restricted Federal authority must give way because the grievances or misfortunes of one segment of our population are more important than limitations on the scope and out reach of the law which honor the liberty of all free men—or at least attempted to do so before the fundamental law was reconstructed by judicial ingenuity into something 'new and strange'" (*RI*, 97).

Tolerance and diversity, the sacrosanct values in contemporary American politics, exalt ideological objectives without regard to the potentially harmful consequences that such commitments may inflict on our inherited way of life. American statesmen, even conservative statesmen whom Bradford maintained should have known better, either adopted the political language of their opponents or else bore silent witness to the violation of hallowed American principles, fearing to besmirch their reputations and, perhaps, to lose the next election. Critical and suspicious of liberal programs, Bradford himself displayed throughout his life a rare courage in repeated encounters with incivility, hostility, ostracism, and unwarranted charges of bigotry, racism, and inhumanity.

Bradford challenged the liberal teleology currently fashionable in American political discourse and accused liberal ideologues of preferring the lesser to the greater social good and obligation. Liberals were, in his analysis, mindlessly determined to pursue various ideological resolutions, such as "liberty and justice for all" or "all men are created equal," to which they gave absolute primacy whatever the cost to the commonwealth or to the supposed beneficiaries, who generally found themselves betrayed. The southern conservative tradition, Bradford was convinced, offered an antidote to liberal hegemony and provided a vital nomocratic force in the public life of the nation.

Southerners persevered in their devotion to corporate liberty and persisted in their skepticism about natural rights and in their suspicion of individual equality. Long ago, Bradford recalled, southerners accepted the idea that only identical persons who had already achieved an equality of condition could enjoy equality of opportunity. The abiding customs and laws of the South took into account the different endowments of different men and yet made it possible for each man to work out his own destiny under God. These felicitous arrangements provided a bulwark against the rise of egalitarianism in the South, just as they quelled southern enthusiasm for abstract notions of justice. Southerners resisted the liberal nostrums of official egalitarianism and distrusted an omnipotent government that bludgeoned them into submission, especially concerning the issue of race.

Bradford conceded that the "color line" still existed in the South and that it would never prove easy to eradicate through legislative action or moral suasion. Racial coexistence, he predicted, would continue to be a process of regular and sensitive renegotiation. Like other contemporary southern conservative thinkers, he sought to reach a moderate and frank accommodation with blacks and expressed pleasure at the accomplishments of black students, black businessmen, and black professionals.

He feared, however, that professions of tolerance and equality too often concealed old assumptions that operated to no one's benefit. Southerners, in Bradford's view, had done well enough in maintaining racial peace, better, in fact, than most others who deplored southern customs, southern institutions, and southern people. If southerners did not solve the racial problems that troubled them and their ancestors and that would, no doubt, trouble their children, Bradford could justifiably feel relieved that it was "no longer necessary to discuss the South exclusively in terms of its racial practices and problems."[14] The guilt of the next generation of white southerners, he predicted, would result not from their treatment of blacks but from their infidelity to the ways of their fathers.

Yet for all his candor and generosity, Bradford never discovered a satisfactory basis of citizenship for black Americans. Then again, neither has anyone else, including the various black leaders, past and present. During the 1890s, for example, Booker T. Washington advocated vocational education for blacks precisely at the moment when the triumph of the corporation had foreclosed the possibilities of upward economic and social mobility for the working class. Similarly, during the 1990s, black leaders such as Jesse Jackson and others have called for a "Marshall Plan for the Cities" in a time of diminishing financial resources, corporate downsizing, and the emergence of a high-tech economy that may render a generation of Americans, black and white, economically obsolete. Even should proposals to create enterprise zones or invitations to invest in the ghettos prove economically feasible, they could not succeed in the absence of law and order. As long as drug abuse, violence, and despair prevail among those whom society euphemistically calls the "underclass," we may entertain no expectations that they will enjoy the benefits or share the responsibilities of American citizenship.

Bradford's interpretation of American history complicated his analysis of contemporary racial attitudes, issues, and policies. He argued persuasively that the Founding Fathers did not intend to grant unconditional equality to anyone. He ignored, though, or at least de-emphasized, the

14. M. E. Bradford, "Not in Memoriam, but in Defense," in *Why the South Will Survive,* ed. Clyde N. Wilson (Athens, Ga., 1981), 217.

historical origins of the United States as a capitalist nation whose early prosperity rested paradoxically on a plantation economy driven by slave labor.

The conservative and provisional liberalism that had assumed ideological prominence by the mideighteenth century advanced the sanctity of private property and the prerogative of capital accumulation, while at the same time it accentuated the subjugation of women and the inferiority of blacks. Thus, not only did the Constitution contribute procedural clarity to the operation of government. It also attempted to facilitate the development of a political consensus among white, male property owners and to reconcile two antithetical notions of property. It secured the rights of propertied men as a class and, as a compromise, accorded to blacks in the southern states a legal existence only as slaves, rendering each three-fifths of a person, specifically three-fifths of a free worker, to enhance the political influence of their masters in the House of Representatives.

Liberals and conservatives who have been critical of Bradford's conclusions, such as the political philosopher Harry Jaffa, argue that the Constitution implies broader rights than it specifies. Their criticism notwithstanding, Bradford's interpretation of the Revolution and the Constitution as conservative remains at least partially persuasive.[15] But the American war for independence, which may have had conservative origins, was also revolutionary, as the eighteenth-century European conservatives who denounced it at the time recognized. Bradford, on the contrary, envisioned a revolution in America that not only was not revolutionary but indeed inhibited the emergence of revolutionary sentiments.

Bradford sought to clear away the rubble of historical interpretation beneath which the genuinely conservative revolution lay buried and to impart its true character to a generation that had lost contact with its collective past. His work was an act of reclamation and recovery, assuming more fully the character of genealogy than of history. His search for the origins and the ancestry of a tradition enabled him to ignore or to dismiss much of the history that interfered with or obscured that tradition.

15. See Forrest McDonald, *We the People: The Economic Origins of the Constitution* (Chicago, 1958), *E Pluribus Unum: The Formation of the American Republic, 1776–1790* (Indianapolis, 1979), and *Novus Ordo Seclorum: The Intellectual Origins of the Constitution* (Lawrence, Kans., 1985).

In carrying out this project, Bradford enjoyed no small measure of success. Yet he still had to explain how, over the next two centuries, the Revolution of 1776 and the counterrevolutionary Constitution of 1787 facilitated the development of the most important liberal, democratic, capitalist nation in history. He could not blame everything on Lincoln's perversion of the Founding Fathers' intentions or on the outcome of the Civil War, for the northern states had adopted bourgeois social relations long before 1860 or 1865.[16]

Like other southern conservative thinkers, Bradford refused to countenance the idea that slavery inhibited southern acceptance of free labor and the world market or that it explained the growing differences between North and South in political, cultural, and religious matters. Instead, he maintained that the generation of southerners who seceded from the Union and fought a war of independence did so not to preserve slavery and the social order based on it but because they thought of themselves as the faithful heirs to the Revolution and the true exponents of republicanism. That southerners fought both to defend slavery and to preserve their republican heritage has given historians ample material with which to fashion imaginative interpretations of the origins, character, and development of the American Republic.

When southerners undertook to defend their heritage against northern aggression, Bradford declared, they were not intent on upholding man's right of property in man. Rather, they were determined to preserve the original character of government and society that their ancestors had won in the Revolution and had codified in the Constitution. "The South," he wrote, "thought and acted in its own way *before* the peculiar institution was much developed within its boundaries"(*RI,* 118).[17]

Slavery, contrary to Bradford's assertions, was vital to the development of antebellum southern society. Moreover, it is impossible not to concede

16. This process, of course, was contentious and fraught with ambiguity and ambivalence. See Jonathan Prude, *The Coming of the Industrial Order* (New York, 1983); *The Countryside in the Age of Capitalist Transformation: Essays in the Social History of Rural America,* ed. Steven Hahn and Jonathan Prude (Chapel Hill, 1985); Charles Sellers, *The Market Revolution: Jacksonian America, 1815–1846* (New York, 1991).

17. See also Walter Kirk Wood, "The Union of States: A Study of Radical Whig-Republican Ideology and Its Influence upon the Nation and the South, 1776–1861" (Ph.D. dissertation, University of South Carolina, 1978), and "The Central Theme of Southern History: Republicanism, Not Slavery, Race, or Romanticism," *Continuity: A Journal of History,* IX (1984), 33–71.

that race bequeathed to the South a decisive and painful legacy. Bradford properly insisted that the Constitution made no provision for universal equality but that it established only limited equality before the law, which was already limited in its scope. The exercise of justice did not, therefore, depend on social, political, or economic equality. Different men could occupy different stations in life and still enjoy the benefits appropriate to their status. However accurate and convincing Bradford's assessment of the Constitution, his judgments, nevertheless, had some distressing ramifications for blacks.

Blacks, like women, have not historically enjoyed full and consistent equality before the law—the kind of equality that Bradford admitted the Constitution legitimately ensured. Even if we disregard the question of civil rights, it is plain that the law did not always protect, or even consider, the legal rights of blacks. Since passage of the Fourteenth Amendment, the Constitution dictated that all Americans as citizens were entitled to "the equal protection of the laws." Nevertheless, the law still did not consistently apply to blacks with impartiality. They did not come before the law as equals. The law, in fact, historically discriminated against their persons, their property, and their interests and thus placed their citizenship on a rather more tenuous foundation than the citizenship of white Americans, especially that of white males.

Bradford always insisted bravely and well that people who began with different endowments would end in different conditions, and that "equality of opportunity" was therefore a sham. But when the law itself conspired to prevent blacks from enjoying the rights to which they were legally entitled, where could they turn for justice?

Another southern conservative thinker, the historian George C. Rogers, Jr., saw the problem clearly enough. He wrote that "we have affirmative action because the South was too slow in ending segregation and race discrimination (and the South should be ready to accept these criticisms)."[18] Rogers exposed one of the most damaging political and philosophical weaknesses of southern conservatism. In principle, southern conservatives have always wanted social and political reform to occur slowly and carefully under the guidance of a benevolent and enlightened ruling elite, but fundamental, structural change rarely takes place that way. Almost always, entrenched interests change course or make con-

18. *Why the South Will Survive,* ed. Wilson, 89.

cessions only when confronted by powerful, external forces. On rare occasions, the national state has bèen less oppressive of liberty and more protective of justice than provincial arrangements.

During the 1950s and 1960s, the generally responsible, decent, and humane conservatives of the South did virtually nothing to encourage white southerners to abandon racial discrimination and to end racial segregation. On the contrary, they often fostered resistance to integration. To their minds, what else could they do? They stood unequivocally for the rights of local communities to decide such issues for themselves. During the struggle to integrate southern society, the communities that they represented were implacably hostile to these measures.

The inadequacy of Bradford's views on race relations not only derived from problems within the southern conservative tradition but arose in part from deficiencies of the liberal perspective on which he fastened his criticism. Affirmative action provides a revealing, if improbable, example. Bradford interpreted affirmative action legislation as an effort to decree an equality of opportunity and condition that the Founding Fathers never intended to bestow and that remained an illusion. Far from protecting a fundamental equality before the law, liberal politicians transformed affirmative action into an instrument to redress past grievances. They created what conservatives with some justification have called a racial spoils system.

The liberal administrations of the 1960s were largely responsible for this situation. Policymakers during the administration of Lyndon B. Johnson sought to organize blacks into "interest groups" to demand their rightful entitlements. Liberals encouraged blacks and the members of other "disadvantaged" groups to lobby the federal government to redress their political, economic, and social problems. Johnson's "War on Poverty," for instance, encouraged blacks and others to represent themselves as an exploited, victimized underclass. Interest-group politics demanded that blacks accept a definition of themselves as a custodial people unable to function as citizens without remedial assistance from the federal government.

The consequences of this approach have become clear in our own day. In opposing civil rights legislation, Ronald Reagan and George Bush argued that blacks were no longer exploited or victimized. Earlier civil rights legislation, such as the Civil Rights Act of 1964 and the Voting Rights Act of 1965, performed so effectively that they severely curtailed, if they did not completely eliminate, racial discrimination. Further legislation was thus unwarranted and would constitute an inordinate advantage for blacks at the expense of whites, who would become the victims of "reverse discrimination." [19] What the state gives, it can also take away.

In broad outline, this analysis recapitulates the essence of Bradford's argument, but he, like the recent occupants of the White House who called themselves conservatives, failed to consider other plausible interpretations of affirmative action. Perhaps affirmative action, special entitlements, and racial quotas did not best serve the interests of blacks. Blacks themselves are now exacting retribution for these shameful peace offerings, despite racial opportunists' unprincipled scrambling for political crumbs. Affirmative action programs, however, did acknowledge and protect blacks from the continuing bias against them, which was frequently sanctioned by custom and practice, if not by law.

Racial injustice was never exclusively southern, however, and southerners have by now suffered enough for their sins. White southerners, especially those who share Bradford's political and moral outlook, have long borne the condemnation of northerners and others who are usually unwilling to examine their own animosity toward blacks. Moreover, in recent years, the outcry for racial equity has become increasingly diluted. The once exclusive claims of blacks have been fused with the demands of a host of other groups that are now routinely characterized—or who routinely characterize themselves—as victims of discrimination and oppression.

Americans have every reason to demand that white southerners at last exorcise the legacy of slavery, segregation, and racism that has troubled their history. Yet the time has come to cease demanding that white southerners disavow their ancestors, repudiate their past, and reject the finest aspects of southern life. They must not forget, and must not be compelled to lay aside, their history, traditions, and identity. Those Americans, black and white, who wish to preserve the relics of segregation because they want everyone to recall its indignities but who do not wish white southerners to fly the Confederate battle flag because it reminds them of slavery, must realize that they cannot have it both ways.

19. For a different view, see Cornel West, *Race Matters* (Boston, 1993), and *Keeping Faith: Philosophy and Race in America* (New York, 1993). See also Eugene D. Genovese, *The Southern Front: History and Politics in the Cultural War* (Columbia, Mo., 1995), 192–98.

In the more than forty years since the Supreme Court outlawed racial segregation in the public schools, it has become all too easy, too convenient, and too inviting for white southerners to abandon their lineage, to fold their inheritance away in drawers, or to keep it locked up in the old trunk that sits in the corner of grandpa's attic. At present, far too many white southerners, young and old, seek to disavow their ancestors and their history or to remember them only with shame. That occurrence is at least as much an atrocity as was the denial of the legal and civil rights of black Americans.

John Crowe Ransom, Allen Tate, Donald Davidson, their contemporaries, and their successors had of necessity to move against, not with, the current of modern history. Censuring those in power, questioning the virtue of the triumphant, the Agrarians and their devotees formulated an alternate political language and moral vision that suited their role as critical adversaries. Their preoccupation as southern conservatives, Bradford wrote, was "to inhabit the wilderness, there crying out against interlopers who occupy the citadel and dispossess the rightful heirs" (RI, 91). They condemned not capitalism, communism, or fascism, not science, technology, or industrialism, not reason, individualism, or progress but the degradation of humanity that these political, economic, and intellectual systems engendered and justified. In short, they denounced the messianic pretensions that these ideologies represented and encouraged.

To twentieth-century southern conservative thinkers, the South had resisted the worst horrors of modernity. Perhaps they were right. Three decades ago James Burnham wrote of the "suicide of the West." There is little reason today to revise his essential conclusion that the heirs to Western civilization are openly defending, and even embracing, the enemies that would see them annihilated.

For the Agrarians, Weaver, and Bradford, southerners seemed the only consistent exception to this attitude in the United States. Southern ways may have been held up to ridicule, and southern virtues may have been out of fashion. But because southerners thought, acted, and lived within an inheritance, conservative thinkers argued, they enjoyed a sense of confidence, faith, and stability that would prove invaluable as the foundations of modern society began to collapse.

Indeed, the American Dream, once synonymous with assurances of inevitable progress and even with illusions of human perfectibility, has been exposed as folly. Men and women now lack confidence in the most basic social and political arrangements. We would thus do well to investigate further the trenchant criticisms that southern conservative thinkers have leveled against modernity.

The Agrarians' opposition to finance capitalism remains intelligent and provocative. Their denunciation of the selfish, possessive individualism that is today disgracing our society was prudent and wise. Their support for widespread property ownership and a market economy subject to socially determined moral restraints still merits sober consideration. Their call for a return to Christian individualism grounded in piety and their condemnation of personal indulgence and egocentrism may help to prevent the irreversible decline of civilization into barbarism. Their rejection of a cosmopolitanism that would eradicate local as well as national cultures may yet enable us to salvage the ideals, values, and aspirations that prevailed at the founding of a great nation. Their reaffirmation of the humane tradition has grown more timely and more urgent with each passing year since the publication of *I'll Take My Stand* in 1930. As Tate wrote to a forlorn Davidson in 1942: "You evidently believe that agrarianism was a failure; I think it was and *is* a very great success; but then I never expected it to have any political influence. It is a reaffirmation of the humane tradition, and to reaffirm that is an end in itself. Never fear: we shall be remembered when our snipers are forgotten" (*LC,* 328–29).[20] History has made a prophet of Tate in this as in much else.

The Agrarians and their successors defended the traditions not merely of the South but of Western civilization. Failure in their eyes meant the lurch toward a new, scientific, technological, and pagan "Dark Age" that would mark a descent into decadence and barbarism. They recognized near the beginning of the twentieth century two problems that have become obvious near its end. First, they decried the mounting pressure for economic growth and material prosperity even at the cost of political stability, social order, and nature. Second, they denounced the resurgence of nationalism, which, like capitalism, also threatened to undo established social and political arrangements and, perhaps, to destroy civilization it-

20. For a summary of the southern conservative critique of modernity, see Eugene D. Genovese, *The Southern Conservative Tradition: The Achievement and Limitations of an American Conservatism* (Cambridge, Mass., 1994), 91–103.

self. They believed that nationalism had animated northern society during the Civil War and observed more sinister manifestations of the same phenomenon in Fascist Italy, Soviet Russia, and Nazi Germany.[21]

Those who have assumed the leadership of the conservative movement in our own day, at least in the public arena, have squandered or ignored most of the Agrarians' penetrating insights and biting critique. The political conservatives who formed the core of the Reagan coalition—a coalition into which southern conservatives like Bradford fit awkwardly at best—embraced acquisitiveness as the key to affluence, applauded self-indulgence as the reward of success, and worshiped money as the source from which all goodness flows. More perilously, they assumed that progress resulted from the victory of wealth over violence and that the international triumph of democratic capitalism would thus solve most of the world's problems. They were wrong on both counts.

The Agrarians' dark pronouncements about the fate of the Republic at the hands of entrenched bureaucrats, untrustworthy politicians, greedy capitalists, and corrupt citizens have come true with a vengeance. The callousness of a government no longer responsive to the needs of its people; the irresponsibility of business in pursuit of unexampled profits; the intensifying racial antagonisms; the mounting violence in the streets and in the home; the widening gulf between vast private fortunes and unrelenting public squalor: all these are only symptomatic of the deeper spiritual crisis of a people and a nation cast adrift from their historical moorings. Under the conditions that now increasingly prevail in the United States, other peoples at other times have looked to a dictator to solve their problems and end their misery.

Liberty, as the Agrarians understood, is certainly not ours by right. Folly, neglect, and indifference may yet deprive us of its blessings. Southern conservative thinkers since the early days of the Republic understood the need for "eternal vigilance." The assumption that modern man had achieved a spiritual emancipation that rendered the ancient restraints and taboos unnecessary troubled those who inherited the southern conservative tradition. The erosion of our political culture was, from

21. It has become commonplace to link the Agrarians to National Socialism. For a thoughtful statement of this argument, see A. James Gregor, *The Ideology of Fascism: The Rationale of Totalitarianism* (New York, 1969). For a discussion and critique of this view, see Genovese, *The Southern Conservative Tradition*, 89–90.

their perspective, only one more indication of spiritual decline: the growing inability of men and women, as Richard Weaver suggested, either to
distinguish better from worse, right from wrong, or to meet the challenges of their world.

But no southern conservative thinker ever suggested that the political
and spiritual crisis of the modern age was inevitable, that it was the
consequence of fate or necessity rather than of imprudent choices and
evil decisions. Ideas, as Weaver wrote, have consequences. Men and
women, these conservative thinkers contended, were not wholly the victims of nature and history. They had at least a hand in making the future.

The Agrarians, Weaver, and Bradford knew that those who had inherited Western civilization faced a momentous choice. It was preemi-
nently a moral, not a political, choice. The men and women of the
modern world had to choose between barbarism and civilization. They
had to decide, as Weaver asserted, if they wished to live and, if they did,
whether they wished to live as men and women, as human beings, in
civilized communities or, to use Weaver's striking image, as rats huddled
in the doorways of darkened buildings amid the rubble of wrecked cities.
It is important at the present moment, when so many of our fellow
citizens feel themselves hedged in by weakness, uncertainty, fear, and
despair, not to let that choice grow dim. Now, more than ever, we need
to elevate the souls of our people, not complete their prostration.[22]

To reverse what Weaver called "the splendid efflorescence of decay,"
all Americans may wish to consider the neglected history and the forgotten traditions of the South. That history and those traditions will not
enable us to unravel the eternal mysteries of nature or even to resolve
the predicaments of the moment. We may, in the end, reject the specific
assumptions, judgments, and recommendations that the Agrarians and
their heirs presented. But the history and traditions of the South, however
troubled they have been, will doubtless provide a fuller understanding of
the human condition and thus better enable us to face the future with
intelligence, wisdom, and humility.

Perhaps it is enough that the southern conservative tradition has survived and that it continues to enlighten, provoke, confound, torment,

---

22. See John Lukacs, *Outgrowing Democracy: A History of the United States in the Twentieth Century* (Washington, D.C., 1984), 368–404, and *The End of the Twentieth Century
and the End of the Modern Age* (New York, 1993).

enrage, guide, and inspire. Ransom, Tate, and Davidson, along with their faithful disciples, Weaver and Bradford, carried the southern conservative tradition into the twentieth century. As the millennium approaches, the present generation of southern conservative thinkers has not given up the struggle. They know that in this world there are no lost causes, for, as T. S. Eliot once sagely observed, in this world no cause is ever fully won.[23] Assembled with friends and countrymen, they honor their ancestral dead and keep their tireless vigil, awaiting the moment when man's fall from grace into history shall be redeemed.

23. This is true even of Samuel Francis, whose recent book of essays is entitled *Beautiful Losers: Essays on the Failure of American Conservatism* (Columbia, Mo., 1993). See Genovese, *The Southern Front*, 261–77.

Index